My American Roadtrip

In Memory for my Mother and Father

Andrew (András) Ludányi

My American Roadtrip

From WWII to the 21st Century

"The road to hell is paved with good intentions."

Foreword to First Edition by
Zsolt Németh

Foreword to English Edition by
Charles Jokay

Copyright© by Andrew (András) Ludányi 2023
All rights reserved
Published in the United States by:

H P

Helena History Press LLC
A division of KKL Publications LLC, Reno, NV USA
www.helenahistorypress.com

Publishing scholarship about and from Central and East Europe

ISBN: 978-1-943596-31-7

Hungarian Edition published by Pro Minoritate, Budapest 2020 as "Amerikai életutam"

Order from Ingram Spark, any on-line bookseller or your local bookstore

Cover Image: Courtesy of Shutterfly
Cover Design: Daniel Németh

Contents

Acknowledgments	ix
Foreword to the English Edition	1
Foreword to the Hungarian Edition	3
Introduction	7
My Background	9
Leaving the Old World Behind	14
Arrival in the New World and the "Old Dominion"	16
A Second Start in New York City	20
The Scouting Experience	21
Changes at the National Level	24
Our View of 1956 from this Side of the Atlantic	27
Back to High School and Political Activism	31
Rope Burn at the New York Coliseum	34
Changing Direction	40
The Alternative Career Path	43
My Graduate Studies in Louisiana	45
Bicycle Ride Through Vojvodina	49
Closing the Circle in my Graduate Studies	59
A Life-Changing Meeting	64
North American Hungarians	65
Our Response via ITT-OTT (Here-There)	69
Our Lives Beyond ITT-OTT	71
Family Events	73
From Louisiana to Ohio	74
Teaching Career Begins at ONU	75
Hereford Pennsylvania: Discussion Group to Movement	78
U.S. Policy and Human Rights	80
Lobbying for Human and Minority Rights	82
Teaching, Writing and Model UN Activities	86
MBK and Hungarian Summer Studies	90
Our Growing Family	94

My 1982–83 Research in Hungary	96
General Transmission of Mission	98
Documenting the Hungarian Community in Toledo	100
Departmental Transformations	102
Canadian Studies at ONU	104
1992–93 Fulbright Professorship in Debrecen	105
Academic Conferences	107
Human Rights Workshops	111
A Model Human Rights Workshop	113
The Subsequent Workshops	115
My Meeting with Márika	119
"Bácsi Bandi" Our Chauffer with a Mission	122
2000 A.D. Human Rights Conference in Bucharest	125
Meanwhile Back in Ada and ONU	126
9/11 and Terrorism	126
Lobbying for Chechen Independence	131
The 2004 Gyurcsány Betrayal and the Öszöd Confession	132
Re-Visiting Vojvodina after Milosevic	134
Showing America to Our Lake Hope Guests	136
The Ludányi András Wine Celler in Gyöngyöstarján	137
Transferring American Experience to Hungary	138
Tamás and Renate Visit Saxon-German Transylvania	140
From Torockó to Graz with Pál, Theresa, Lizy and Lona	144
While Back at ONU	146
The American Macro Political Scene	148
Kossuth-Lincoln-Obama	149
21st Century Profile of the USA	151
The Coalition (HAC) and White House Briefings: Shades of the Indian Treaty Room	153
Decision After Retirement	155
My Revised Perspective of Our Global Role	157
The Global Corporate Power Structure	159
At the End of my American Roadtrip	160
Csilla and Anikó and the Vastness of the USA	161

Adjusting to Budapest 162
Registering the Past in Black and White 167
Fulbright, AHEA and Final Academic Activities 168
Facing the Coronavirus! 170
Conclusion to my road trip (Some Afterthoughts) 172
Afterword 177

A P P E N D I X: *Is Viktor Orbán a Populist?* 181
Historical Roots 182
Hungary's Népi/People's Movement 184
Orbán's Political Socialization 185
Populist Revival? 187
Elections and Media 189
CEU / KEE 191
LIBE Accusations and NGO Activities 194
"Bad Word" Populist or "Popular" Populist 196
Concluding Observations 203
Index of Names 205

Acknowledgments

This reflection on my life would not have seen the light of day without the encouragement of Shelleigh and Robert Alexander, Anna (Nusi) Gábor Cseh, my daughters Csilla and Anikó, my former wife Julianna (Panni) and my present wife Anna Mária (Márika) as well as Béla Bognár. I would also like to thank all those individuals who read the first draft of this book and made corrections or provided suggestions for improving the content including my brother Pál (Paul) Ludányi, my sister Narcissza Ludányi Layton, Anna (Nusi) Gábor Cseh, Szabolcs Kálmán, Zsolt Németh, Viktor Fischer, Ildikó Bodoni, Antal Bozóki, Zsolt Szekeres, Ildikó Forgács, Huba Brückner, Kálmán Magyar, Edith Lauer, John Lomax, Károly (Charles) Jokay, Krisztina Kos, and Katalin Kádár Lynn.

Foreword to the English Edition
Parallel and Twisting Roads

Andrew Ludányi and I have lived parallel, similar, phase-delayed and interesting lives with many twists of fate in common. To start with, "what is in a name?" asked Romeo, and we can ask the same. Are we talking about Charles Jokay writing a foreword for Andrew Ludanyi, or is it Jókay Károly doing the same for Ludányi András? The answer: both, and it depends on the context and timing.

Andrew was born 23 years before I was, in Hungary, to a middle-class family, becoming a refugee at the age of 4. Andrew is almost my mother's generation, the generation of middle and upper class Hungarians who became refugees, spent 4-5 years in camps or makeshift housing in Austria and Germany. They reached the United States as "DPs" or displaced persons, only to enjoy the vagaries of being "fresh off the boat" members of the Hungarian emigrant community. I was born in 1963, to a family with a similar story. They arrived in the US 1949-50, and met in the Hungarian community of Chicago, the city that became my birthplace. Andrew had to "learn" life in the US, as did my parents, as I had to "learn" about being Hungarian-American by birth.

Our parallel and twisting paths crossed, unbeknownst to me at the time, when Andrew's sister and my mother became best friends at Elmhurst College almost a decade before I was born. I first met Andrew, or "András bácsi" (Uncle Andrew) when I sat in his lap as a toddler in the mid-1960s. My mother's family and his family became lifelong friends.

While Andrew had a head start, his pursuit of Political Science as an academic field, teaching, and engaging in human rights activities on behalf of Hungarian minorities in the countries that encompass parts of historical Hungary. Supported by Hungarian scouting and weekend Hungarian school, the two of us were on the same path. Andrew and I met often at Hungarian events, conferences and professional gatherings while I pursued my own PhD in Political Science. I had hoped for an academic career similar to Andrew's, but in 1989 the so-called "end of History" ended my dreams of an academic career.

As our lives and fates predestined us to meet and support one another, sometime in 1990 Andrew asked me, his junior, to write a letter of recommendation for him supporting his Fulbright application to teach in Debrecen, Hungary. (He got the grant). As in any folk tale, "expect a reward for your good deed," in 2012 he proved to be very supportive of my own application to become Executive Director of the Fulbright Commission, and volunteered to help in many ways ever since.

The parallels and common twists in our separate, yet intertwined life journeys cannot be accidental: this has to be an example of predestination or Providence.

Andrew, as a young refugee, had to become American while staying very much Hungarian at heart, while I, born in the US, had to become Hungarian while staying American of mind. In this sense, our paths headed in the opposite direction, for a while. However, in the end, Andrew ended up living and working most of the year in Hungary, involving himself in many academic and service projects, and I moved to Hungary in 1994, and promote educational and cultural exchange between the land of my birth and the land of my heritage.

Parallel lives, Andrew and Charles, Károly and András. With this background in mind, gentle reader, you will understand and respect Andrew Ludányi's achievements even more, as his was not an ordinary road trip.

Revised November 2022
Charles (Károly) Jokay
Executive Director, Hungarian Fulbright Commission

Foreword to the Hungarian Edition
A Personal Chronicle of Life Lived Here and There

In this personal chronicle, the reader meets András Ludányi, a university professor of political science and a scholar of Hungarian history and culture who turned 80 this year.

This journey began when Ludányi was born in the town of Szikszó in eastern Hungary on February 12, 1940. The storms of fate drove his family to flee the country of his birth during the siege in 1944–45 and find a new home in the new world in 1949. For the next several decades, Ludányi strove to integrate into American society while at the same time preserving his connections to the culture and traditions of his homeland. After having spent well over a half century in his adopted homeland, in 2009, Ludányi returned to Hungary, where he remains a prominent figure in intellectual and political life.

These milestones, however, offer merely a sense of Ludányi's physical journey. The stands he took in support of values dear to him go far deeper. When the 1956 Revolution broke out in Hungary, he protested in the United States in support of the struggle, and after the defeat of the Revolution, he worked to encourage support for Hungarian refugees and protested against Soviet oppression. He always took a firm stance in support of the rights of the Hungarian minorities in Central Europe and human rights in general, and he was a leading figure in efforts to nurture and support Hungarian cultural life in his new homeland. And all the while, the rhythms of his everyday life were set by his creative and intellectual pursuits, his work as a pedagogue who trained generations of students, and his many publications and presentations at prestigious conferences.

In 1956, as a teenager in high school, Ludányi actively participated in the demonstrations outside the headquarters of the Soviet Mission to the UN in New York, demanding that action be taken to stop the bloodshed. He found it appalling that, while Radio Free Europe was encouraging Hungarian freedom fighters to hold out in their struggle and offering assurances that help from the West was coming, the Americans were officially informing the Soviets that they were interested in maintaining the status quo, appearances notwithstanding. Ludányi was motivated by a sense of desperation and a desire to do something for his homeland in his adopted country to join the "Riflemen" volunteer fighting group, which was organized by Zoltán Vasvári to "be at the ready should 1956 be repeated in the future."

In August 1959, Ludányi landed on the front pages of the newspapers when he endeavored to disrupt a Soviet exhibition at the New York Coliseum which was being held in the spirit of US-Soviet détente. Ludányi tried to remove the Soviet flag from the roof of the building as a gesture of protest in commemoration of the brutal suppression of the 1956 Revolution and freedom fight. He was unsuccessful in his efforts, and he almost paid for this bold act with his life. Charges were brought against him, and he spent eight weeks in a hospital.

His studies at university had something of a sobering effect on the young Ludányi. Though he was tempted to pursue a career in the military or the world of sports, he decided in the end to study political science and international relations, and he emerged as both an important scholar and university professor. As he mentions in his recollections, during a boxing match in Chicago in 1963, he took a right hook from a boxer named Robert King, and the blow was enough to dissuade him from making a career out of boxing, a decision for which he remains grateful to this day.

Ludányi could not help but note with some frustration that Hungarian culture among the émigré communities in the United States was fragmented at the time. Together with other members of this dispersed community, including his friend Lajos Éltető, Ludányi began seeking solutions that would help nurture and preserve this culture for the next generations of Hungarian Americans. As he notes, "we had to bring into being a network of communication that would successfully reach out to the next generation, or those who had not yet been infected by the ideological extremes and struggles of the émigrés. To this end we would have to deal with real problems that would address Hungarian survival in an assimilationist setting. We had to give up the idea that we could liberate Hungary from the Soviet yoke. Instead, how could we preserve Hungarian identity over time, how could we contribute to the cultural survival of Hungarians living scattered throughout the world, but particularly on the North American continent?"

The information network was based on an array of articles and an ever-growing circle of people who took an interest in Ludányi's efforts. As Ludányi recalls, it was called "ITT-OTT," or "HERE-THERE," borrowing the words from the lines of a poem by Hungarian poet Endre Ady. Ludányi and his colleagues shared the first collection of articles with some 30 other people, and on October 23, 1967, the eleventh anniversary of the revolution, they sent them out by mail. Out of this discussion group grew the Hungarian Communion of Friends, which by 1975 had grown the wings of a structured organization. Since 1976, the Hungarian Communion of Friends has organized ITT-OTT Conferences every year at Lake Hope in Ohio for members of the Hungarian-American community and beyond. I myself had the pleasure of attending the conference twice, once in 1987 and once in 2019.

Ludányi defended his dissertation, entitled *Hungarians in Romania and Yugoslavia*, at Louisiana State University in 1971. He then taught political science at Ohio Northern University in Ada until 2008. As a university lecturer and researcher, he won considerable professional recognition and organized a far-reaching network. For decades, he was an active participant and organizer in Hungarian-American public life, and for many years he was an enthusiastic participant in the Scouts, one of the most effective organizations in American-Hungarian cultural life. He was also one of the founders of the Hungarian American Coalition, and he served as a member of the American-Hungarian Educators Association. He was a promoter and active supporter of the Hungarian Fulbright Commission, and he supported the work of the Hungarian Human Rights Foundation on behalf of the rights of Hungarians living outside the borders of Hungary and other minority communities.

Ludányi's memoirs offer a broad overview of the lives of Hungarians living as members of the émigré community in the United States from the end of the Second World War to the present day.

In addition to all this, Ludányi's recollections offer a rare and valuable contribution to our understanding of American domestic and foreign policy and American-Hungarian relations. It has never been an easy task to arrive at a simple assessment of US policy, and this task is perhaps more difficult today than it has ever been. Ludányi nevertheless makes at attempt to do just this, and he does so without ever ignoring his own mistakes and disappointments. His insights are particularly engaging in part because he writes both from the perspective of a loyal, even patriotic American citizen but also from the viewpoint of an outsider, a concerned Hungarian who is committed to Western values. As someone who has lived both "here and there," he offers an innovative analysis of the development of the United States, including both its present state and its role in the international community, up to and including the 2020 presidential elections.

The volume which the reader has now taken in hand is being published both in English and in Hungarian, as it will be of interest both to American and Hungarian audiences, not to mention to Hungarian Americans. It will serve to foster an increasingly nuanced understanding of Hungarian-American relations, while also appealing to readers who are simply enrapt by the thoughts and insights it offers, which are shared in a light style which will often bring a smile to the reader's face.

December 2020
Zsolt Németh
Chairman of the International Relations Committee
of the Hungarian Parliament

Introduction

This is an essay about my personal encounter with the United States of America. I'm writing it in the autumn of my life and hope I can finish it before the grim reaper includes me in his annual harvest. Because it is in a sense an end of the road reflection, I feel I can be absolutely honest. This means that I will be critical as well as complimentary. I hope no one takes my comments as the reflections of an ungrateful ingrate. It is rather the concern of a first generation American who sees dark clouds gathering in the not too distant future. It is also based on a lifetime of reflections on my personal and American experiences. Indeed, if anything I'm truly very grateful that I could spend most of my life on American soil. My personal career as a university professor has been rewarding in every sense of the word. From the Fall Quarter of 1968 when I began my teaching adventure at Ohio Northern University (ONU), my contacts with students in the classroom, on the soccer field or in the Model UN simulations, enabled me to see and experience the American world in all its complexity, with its promise, its problems and its challenges. The same applies to my colleagues in the Department of History, Politics and Justice with whom I shared many years as the senior and later also the longest tenured member. This essay will deal with my life and its immersion in the American experience from World War II to the present. These seventy odd years also provide the opportunity to reflect not only on America's recent past but also on our probable future. I follow my life on four parallel tracks, my personal family life, my communal ethnic life, my professional career path, and finally how I have experienced American life and American foreign policy. The tracks constantly converge and frequently I have to switch tracks, but toward the horizon the four tracks seem to merge in the evening haze. This is **not** a scholarly summary of my life, but an impressionistic and personal testimony.

My Background

I was born on February 12th, 1940 in Szikszó, Hungary. World War II was already moving into its murderous 6th month. I was the third child of Erzsébet Prileszky Ludányi and vitéz[1] Colonel Antal Ludányi, the commander of the proud Infantry Brigade of Somogy county, Hungary, which participated in some of the most dramatic and bloody encounters with the Soviet Red Army. The other members of our family were my older sister, Narcissza (Ciszka), older brother, Tamás, and younger brothers, Antal Jr. and Pál.

Until 1941 the Hungarian military was not engaged in conflict against the Red Army. It was mainly engaged in consolidating Hungarian control over regained territories that had been lost after World War I, and the 1920 Dictate of Trianon.[2] Thus, until 1941 we saw more of our father than later

---

1   *Vitéz* is the title given to those who belonged to the "Vitézi Rend"(Order of the Valient/Brave) a Hungarian military order of merit founded in 1920 in recognition of outstanding courage and service on the battlefield. It was established to provide Admiral, later Regent Horthy with an order that would provide him with a committed support group in the military. The "Order" has been stigmatized by some rabid anti-Hungarian bloggers in the West, who have accused it of being guilty of collaboration with Nazi Germany during World War II. This collective accusation is a distortion of reality. While individuals in the "Order" supported Hungary's war against the Soviet military to the end, many vitéz officers loyal to Horthy were in favor of withdrawing from the conflict as soon as this was feasable, including the Chief of Staff vitéz Vilmos Nagybaczoni Nagy, vitéz Ferenc Koszorús and my own father. In this they received no tangible Allied support/encouragement.

2   *Dictate of Trianon* is my perspective on the "Treaty of Trianon" which was imposed on the Kingdom of Hungary following World War I on June 4, 1920. It was both a punitive and dictated "peace treaty." The Hungarian representatives were not given the oppertunity to present their case to the framers (France, Great Britain, Italy, the United States and their representatives) of the treaty. (The USA never ratified this treaty and concluded a separate treaty with Hungary in

during his service on the Russian front from the winter of 1941 to the fall of Budapest in the winter of 1944–45.

As a child I did not really have a conscious understanding of what was going on in the world around us. Most of my "recollections" are probably the memories of my mother, my sister and older brother which they shared with me in later years. During the last year of the war our family stayed near the little village of Bagola in Western Hungary on a small plot of land that my father acquired with his status as a vitéz. Here we could avoid the bombing raids which hit larger cities, like Kaposvár or Győr. On this vitézi plot I had my first serious encounter with the effects of wine. As my sister Ciszka told me, I must have seen how the grown-ups siphoned the wine from the barrels in our wine cellar. When the grown-ups left the cellar, I simply followed their example. However, like the wizard's apprentice I overplayed my part and could not turn off the wine flow from the siphon. I had drunk enough of it, and was drenched in it, and I could not make it up the stairs. Instead, I left a barefoot trail from the wine puddle to the corner of the basement where they found me, a four-year-old vino, sound asleep.

More directly tied to the war was the dogfight that was fought in the skies above us by a bomber and a small fighter plane during this period. Those American bombers that were returning to Northern Italy after a bombing run over Budapest, Kaposvár or Győr, would drop their remaining bombs on the small oil producing facility near Nagykanizsa. On this particular day, however, a small fighter plane from one of the nearby airfields rose to challenge the bombers. We witnessed how this small plane flew below the last bomber in the fleet and machinegunned its underbelly. Almost immediately a plume of smoke enveloped the back end of the bomber. As the plane began to descend toward the horizon, two parachutes left the bomber. Of those who witnessed this on our hillside, cheers of admiration erupted for the fighter pilot.

However, my first real memory was already linked to our long flight from Kaposvár, through Csalóköz, to Austria. What I remember is not the actu-

---

1921.) This dictated peace deprived Hungary of 71% of its historic territories and 60% of its population, including three and half million ethnic Hungarians who became the hostages of the newly created successor states of Czechoslovakia and the Kingdom of Serbs, Croats and Slovenes, later renamed Yugoslavia, and the newly enlarged Romania. This treaty automatically made interwar Hungary and its foreign policy a potential ally of all other revisionist states.

My Background

From l. to r.: Tamás, Toni in our mother's arms, András in our father's lap and Narcissza (Pál is also present in our mother's womb) 1943.

al path we took, but how we travelled. We kids were all crammed unto the back seat of my father's service car pulled by two horses, since the car had long run out of gasoline. The names of the horses were Duci and Dália, two beautiful saddle horses, that now had to become the two-horse powered motor of an otherwise useless military vehicle. These four wheels and these two horses took us from Kaposvár to an Austrian farmstead close to Salzburg. There we rested, because we had made it far enough West to be in the American rather than the Soviet zone of occupation.

However, my father was still in the uniform of a Hungarian army colonel. His men were also still in their uniforms rather than civilian clothes, but they were now all part of our refugee caravan. Even though the war had officially come to an end on May 4th, there were marauders who used these uncertain times, to settle scores with their former enemies. Thus, one evening as we sat down to eat with an Austrian farmer and his family, the door flew open and in burst a group of Serb Chetniks, armed to the teeth, who wanted to arrest a "Hungarian war criminal." Our family stood in shocked bewilderment as they took our father and some of his men away. For days we did not have any news of their whereabouts. About a week after the Chetniks took them away, we heard that they had been handed over to the American occupation authorities. They were put in a prisoner of war camp, wherein the American officer in charge appointed our father (presumably because of his rank) to be the person to keep order among the prisoners. Since he knew that they would be soon returned to Hungary under Soviet control, he arranged a nocturnal departure from the camp for all the Hungarian prisoners.

This experience led my father to rethink our options and our family moved to the little town of Hochburg, where he took a job as the assistant gardner of the Countess Kastell. This kept us from being deported back to Hungary until the attitude of the Western Allies changed regarding the former enemy peoples. (Until the end of 1948 former enemies were defined as undesirable "D.P.-s" /Displaced Persons/ for emigration to the United States.) Thus, many Hungarian families opted to emigrate to Argentina, Brazil or Venezuela, or even Australia. When in 1948 the official American attitude changed, our family applied for admission to the United States. After a strict vetting process to check that our father had not been a member of fascist or communist organizations or parties, we were given the green light to emigrate to the United States.

Saying good-by to the kind people in Hochburg who had taken us in was no easy task. This little Austrian town, the home of Karl Gruber, the composer of "Silent Night," had become a secure home for us for two years during very uncertain times. (It also provided us with an opportunity to attend two midnight masses at Christmas with the village chorus singing "Silent Night" - an unforgettable experience!) Before we left to move into the refugee center of Weghscheid where we received final clearance for our travels to the United States, the Countess Kastell had the local tailor provide us with true Austrian "lederhozen" sewn out of the U.S. army blankets that we received in the refugee center. These short pants were held up by suspenders just like those used by Austrian peasant youth in the Alps. (You can imagine how distinguished we would look and feel when we attended school in Victoria, Virginia soon after our arrival in the United States. For our classmates who wore jeans, not short pants with suspenders, we looked like weirdos from Mars!)

Being admitted was just the first step. The next step was to get the sponsorship as a family from someone in the United States. NCWC[3], a Catholic organization, came forward to sponsor us. However, we had to wait our turn. This meant that we had to continue being refugees in a former *láger* which had previously been used to house military personnel during the war. This meant mass housing conditions with families using blankets to establish "walls" between themselves and their neighbors, as well as public toilets that allowed for minimal privacy. The food services were also limited and had to be supplemented with mushroom gathering in the nearby woods after a good rain. This improved after UNRRA[4] sponsored food deliveries became regular to the refugee camps. One of the least popular meals was the "Truman potato." It was nicknamed after the American President of the time because it came from the USA and was labeled on the cans as "sweet potatoes." Unfortunately the camp cooks did not know how to prepare this healthy delicacy. They assumed that a potato is a potato, and fixed it the way they learned to fix regular East Central European potatoes, fried in a lot of grease with chopped onions. The result was not the same and poor Harry Truman got credit for this culinary delight. On days when this was served, the ditches from the mess hall to the barracks reeked of "Truman potatoes." In the camp our assessment of the Truman administration and American policies were very mixed, and not just because of the potatoes which were credited to him. It came as a shock to most of the grown-ups that the United States had used the atomic bomb in Hirosima and Nagasaki. For most of us who were not yet teenagers, the gravity of this destructive force had not sunk in. However, overhearing the assessment of our parents, we knew that a new age dawned on mankind and that the United States had become the most significant power in the world. Some of them worried that the tie salesman from Missouri may not be able to handle "Uncle Stalin." This first impression was reinforced by the rapid American troop withdrawals from Eu-

---

3   NCWC was the National Catholic Welfare Conference that existed between 1944-1971 and provided refugee assistance in the form of relief and resettlement from/in war-torn areas of Europe.

4   UNRRA was the United Nations Refugee Agency that was created to provide for the millions of refugees that inundated Austria and occupied Germany following World War II.

rope while the Soviet Red Army was still at full strength and stationed in the heart of the continent.

The lively political discussions among the D.P.-s revealed a great deal of trust and hope concerning the ability of the USA to keep the Soviets at bay. Some of them argued that the bombs dropped on Japan, had actually been meant as a warning to the USSR. Others countered that the agreements hammered out at Yalta and Potsdam between the Big Three indicated otherwise. At any rate, most of the people seemed to think at that time, at least among the refugees in Weghscheid, that a Republican president would be tougher than the Missouri tie salesman. Later in life I would question this assessment on the basis of Kennan's containment policies which led to US economic and military support for Turkey and Greece, and eventually also the establishment of NATO and American involvement in the Korean war. At any rate, as refugees from 1946 to 1949, we were merely the worried observers of global politics.

Leaving the Old World Behind

In the late summer of 1949 the day finally arrived for our departure to the New World. This was preceded by a final health screening for all of us, as well as saying goodbye to all our friends in the camp. We had made friends in the *láger* school which was run by priests, ministers, and teachers who were also refugees. This school was like a small country school where at least three grade levels were clustered together in one room. Consequently, the instruction we received was very rudimentary in Hungarian as well as German. Yet some solid friendships came into being among classmates, which were reinforced as we played soccer in the empty lots of the camp. Another important unifying camp institution became the exiled scouting movement which our teachers and some former army officers established. For the youngsters, both boys and girls, this provided a great opportunity to become members of a community that led us to enjoy the outdoors with hikes in the beautiful Austrian Alps. It freed us for weekends from the dreary, and often depressing existence of the refugee camps. At the same time, it too strengthened our group solidarity and our friendships. Now we had to say goodbye again, but we made promises that we would keep contact with each other.

Our train left Salzburg for Bremenhaven in northern Allied-occupied Germany, where we were housed for a few days before our voyage across the Atlantic Ocean. I do not remember much of this trip, since I spent three or four days in the ship's infirmary with a high fever. The "General Blatchford" was the former troop carrier that now served as a refugee or D.P. carrier. Aside from the American naval personnel on board, everyone else belonged to the former category totalling about 400 people. (I'm not certain of this number, it is the guesstimate of my sister Ciszka!) At any rate, one of my most memorable experiences in the infirmary, was my first meeting with a black man, that is an Afro-American. He was a tall, thin medical orderly or male nurse, who came in to take my temperature. My feverish condition put me into panic mode, I assumed that perhaps I was no longer alive and was now facing my after-life handler. He must have read the fear on my face and returned with a big glass of cold orange juice. This convinced me that he could not be all bad. This was an important first lesson since our destination in the USA would include many more Afro-Americans. After they released me from the infirmary, I realized that he was one of many blacks among the crew of our ship.

The voyage lasted about eight or nine days and our family was not housed together. I was in the infirmary and my mother and sister with our youngest, five-year-old brother (Pál), were located in the women's section of the ship. Meanwhile my brothers Tamás and Antal Jr. were housed with my father in the men's dormitory section. For all of us the sight of the Statue of Liberty and the Port of New York City was the moment of family reunification. We could watch together, with relief and anticipation, as the General Blachford docked in lower Manhattan. We were let off the ship and guided toward a great hall where we were also reunited with our limited personal baggage. There we had to wait until our papers were checked and our Catholic sponsor arrived. We spent one night in a downtown New York City hotel. From there the representative from NCWC took charge of us and took us to the Pennsylvania Railroad Station in the middle of Manhattan where he bought us tickets to Richmond, Virginia.

Arrival in the New World and the "Old Dominion"

The train ride to Richmond was also a learning experience. At Penn Station our NCWC representative handed us over to a conductor in a neat uniform with a red cap. He took us to the end of the train that was scheduled to leave for Richmond. As we settled into our corner of the coach and began to look around, we realized that all the people in the coach were not Hungarian D.P.-s, but Negroes, that is Afro-Americans. Just as we were labeled by our D.P. status as not yet true Americans, our travelling companions were labelled by their skin color. As our train lurched forward and left New York City, we were overcome with apprehension: are we going into a world where everyone else is black and our family will be a very visible minority? No, it was simply the established pattern of 1949 that a segregated America made its citizens with destinations south of the Mason-Dixon line travel in different compartments based on their skin color. As we crossed New Jersey, Pennsylvania, and Maryland we saw that the actual population was both black and white and shades in between. As we watched our traveling companions, we also learned useful things from them, as for example obtaining drinking water from a fountain that had little cone-like disposable cups. By the time we arrived in Richmond we had developed some awareness of the contradictions that existed in our new homeland.

A young Irish-American priest, Father Silk, was waiting for us at the station, he represented NCWC in Virginia. He took us to a hotel near the station and explained on the way that unfortunately the gardening job in Richmond was no longer available, it had been filled by someone else. He would come back for us the next day, to take us to an alternate job site near Victoria, Virginia. The trip next day involved a 35-mile ride south of the state capital to our alternative employer, Mr. Forester's farm. We had all dressed in our Sunday best including our short pants held up by suspenders. Mr. Forester was not impressed, he thought that the suspenders were body braces, and muttered that he had not bargained for cripples. The priest had to explain that we were not in body braces and would surely be capable of farm work that other youngsters our age could perform. So Mr. Forester got all seven of us for seventy dollars a month, but from which he deducted eight dollars to cover the cost of the milk our family consumed. Our father would be the farm hand, but my mother and sister would help with milking the 21 cows, and the three smallest members of the family (with the body-braces) would be responsible for herding the cows out to pasture and bringing them in for milking. My older brother Tamás, now called Tom, would help with cleaning the stables (for the cows and two draft horses, Prince and Dolly) and harvesting the tobacco.

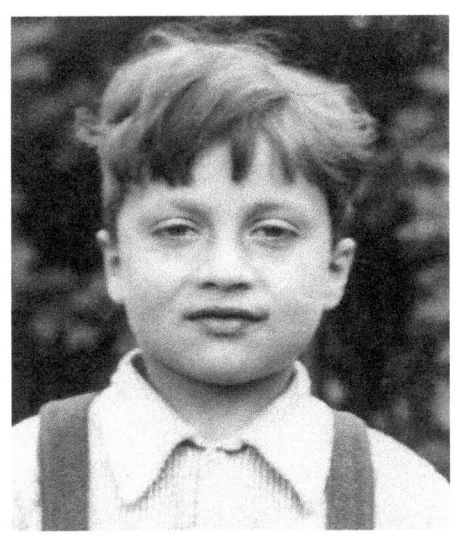

The terror of the Victoria VA school yard: András with hozentrager suspenders

The school year was just beginning, so four of us, Tom, Tony, Paul and myself got ready to get on the school bus that picked us up early in the morning. On the opposite side of the road were the Afro-American kids waiting for their own bus. We went on different busses to different schools. Again we came face-to-face with the custom of segregation that we had encountered on our train ride to Richmond. As soon as we got off the bus we faced an even more daunting challenge, trying to fit into our new setting in short pants with Austrian suspenders. Our classmates giggelled and pointed at us, with comments on our appearance, comments that we could not understand. The intervention of the teachers was only a temporary reprieve. During recess and lunch time, the harassment continued. As the oldest of the three, I had to stand up for my brothers as well as myself. This got me into a number of fights in the school yard. Fortunately the supervising teacher saw that the confrontations were not really the fault of the foreign kid. But after the first few days we begged our parents to get us the kind of jeans our classmates had, so we could fit in.

I do not know how our parents were able to do it, since we constantly had cash flow problems, but after about a week of suffering we were outfitted with worn clothes which we received from the church. These were like those worn by our classmates. By then, however, our youngest brother had become so traumatized that he did not want to go to school. Every morning Tony and I had to drag him to the school bus, and force him to get on the bus to the jeers and cheers of the other students. Once we got to the school, we went our separate ways, to different grades and classes. My teacher saw that one of my main problems was learning English and spelling. She sent one of her best spellers, naturally a girl, to sit in the hallway with me and review the words we had covered that day. I was a slow learner, because the words were not written phonetically, like in Hungarian or German. Furthermore, she was a cute instructor.

The lunch breaks continued to be my favorite time at school. Partly because my language instruction continued in a less formal context, with my lunchtime friends, teaching me words that were not part of the curriculum. For example, as we played football, they always called it that "f___ken ball." But the game itself was a new adventure, since it was more of a contact sport than soccer (another contradiction, since they called it football, yet the passing, running the ball, the tackling, required a constant use of your hands.) And if you were'nt aggressive enough you didn't have "f___ken balls." Somewhat confusing at first, but I got the hang of it and was an aggressive player, perhaps too aggressive because in one play I knocked over a guy who was a head taller than myself. His name was Jackson, I remember it well because he gave me a trouncing that was memorable. Fortunately the playground supervisor saved the foreign kid from being totally decimated.

That first year in Virginia was not easy for any of us, particularly not for our parents. My father had not really had to do too much physical work before Mr. Forester's farm. While we were in Austria he had been a gardner on the Countess' estate and he had also done some logging work where he was injured by a loose limb. The injury was the cause of a stomach ulcer which was with him to the end. However, the work on the farm involved long hours, doing a whole variety of tasks from stump removal, haying, stacking tobacco to all the assorted work with milking the cows and keeping the barn clean. This hit him at the age of fifty-five, after service on the Russian front in winter, with multiple shrapnel injuries in his legs. But the most difficult part psychologically was to accept the role of being a hired hand and taking orders from those who had much less education or wisdom. He adjusted to these difficult life changes to feed his family and to survive. For my mother the adjustment was just as difficult. Besides assisting with the milking she also put food on the table for us from limited resources and with a wood-fed stove that did not have adequate cooking surface. Our water supply was a 55-gallon drum in front of the house that Mr. Forester would replenish as needed. Our mother also had to hand wash our clothing and dry it on the clothes line when weather permitted.

Although my parents realized that this was a dead-end for the whole family, my sister Ciszka's communication skills (she was the only one to this point with good English language skills) enabled us to break out. She let the NCWC authorities know that our situation was desperate. With their help we found another dairy farm near Amelia, Virginia with better living conditions and somewhat better pay. This farm was owned by the Watkins brothers, Marvin and Jimmy. Here we had our own little three-room house, separate from the farmer's residence, but also without indoor plumbing, but with a hand-pumped well just outside the kitchen. Furthermore, the salary of my father increased to eighty-five dollars per month. My mother could also diversify our diet because she was given access to the farmer's vegetable garden and her kitchen finally had a real stove, although still wood-fed. Our lives improved, our improved existence also opened the door to further developments. Our sister Ciszka began to complete her high school education by correspondence. The rest of us also began the new school year with an improved English language preparation and in jeans. The Watkins farm was our first step up on the American ladder of opportunity.

The history instruction in this Amelia grade school led us to sense the foundations of American national consciousness. In this new school our teachers also organized class field trips to Jamestown and Williamsburg. The story of Captain John Smith and Pocahontas captivated our imagination as did the early struggles of the Virginia settlements. It is surprising how fast the sense of American identity became part of us. However, our heroes became not only George Washington, Thomas Jefferson and Patrick Henry, but also Robert E. Lee and Stonewall Jackson. (The latter two heroes became a problem for us later when we learned the New York City version of the Civil War in P.S. 122 in Astoria, Queens.) However, while in Virginia, I could voice the patriotism of Patrick Henry and standing near our woodshed could proudly proclaim "Give me Liberty or give me Death!"

It was this quest for liberty that convinced Ciszka that we must reach for the next rung in the opportunity ladder. Through letters she and our mother wrote to relatives in Astoria, Queens, we learned about job opportunities in the New York City area. Ciszka was able to say good-by to farm life and moved to Greenwich, Connecticut where she found a baby-sitting and housekeeping job. Here she saved up enough so she could cover Tom's move to Astoria with our relatives. Tom got a job as a messenger-boy and this got the two of them to save up enough to pay for the whole family's transportation back to New York City. Here, both my father and mother found factory work with Swingline Staples in Long Island City. With their joint salaries, we could then afford to move into an apartment near our Astoria relatives.

A Second Start in New York City

In New York City the family's economic foundation was established to enable us to think of alternative futures. The Big Apple also provided us with contact with other Hungarian D.P.-s who had recently settled there. This meant that on week-ends we could meet with ethnic kin at the Jewish owned "Paprikás Weisz" store in Yorkville on the East side of Manhattan. There we could replenish our Hungarian tastes for plum jam, gyulai kolbász, szalonna and assorted other foods that had not been available in Virginia. New York City also had other East European and South European ethnic communities, whose bakeries provided real bread as opposed to the packaged factory made "Wonder Fluff" that was called bread in Richmond and Amelia. At the same time, we made contact with other D.P.-s who informed us about the existence and the location of St. Stephen of Hungary Church as well as Árpád Hall and other institutions that had been established by the "old time" Hungarians, i.e., those who had come to the United States before the passage of the Johnson Act in 1924.[5]

---

5 **The Immigration Act of 1924 (The Johnson-Reed Act)** put a limitation on immigration based on national origin. A quota provided immigration visas for two percent of the number of each nationality already in the United States according to the 1890 national census. It was completely discriminatory toward Southern and Eastern Europeans who had only come in large numbers to the United States after that date. Furthermore, it was almost totally exclusionary for Asian immigrants (Japanese and Philipinos excepted!)

Ciszka's 1951 snapshot of our family in Astoria: l. to r. Tamás, Toni, András, mother Erzsébet, Pál and father Antal

At any rate, these occasional contacts enabled us to become part of the New York City area Hungarian D.P. network. This meant that we could meet after church services at Miklós Taliga's book store on First Avenue and also started to attend the week-end Hungarian school that he supported. It also led to organizational activities including the establishment of the Szt. Imre (Saint Emeric) youth club on 81st Street between First and Second Avenue on the East side. In other words, we established a dual existence: during week-days we worked or studied within the context of American institutions while on week-ends we reverted to an existence that took us closer to our roots in entertainment and friendship circles.

The Scouting Experience

After this, the most significant change among the D.P.-s in NYC was the establishment of scout Troop #7, named after Gusztáv Erős.[6] Zoltán Vasvári

---

6   **Erős Gusztáv** was the troop leader of the scouts in the High School of district # I in Budapest. He was inducted into the Austro-Hungarian Army at the beginning of World War I and died in battle. In his honor at the beginning of 1919 the district # I scout troop was renamed Erős Gusztáv Scout Troop #7. This number and this name was also adopted by the Hungarian exile scout troop in New York City in 1954 after scouting was disbanded by the communists in Hungary.

Zoltán Vasvári our #7. scout troop leader, giving instructions near the tent of the Turul patrol

Morning inspection of the Turul patrol by Péter Mauksch and Viktor Fischer

organized the first patrol in 1951 and had the support of the Scout Federation in Exile for the establishment of the New York City Troop #7 in 1954. This exile Hungarian Scout troop provided the organizational center for a generation of young emigre Hungarians. As had been the case in Austria, now in NYC my two younger brothers and I joined this troop and acquired the connectedness that P.S. 122 could not provide. Our first meetings were held on the roof of a warehouse in lower Manhatten where our troop leader was employed as a truck driver and mover. He too was a former army officer who had served on the Russian front. Zoltán Vasvári (or Zolibá) had been a captain in a Hungarian armored division. He was in his early forties and about ten years younger than my father. With his two assistants (Péter Mauksch and Viktor Fischer) he organized us into a disciplined and active group within the Hungarian ethnic community in NYC. About every three months we took a

On Fifth Avenue the Erős Gusztáv troop is led in parade by
Viktor Fischer and Árpád Makay. András is immediately
behind Árpád

week-end hike in the Catskills or the Adirondack mountains and every summer we spent one week or ten days camping in upstate New York or Eastern Pennsylvania. More important, we held weekly meetings on the warehouse rooftop, where we practiced our language and learned scouting lore in the tradition of Lord Baden-Powell. These experiences, particularly the hiking and camping experiences provided us with a strong group solidarity. I believe the campfires were the most important catalysts! They provided a mystic, almost spiritual experience for all of us. Tibor Cseh formulated this best in passing the lore on to future scout leaders. He said: "Every fire becomes ashes and embers, but the embers of a campfire remain with us until we live, and its flames warm us throughout our lives. A good campfire is a cosmic experience. Time stops! The fire blocks out the outside world. Anything beyond the circle of light that is the campfire... becomes non-existent. The problems of our workplace... the chaos and noise of the marketplace, the clutter and congestion on the highways during rush hour! Within the circle of light is the fire, the flames, the scent of burning wood, the songs springing forth from our souls, the ballads, the stories, the dances, the jokes, the poems, the battle cries, the songs of the fugitives and refugees, the voices of those living and dead, the joy of youth and the centuries old wisdom of ancestors gone; the mysterious fusion of dreams and reality! Our faces glow in the fire's warmth and we are transformed in communal unity."[7] The embers and warmth of those campfires have remained with us through good times and bad times.

Changes at the National Level

While our family was adjusting to life in New York City a major change also took place at the national level in the United States. The war in Korea dragged on and casualties mounted, General Douglas MacArthur was recalled. Truman's popularity dipped and the Republicans began to regain their confidence after the close but lost election of Thomas Dewey against the incumbent President in 1948. However, they were divided in their support of the two front runners in 1952, that is between Robert Taft and Dwight D. Eisenhower. In the Democratic party, on the other hand, Adlei Stevenson seemed to have his nomination assured. In the end, Eisenhower won the Republican nomination at their party convention. When Eisenhower won the election most Hungarian D.P.-s felt that this would mean more than just "containment" of Communism, but would lead to "roll-back," and perhaps we could then return to a free Hungary. This naive perspective was based on putting too much faith in the electioneering promises of the winners who had been castigating the Democrats for "losing China." The activities of Senator Joseph McCarthy also added to the false hope that the anti-Communist momentum would lead to liberation rather than the continuing nuclear stalemate. It was in this context that my older brother Tom joined the Marines. He did his boot camp training at Parish Island in South Carolina in 1953

---

[7] ***Scout Campfires*** were a central element in building group solidarity in the lives of young and old. Tibor Cseh describes this best in an article in which he wrote what makes "The Good Campfire." My enclosed translation is based on our memorial service for Tibor. See: *ITT-OTT/ MBK Évkönyve* (Yearbook), 2005, p.16. (sec.6)

"Rapszodia" dance group led by Mária Molnár (kneeling). Front row l. to r.: Erzsi Horváth, Ilona Sala, Csilla Makay, Éva Szuchy, Viola Gombos, Rima Sala. Back row l. to r.: Viktor Fischer, Péter Tarköy, Árpád Makay, Péter Némethy, Huba Taliga, András Ludányi.

and underwent additional training in Camp Pendleton in California before he was sent to Japan and Korea as part of Uncle Sam's commitment to stemming the expansion of Communism.

In Astoria where the three youngest Ludányi's attended P.S.122 our socialization in American urban culture moved ahead rapidly. During release time once a week we attended cathecism classes at Immaculate Conception Church. In our spare afternoons, after each of us reached the age of twelve, we delivered the daily "Long Island Star Journal," and this provided all three of us with some spare change. Our neighborhood was mainly Italian-American, and the old-timers would play bocci ball just a block from where we lived. However, the neighborhood already began to change ethnically while we lived there. The newer population was made up mostly of Greek-Americans and Maltese-Americans, but a smattering of East Europeans was growing as the Hungarian, Polish, Croatian and Ukrainian D.P.-s started to move in. In the park near our home under the Hellgate bridge (just north-east of the Triboro bridge) we played soccer with many of these first-generation immigrant kids. Two Maltese brothers, Ronnie and Savier were our best friends. The student population at P.S.122 reflected this cross-section of the over-all population.

Just about two years after we moved to Astoria, we had an interesting and life-changing meeting with one of our fellow Hungarian D.P.-s. It was already getting dark and my brothers and I were on our way home from church with our father. We brothers were arguing about something and one of us threatened to use physical force to back up the point that he just made. Our father then laudly scolded us in Hungarian and he said if we did not quit, he would pull our ears. At that point a voice out of the darkness behind us said: "Te vagy Toni bácsi, Ludányi Antal ezredes Úr!?" (Is that you 'Uncle' Tony, Sir colonel Antal Ludányi!?) They embraced and could not believe that they would see each other ever again. Captain László De Simon had served as my father's adjutant on the Russian front. Both had assumed that the other had been killed or captured. The two summerized their lives from the Russian front to Astoria, Queens. At the end of their discussion the former adjutant offered his former commander a job in his dental laboratory, a job that paid more with better conditions than his present position in the Swingline Staples factory. This was our next step up in the American land of opportunity.

By 1957 my brother Tom, now a Korean War veteran, had received his honorable discharge from the Marine Corps. He received a job at a tool and dye making shop in Woodside. This job helped Ciszka and Tom to purchase the family's first car, a 1959 Ford Fairlane 500 with attractive tailfins. (Actually, we already had a car earlier, a 1928 Model T Ford, on loan from the Catholic church so that we could make it to church services on Sundays in Victoria, VA. But we had to return this car to the local church when we left Virginia.) Now we became mobile, and Tom or Ciszka could now help transport the scouts of the Erős Gusztáv Troop #7 to their summer camps. Our American dream world was heading in the same direction as the rest of our "new country:" more development, more highways, more consumer goods.

But this was all preceded by 1956. This year changed all of our lives dramatically. Already on one of our scouting excursions in August to the Adirondacks, Gábor Brogyányi told us that according to Radio Free Europe reports there was a great deal of unrest in Poland and Hungary. He also mentioned that Nikita Khrushcsov had given a speech at the 20th CPSU Congress in February which criticized Stalin and the cult of personality. (Stalin died in March of 1953 and was replaced by a collective leadership in the Politburo, including Bulganin and Khrushcsov in the two most influential positions.) All of us paid close attention to what Gábor said, because his father followed events in Eastern Europe closely. And sure enough, things began to unravel in our former homeland as the Stalinists and the "reformers" faced off in early October when László Rajk, who had been executed after a show trial in 1949, was reburied in a demonstration against the AVO[8] and the brutality of the Hungarian Stalinist, Mátyás Rákosi! The tensions in the Hungarian Communist party spilled into the streets and a fullscale uprising erupted on October 23rd. University students marched through the city with demands for reform, workers and the general population joined them. They gathered in large numbers in Kossuth square in front of Parliament and also the radio station to have their demands broadcast. When the AVO opened fire on them to disperse them, they instead fought back with whatever weapons they could get their hands on. In New York, Pittsburgh, Chicago and Cleveland Hungarian-Americans were glued to their radios listening to the reports coming from their homeland. What would their new homeland do now?

Our View of 1956 from this Side of the Atlantic

Their new homeland was in the midst of an election campaign and both Eisenhower and Stevenson tried to skirt the issue of American responsibility. However, for us Hungarian-Americans, whose friends and relatives had their lives on the line, this was not an option. We went out onto the streets of New York in front of the United Nations and the Soviet Mission to the Unit-

---

8   *AVH/AVO* stands for Álamvédelmi Hatóság/Álamvédelmi Osztály which was the security apparatus/secret police of the Communist order, roughly translated as the State Defense Authority/State Defense Division, under the direction of Péter László, carried out the terrorizing, imprisonment and execution of people after the Communists captured state power.

András with parents Antal and Erzsébet Ludányi in 1956

ed Nations demanding action to stop the bloodshed. For the next two weeks we participated in street demonstrations wherever we could draw media attention to the Hungarian question. I remember well the demonstration in front of Madison Square Garden where the Republicans were holding their final big campaign night for Eisenhower's re-election. We held up signs saying "What About Roll-Back Now!!" and "Freedom for Hungary." I remember one irate Republican lady running up to me and yelling "Not one drop of American blood, not one drop of American blood!"

Our tragedy was not only the upcoming American elections, but also the Suez crisis that was coming to a head at this time. Israel-France-the United Kingdom used this moment to unleash an attack on Egypt. With the attention of the world rivetted on the crisis in Budapest and the Soviet Union kept busy on the banks of the Danube, the Israelis, the French and the British could move unhindered to discipline Gamal Abdel Nasser for daring to nationalize the Suez Canal. The Israelis gained control of the Sinai Peninsula, destroyed the Egyptian air force and insured their military predominance. The French and the British re-gained their colonial influence temporarly in the region, at least in the Fertile Cresent (Jordan, Lebanon, Syria and Iraq). The Americans soon replaced them in this role, after giving them a thorough scolding in the UN for their old imperialistic ways. Yes, as Clemanceu had said during World War I, "one drop of oil is worth one drop of blood of our soldiers."

We Hungarian-Americans simply did not have the appeal of the Suez Canal to support our pleas. Nor did Hungary have significant quantities of oil. The "Blue Danube" only had aesthetic and emotional appeal, an appeal that at best could receive majority votes in the General Assembly of the UN, but could never get past a veto in the Security Council. So we grit our teeth and continued our demonstrations, which caused problems mainly for the NYPD and ourselves. In one demonstration on 68th street close to Hunter College I almost invaded the Soviet UN Mission. The Mission was surrounded by a defensive ring of New York's finest, plus a row of wooden horses between the police and us the demonstrators. As we walked up and down in front of the mission, shouting anti-Soviet slogans, one of the mission representatives looked out a side-window with a broad grin. I jumped unto the top of a nearby wooden-horse and reached the terrace below his window. The nearest police officer was able to catch hold of my left leg and janked me back down. This led to a brief stay in an overnight holding cell until my father came to pick me up with the promise that I will be kept far away from the Soviet UN mission. This promise was kept, but I kept demonstrating in other parts of the city, including the UN building itself.

World politics is rarely influenced and never decided by street demonstrations. In spite of the aggressive language of the Republicans in the political campaign, they followed the *status quo* policies of their Democratic Party predecessor regarding the power distribution on the European continent. Secretary of State John Foster Dulles actually reassured the Soviet Union at this time that the United States did not think of the East European states as potential allies. At the same time American pressure was exerted on both France and the United Kingdom to cease and desist their intervention in the Middle East. This provided the Soviets with a green light to send in their military to crush the Hungarian Freedom Fight on November 4, 1956.

Between October 23 and November 4, Hungarian-Americans actually believed that some sort of intervention would be possible from the West. Some Radio Free Europe broadcasts encouraged the Freedom Fighters to hold out until paratroopers could arrive from the "West." I know that in New York City at the St. Emeric Club on 81st street, some former Hungarian Army officers set up a recruitment center for people to sign up if they would be willing to serve in some units that might be sent to Hungary. As a sixteen-year-old idealist, I put my name on the dotted line with about eighty other volunteers. I still do not know who was behind this recruitment drive (CIA?), but we were never called up for service. (However, at the time it was a serious effort, perhaps part of a contingency plan, because the recruiters checked our physical condition and our ability to speak Hungarian.) At any rate, the 1956 experiences became seered into our psyche and we felt that our Hungarian identity was not something that we would want to, or could, easily abandon.

In November and December of 1956 our activism changed to refugee assistance. Even official U.S. Government circles took the lead in helping to establish refugee centers near Vienna, Austria. Vice President Richard Nixon visited some of these refugees and promised them assistance to emigrate to the United States. Of the roughly 200,000 people who fled Hungary at this time, about 35,000 were welcomed to the United States. We were extremely proud of these new arrivals to America. They were the Freedom Fighters (or at least some of them) who had put their lives on the line and rose up against great odds to fight Soviet power. In this struggle they had shaken the very foundations of the Communist empire. In their desperate struggle they had revealed the true face of the Soviet empire with reverberations in every communist party as party members left the movement in droves in France, Italy and other Western countries. They also revealed how totally unprepared the West, including the United States, was in the face of dramatic change in the East.

We Hungarian-Americans also felt that we had come up short and not been able to provide our fellow Hungarians with the kind of tangible support that would assist their drive to national independence. So we did our best on this side of the Atlantic to welcome and assist the 1956 Freedom Fighters in their changed status as refugees. I remember how our New York area scout troops went to Camp Kilmer, the army base in New Jersey, which had been transformed into the reception center for the refugees. We distributed toys, sweets and clothing to the newly arrived. We also provided a program with Christmas carols and Hungarian folk songs to make the transition easier for the residents of the camp. Finally, the older volunteers from the scout troops assisted with translating and filling out forms and providing information about employment opportunities or contacts with Hungarian-American communities throughout the United States.

Back to High School and Political Activism

For all of us it was difficult to go back to the hum-drum activities of our schools or jobs. By this time I attended Long Island City High School near the Queensboro bridge. But my heart was not in my studies and I was at best only an average high school student. Had my sister Narcissza, not prodded me on certain critical occasions I might have veered far from my school studies. In fact she intervened in my educational life a number times and helped me to become the college professor that I became. Not only did she help me understand the math assignments that I feared and avoided, but she actually visited Long Island City High School to help determine the route that my educational career would take. My school adviser was Mr. Warrenoff, a Social Studies teacher who disliked me very much. We had run-ins over his interpretation of both European and American history and he was not used to being challenged by a fifteen-year-old high school student. If I remember correctly, it was in our sophomore year that we had to firm up our choice of studies, whether we would be on the "academic," "vocational," or "general" education track. He said that since my math grades were not very good ("C" and "B") he recommended that I follow the "general education" track. This meant that I would not have to worry about going to college, that is I could pursue a career in "boxing" or other professional sports. At the time, I almost felt good about this decision, until I shared it with my family. Narcissza immediately made an appointment with Warrenoff, and because of her "meddling," I was put on an academic track which led to preparation for college studies. Thank you Ciszka, for being my "tough love" sister!

 I had other confrontations at L.I.C. High School that were memorable for me personally, but I will not dwell on most of these. My teachers, including

Mr. Irwing, Ms. Glasser and Mr. Cohn probably remembered these long after I graduated in 1958. Here I will only discuss my Trianon Report in Ms. Glasser's class. She had given us the assignment that we should prepare a written report on an issue that we had strong feelings about. We should be prepared to present these to our class in a 15–20 minute oral report as well. I spent a great deal of time on the Treaty of Trianon and its impact on the future of East Central Europe. I consulted some of the best sources on this question and prepared a report that many university students would be proud of. I poured my heart and soul into this analysis, prepared maps and tables to back up my major points. While the facts were all included I also wrapped these with my emotional commitments. When I presented the findings, my classmates were unprepared to absorb all that I wanted to impart. They could not imagine why I spoke with so much emotion about an issue that they knew nothing about. And the twenty minutes were not enough to provide the background to the injustice that I wanted to share with them. This failure was a great learning experience for me. While Ms. Glasser gave me an "A" for preparation, she let me know in no uncertain terms that I was not able to do it justice in the time alloted, and I had not separated my opinions from the facts. This was worth only a "C."

Aside from my school work, class assignments and lessons, I did not participate in extracurricular activities at L.I.C. High School. These belonged to my second, or week-end life, which had become my scout troop and the St. Emeric Club on 81st Street. Now with a new infusion of 1956-er Hungarians we tried to integrate them into our established activities. We had less success in involving them in our scout troop activities and more success with participation in the St. Emeric soccer team and the "Hungaria Rapsody" folk dance group established by Mária Molnár and Naca (Mrs. Joseph Sagan). Since I was a good athlete I participated in most of these activities besides the scouts. But around this time I dropped out of the soccer team and began to be active in the boxing program established by István Verseghy at the club. It was also at this time in early 1957 that our Scout troop leader, Zoltán Vasvári, got me involved as his English language correspondence secretary in the Hungarian branch of ABN (Anti-Bolshevik Bloc of Nations), a distinctively emigré organization including all the nationalities that had been incorporated into the Soviet empire and its satellites. This activity was able to get me to overcome some of my frustration at not being able to do anything about the continuing oppression in Hungary. With Zolibá and some of his associates, including Károly Andreánszky, I was able to talk about Hungary's options in the Soviet Bloc and also issues of American foreign policy. They too felt that American commitment to the global *status quo* made the liberation of Hungary very unlikely in the forseeable future.

In the meantime what could we do? The young 1956-ers who now joined the debate, saw our role mainly as becoming the voice of oppressed and silenced Hungary. They clustered into an acronym organization called ÉMEFESZ, whose English equivalent would be North American Hungarian University and College Student's Federation. They were in competition with a variety of Freedom Fighters Organizations which received some support from U.S. agencies that funded the Kossuth Club (led by János Horváth) in Mid-Town Manhattan for scholarships and UN lobbying activities. These organizations were in a loose alliance with the Magyar Nemzeti Bizottmány (Hungarian National Council) of the former center-left parties that were forced into exile in 1948–49 by the Mátyás Rákosi Communist power consolidation. In the world of the D.P. Hungarians all of these groups were somewhat suspect and seen as compromised by their previous coalition with the Communists. Overall this meant that on a political level emigrant Hungarians were fragmented into at least three large clusters, with the 1956 and 1947–49-ers in one group, the "old-time" Hungarians of the American Hungarian Federation in another group, and the 1945–47 D.P. Hungarians in the third group. Only the exile scout movement was able to rise above this fragmentation under the leadership of Gábor Bodnár.

Still, as a young activist I was frustrated not only by this fragmentation, but by the seemingly passive stance of the scout movement. After graduating from high school this frustration became even more pronounced since I was only able to find a two-bit factory job as a packer in down-town Manhattan near Canal Street. It was during this time that I began reading political journals and publications of fringe rightist groups. While there were many things that I disagreed with in the publications, for me its appeal was the strident call to action. Unfortunately, it gave me a false self-confidence that led me to think that action of any sort was to be preferred to inaction. Thus, I began to look for opportunities to test my ability to challenge the *status quo*. Just one example was my effort to sabotage the showing of a pro-communist film glorifying Communist China under Mao. The projection was to take place in a movie theatre near 47th street on Broadway. I bought a ticket and went to the back of the theatre and sat in the gallery until the film started and the audience was settled in. Since there was no-one else in the gallery, I quietly unwound the fire-hose from the staircase and wedged its snout between two seats aiming it high at the screen. Then I turned on the water and ran down the back stairs. I heard the screams just as I walked out the door to lose myself in the crowd on Broadway. In retrospect childish perhaps, but it was action and at the time it felt good.

This and other minor acts of sabotage against the world "communist conspiracy" increased my confidence in my ability to fight the bastards who oppressed my people. Then in 1959 a major opportunity offered itself for my activism. As part of the *detente* opening toward the Soviet Union an exchange of exhibitions was agreed to between the USA and the USSR. The Moscow exhibit became famous because it put Richard Nixon in the spotlight in his "kitchen debate" with Nikita Khrushcsov. The return Soviet exhibit was to be housed in the brand new New York Coliseum exhibition center facing Columbus Circle. This became the scene for my next confrontation with the Russian bear. However, because I wrote about this in another context earlier, I will hereby simply quote that summary, albeit in somewhat abreviated form:

Rope Burn at the New York Coliseum[9]

When the police (NYPD) and ambulance picked me up behind the New York Coliseum my mind was still a blur. A dull pain gripped my back where I had tied the end of my "escape rope" to my scout belt. But my hands, my fin-

---

9 *The New York Coliseum* was built between 1954–56 and was demolished in 2000 and replaced by the Time Warner Center on Columbus Circle. The Coliseum housed the Soviet Exhibit in 1959. The picture postcard of the Coliseum, on the webpage, still carries the image of the Soviet flag as it hung on its front in 1959. See: https://www.cardcow.com/29632/coliseum-circle-new-york-city/

gers were aflame. As I slid and fell off the back of the Coliseum, I had held on for dear life to the rope. It pealed off the skin from the inside of my palm and my fingers. The pain was intense!

After I hit the ground, just inches from a cement sidewalk and a bench, "the rope" gently pulled me back to a hovering position two-three feet from where I had dented the grass and the flowers. If I blacked out it was only for a few seconds. Instinctively I pulled out my pocket knife and cut myself off from my life-line. Then slowly, on all fours, on my elbows and my knees, I crawled to the back entrance of the closest apartment house that enclosed the garden behind the Coliseum. The crawl seemed like eternity even if the distance was not more than about thirty yards.

At the entrance I summoned all my strength to knock on the glass door with my fists and my knees. As I remember I also let out a few cries for help. The porter, doorman or night watchman, probably a Hispanic on the basis of his accent, asked "how the hell did you get here?"—"Did you try to break in? Who are you?" "I fell off the Coliseum" is all I could answer. "Would you please call an ambulance and the cops?" In disbelief he left me on the back steps and turned to call the police. The ambulance and police arrived almost at the same time.

The two cops asked how I had gotten into the enclosed space behind the Coliseum and the apartment buildings. Without asking for my rights, I told them that I had tried to cut down the Soviet flag facing Columbus Circle. Then, when this failed, I tried to leave the roof of the Coliseum without being detected by the police. On the Columbus Circle side the police guarded the flag all along the front. So I chose to let myself down on the back wall in relative darkness. "If you check the back wall, you'll find my escape rope hanging there from the roof." One of the two went to check out my story and came back just as the ambulance took me to Roosevelt Hospital "around the corner."

In the emergency room as the orderlies were examining me, taking X-rays of my back and inserting a catherer to check my urine, the cops were held at bay for a few minutes by the nurses bandaging my hands. But after these preliminaries, they returned to the questioning. In the meantime as my pants were removed for the catherization, my pocket knife and razor blade collection fell to the floor. " What are these for?" one of them asked. "These were my tools to remove the Soviet flag!" "OK—tell us what you were up to!?"

I told them my name and that I lived in Astoria, Queens. I also asked them to contact my father or my brothers on the phone number in my wallet. (Fortunatelly my mother and sister were out of town on a road trip in Virginia's Blue Ridge mountains, so the shock of my arrest and hospital stay would reach them, in a toned down second wave.) At any rate, I stressed that cutting down the flag was all my idea and that I had no accomplices with whom I carried out the aborted mission. "How did you get to the roof and why?"

Getting to the roof was easy, I just bought a ticket to see the Soviet exhibit on the ground floor. Once I was in, I just strolled around and looked like one of the other visitors interested in Soviet society, agriculture and technology. It was late afternoon when I entered so I did not have to wait long before it was closing time. When they started ushering people out of the hall, I simply hid behind one of the exhibit displays until all was quite and the front door was locked. Then I went to a back door where I had seen service people go in and out, and used that exit to find the staircase that led to the roof.

Your second question is harder to answer. The short answer is that I'm Hungarian and just three years ago the people who put on this exhibit, buchered my people on the streets of Budapest. I really wanted them to know that not everyone has forgotten their brutality. But I miscalculated, I did not realize until too late, that the four-story long flag was attached to the roof by bolts and steel cables and not by ropes. My pocket knife and the razor blades would have been able to cut through the ropes, but the cables and bolts held the flag fast even after four hours of relentless effort on my part. Only my hands suffered, the flag was still in place as the first flikkers of sunlight indicated the arrival of dawn.

I panicked and began to look for a place where I could attach my escape rope. My plans had included it from the beginning, but I did not know that it was not amateur user friendly. Just before I entered the Coliseum, I did have second thoughts for a moment regarding my ability to descend from the top of the exhibit building. As I was walking along Central Park toward Columbus Circle with one of my friends, I even asked him if he had gloves that I could borrow for a few hours. Not knowing what I wanted to use the gloves for, he looked incredulous, what the hell do you need gloves for in August? I avoided answering him and diverted his attention by asking him if I looked fat, whether he thought that I needed to lose weight? He looked at me again in a suspicious way and said: what the hell is your problem András? Just that fucken four stories tall Soviet flag hanging down the front of the Coliseum! Its distracting!

Now that I couldn't cut down the flag, I took off my shirt and began to unwind the parachute rope wound around my body. I was now at the back of the building, looking down into the dark courtyard into which I had to descend. I tied the rope to one of the ventilation ducts close to the edge of the roof and attached the other end to my scout belt around my waist. Then without looking into the abyss again I first lowered the length of the rope into the darkness and then threw my left leg over the wall. This was the point of no return, my weight was now drawing me, over the parapet.

The next few seconds seemed like eternity. Although I held the rope with all my might, it began to slip from my grip. At first I tried to brace my legs against the wall, but the rope continued to slip. It flashed through my mind that I should have knotted the rope. Too late now! So I tried to wind my right leg around the rope. This did not slow the momentum of my descent. By this time I knew that the skin was peeling off my hands. But I also heard myself talking to myself: " HOLD ON! HOLD ON! You are slowing your fall." At this point I knew that nothing could stop my fall! I just yelled: "Isten segíts" (God help me!) not once but three or four times. My mind was racing and I saw my life flashing before me. Then I felt the rope jank my body just as I hit the ground. A dull wave of pain ended the fall. I was still alive.

Reflecting back on this fall from the hospital emergency room, my thoughts were now constantly interrupted by the cops who were trying to fill out their crime report and the doctors who were attempting to assess the extent of the damage to my backbone and my spinal column. The doctor in charge, told me that it did not look like I had damaged my spinal cord, since I had not lost feeling in my legs. However, since I had fracktured my disks in two places, they would put me in a rotating, restraining bed which would keep me from moving my backbone until the fracktures healed. This was like putting my body into a body-cast without a body-cast, but with two open sides. About every two hours, nurses would strap me in and rotate the bed, so that I would not remain in the same position too long, two hours face down, three or four hours face up. This was to insure that blood circulated to all parts of my body.

I was to be confined in this helpless and humiliating position for the next three weeks and then swiched to a regular hospital bed for the remainder of my stay at Roosevelt Hospital. This stay was anything but dull! Since I was technically a prisoner of the NYPD, there was a police officer on constant watch outside my hospital room. They frequently came into the room to talk. From them I learned a great deal about police work and they in turn learned a lot about Hungary and why the Hungarian uprising took place in 1956. They also were the ones who informed me that another Hungarian demonstration was successful just before the upcoming Krushchev visit. A group of Hungarians led by István Serényi climbed up onto the Statue of Liberty and blindfolded her so she could not be part of the shame of the upcoming visit of the butcher of Budapest.

This "seminar" in law enforcement and recent Hungarian history came to an end with the addition of another patient to my hospital room. He too was a prisoner. However, he was the real MacCoy, he had been shot in the upper leg just as he was attempting to break into someone's apartment from a fire-escape. The shooter was a neighbor who used a 357 magnum hunting rifle with a hollow-point bullet that had devastating bone-shattering results. The poor would-be burgler was encased in a large plaster cast that covered him from neck to knee. His immobility was linked to weights that kept his leg raised above his torso.

The physical limitations of both of us were overcome by extensive background stories that we shared about ourselves and with increased mobility by the third week the nurses moved our beds closer to each other so that we could play chess. He was a master of this game and enjoyed the game even when he faced a weak player. I certainly was no match for him. Of the forty or fifty games we played, with one exception, he defeated me at every turn. It was frustrating but it killed the boredom of our hospital stay. After about four weeks he moved to another room, since his lawyer came in and paid bail until he would be well enough to go to court. For me the police continued to stand guard outside my door. (I did not realize it at that time, but because I was a prisoner of New York law enforcement, the city covered my stay at the hospital.)

The constant police presence, kept my visitor list down to a minimum. In theory only family members were to visit me. In fact, I had a number of visitors who were not family, but who pretended to be. Three were girls from our "Hungaria" dance group.

In addition to the dance group visitors I had a number of other visitors as well. These were people less able to claim family relations, so they pretended to be men of the cloth, that is one was a Lutheran minister, while the other claimed some affiliation with the Calvinist Synod. Both really visited me for "political" reasons. The former to award me with a medal for my "heroism," the other to involve me in the future activities of a Hungarian Emigré group affiliated with the Hungarian National Council. I accepted the medal, but I did not commit myself to any future political activism.

From my family, my most frequent visitor was my sister Ciszka. She visited me on a regular basis and always brought me reading materials. These were mainly history and literature textbooks that she had used at Elmhurst College. Her hidden agenda was to get me hooked on reading some of these books so that I would re-think my commitments and want to attend college. Her glowing presentations of Elmhurst College would have made the admissions people proud. My concern with college, however, was that I had very little confidence about my math and science skills. On the other hand, the scars on my palms and fingers reminded me that perhaps I should consider other options. And I had plenty of time to think about these different life careers.

My idealistic and romantic self-perceptions received a rude awakening with the fall. The tingling reminder of the rope burn and confinement in a hospital bed with the humiliation of dependence on nurses to assist my elementary bodily functions brought home the fact that I was not Schwarzenegger. My subsequent fate and experience with the American legal system also helped me reach the conclusion that the **other** path had a greater prospect for survival both in the short term and in the long run. Thus, at this juncture my academic career was charted for me by my sister's persistent lobbying and the trauma of my rope burn. Having read this remembrance **YOU** may avoid the rope burn and go directly to college!"

Changing Direction

The 1956–1959 time period was a turning point in the lives of all of us. My sister had gone off to Elmhurst College at the behest of Professor August Molnár, who had established a Hungarian studies center at that institution. The influx of many 1956-er young men (and a few women) was ideal for starting such a program. Ciszka became a chemistry major at Elmhurst and her subsequent career was defined by this choice. While at Elmhurst she established life-long friendships with the Zoltáni family in Evanston and many other Chicago area Hungarians of her generation, including Lajos Jókay, József Kovács and Mihály Csíkszentmihályi.

After my eight weeks in the hospital, my case came up for trial in New York City. I was charged with illegal entry. Senator Clifford P. Case of New Jersey also put in a good word for me after his Hungarian-American constituents lobbied on my behalf. Finally, my lawyer (who defended me on a pro bono basis) appealed to the sympathy of the judge contending that the "poor boy had suffered enough." The judge agreed, but put me on six months probation, during which I had to write weekly reports to a probation officer. For practical purposes my case was dismissed. This cleared the way for my application to Elmhurst College for the Spring semester of 1960.

Before I started my college career, however, I made one more attempt to revive my ambition to be part of Hungary's liberation from János Kádár's dictatorship. Our scout leader, Zoltán Vasvári, of Troop #7, had a falling out with Gábor Bodnár and the central leadership of the exile Hungarian Scout Association. Vasvári would have liked to incorporate into the scout program some more active political and military training materials. There he encountered a stonewall of resistance. So Vasvári decided to organize a para-military organization called the "Shooters."[10] My brother Pál and I were his first recruits. Soon we recruited others, mainly in New Jersey in towns like Passaic, Garfield, Clifton and Newark, but also some from the Philadelphia, PA area,

---

10 ***Shooters*** is the literal translation of "lövészek." It was a para-military organization founded by Zoltán Vasvári in 1959. It included ca. 100 young Hungarian-Americans and remained active to about 1989. During its first decade it was mainly a para-military organization, but afterwards became a social-cultural organization for young Hungarian-Americans.

Emblem on uniforms of the "Shooters" with the American Liberty Bell embedded with the crowned Hungarian Crest between the Cross and the Sword

the Danbury, CT area and the Cleveland and Youngstown, OH areas. It remained a relatively limited organization in numbers, with about 80–100 active members in its prime. However, it was a very committed organization. Vasvári's farm in Pennsylvania, in the beautiful Susquehanna river valley, was our base of operations. There we had target practice sessions, occasional paratroop jumps and nightime and daylight military exercises of various sorts. Many young 1956-ers who had not joined the scouts in exile became "Shooters." In terms of their background a large proportion were employed in housing construction. Since I began my studies at Elmhurst College in Illinois, I participated only in the summer activities of the organization and after I continued with my graduate studies in 1963 at LSU in Louisiana the geographic distance made it impossible to continue as an active member. Some fifty-eight years later Réka Pigniczky and Andrea Lauer had been interviewing Hungarians for some years, who had to leave the country right after the Revolution of 1956 or at the end of World War II. In this "Memory Project" they videotaped more than a hundred individuals, including some people who remembered the activities of a group called "Lövészek"(Shooters). This intrigued both interviewers, and they collected more and more memories about this

Showing of the Réka Pigniczky and Andrea Lauer "Shooters" documentary at the Urania Theatre in Budapest, November, 2017. l. to r. András, Katalin Szilágyi-Ovaitt, Enikő Vasvári-Warren and Dr. László Varjú

group. The story that emerged, centered around Zoltán Vasvári, who was the founder of the New York City Hungarian Scout Troop #7 in 1951. Then after 1959, Vasvári broke with the Scouts and established a para-military organization of young men and women to train them to be prepered in case 1956 was repeated in the future. As a follow-up to these interviews, Réka and Andrea located those individuals who had been part of the "Shooters" and planned to do a short documentary film on this Cold War phenomenon. Since my brother Paul and I were both members of this group we were also invited to a reunion of the "Lövészek," at the former Vasvári Farm, near Towanda, PA on Labor Day week-end in 2016. This reunion, with re-enactments, recollections, old photos, and some old film strips, became the basis of the documentary on "Cold Warriors/Shooters" which is now also on YouTube, but which was previewed in a documentary film festival near Cleveland and also in Budapest at the "Uránia" theatre in November, 2017. Those of you interested in an idealistic snippet of Hungarian-American history, can find this at the following internet site: Vimeo.com/215506258 and the code word "Loveszek"

The Alternative Career Path

Academic studies had a sobering effect on my world outlook. Initially I was a very humble student because I was not sure that I was really meant for college. Even my arrival and my physical appearance on campus reflected this uncertainty. I had one winter overcoat which I had inherited from my father and other hand-me-downs constituted my wardrobe, including one pair of dress shoes and one pair of sneakers. All of these fit into the Marine Corps duffel bag that I inherited from my brother Tamás. From New York City I took a Trailway bus to Chicago where Ciszka and Mihály Csíkszentmihályi were waiting for me. The next day Mihály drove me to Elmhurst where I registered for my courses at the college and received lodging in the barracks near the Gymnasium. My roommate became Walter Bellemore a staunch Republican from Connecticut. During that first semester I took general education courses and ended with three "B," and two "C" grades. But most important I learned to study effectively before examinations and became part of the janitorial staff in the college library. The revenue from this "student work study" position enabled me to make it on a dollar a day during that first semester. Government student loans and summer earnings let me return to Elmhurst in 1960–61, and supplemental scholarships helped me to continue my studies until graduation with high honors as a history major in 1963.

By the time I arrived at Elmhurst, the Hungarian Studies center had moved to New Brunswick, NJ and Rutgers University. Most of the Hungarian students who had followed Professor August Molnár to Elmhurst, had graduated by this time. The Egyed sisters, Csilla Makay and Steve Danko were there to the end of my first academic year, but only Steve and I remained until 1963. This meant that my non-curricular activities were less Hungarian related and more closely linked to sports and to the ongoing political debates on campus.

Initially I planned to paricipate in the "Golden Gloves" competitions in Chicago. Wally Bellemore became my agent/coach in this undertaking. I entered the competition as an unattached boxer. For my training I utilized the basement of Irion Hall which was at the same time the laundry room for the dormitory. There I jump-roped for hours and shadow boxed when the place was available. I was confident that my previous training with István Verseghy at the St. Emeric club would now start paying off. When the big day came and we went to ring-side on Chicago's south side, I realized that the competition would be tough. Most of the entering boxers had a club affiliation like the CYO which gave them an edge in both training facilities and trained professional coaches. Still, when it was my turn to enter the ring, there was no hesitation on my part and the adrenalin rush combined with the cheers in the stadium gave me an excellent first round. But dreams of becoming a second László Papp[11] or Rocky Marciano can be shattered with one lucky or one well aimed punch. Robert King – I still remember his name – delivered such a right hook to my temporarily unguarded jaw. The Referee imagined that my legs wobbled and my eyes became glazed. He passed his hand before my eyes and said that the contest was over and Wally threw in the towel from our corner. It was over! Thank you Robert King for ending my boxing career.

Now I turned to college wrestling as an Elmhurst College Bluejay. The daily training sessions and instruction from Coach Langhorst led to success in the long run. Although my first year on the team was less than sensational, with three wins and three losses, my subsequent endeavors on the mat led to winning seasons and in my senior year I was even voted "most valuable" wrestler by my teammates, including our team captain, Jim Leamon. At any rate, the personal and individually focused confrontation that is part of wrestling, leads to satisfaction that can rarely be attained in team sports.

The personal challenge was also present in the political debates that divided our student body on the issues separating college Democrats and Republicans and Liberals and Conservatives. From a socio-economic perspective I should have automatically been a Democrat rather than a Republican. But my family background and my D.P. status made me into an automatic rock-bottom Republican. At that time I could not imagine affiliating with the party that had any responsibility for either Trianon or Yalta. In the debates American involvement in Vietnam was a central issue at this time and I always represented the strong anti-Communist position. I was a good debater and this

---

11 *László Papp* was the best-known and most successful Hungarian boxer, who had won three Olympic gold medals in his weight class.

led to some recognition from many of my fellow students, particularly the "jock" Conservatives as opposed to the "pre-theo" Liberals. This also led to the creating of our own organization on campus, called "The Mossback Society" with close affiliation to the Young Americans for Freedom, which at that time was active nationally. At the same time, my political stance was never really challenged by any of my instructors although I did actively present my position on issues in the student newspaper "The Elm Bark." Neither Professor Royal J. Schmidt, nor Dr. Rudolf G. Schade ever intimated their displeasure about my perspectives, even when I knew that some of my views clashed with what I heard from them in class. It did not show up in their grading either and both provided me with outstanding recommendations when I applied for graduate studies at Louisiana State University.

In my family's life other significant changes also took place during my college years. Our father, vitéz Antal Ludányi died during the summer of 1961 after a long struggle with stomach and pancreatic cancer. His death left a void in our lives, he had always been the link in our family to tradition and historical Hungary. He was a devout Catholic and had a strong influence on our values and religious lives. Almost as a symbolic contrast, our sister, Narcissza, left the family just one year later via marriage to Howard Manton Layton, with whom she had been in contact through the Coulter Company. All four of us brothers took her to the alter before Reformed Minister Harsányi in Cartaret, New Jersey. (Secretly, I had hoped that she would marry one of the men she had met while at Elmhurst, so that the family's Hungarian links would be re-inforced. Well this was not to be, but life must go on!) Ciszka and Howard then established their own corporation called Interlab Inc., which produced ultrasonic cleaning machines and provided many of our family members with employment.

My Graduate Studies in Louisiana

My encounter with America at the social and academic level next moved South to Baton Rouge, Louisiana, in September 1963, where I received a three-year NDEA Fellowship in the Department of Government at Louisiana State University. My graduate studies advisor was Professor Peter Fliess a specialist in International Law and Politics. The next five years were some of my most rewarding years in concentrated intellectual development. At the same time the atmosphere and setting of LSU's campus was ideal for learning more about the variety and richness of American civilization. It was my good fortune to be present in this part of the country after having already inbibed in the nature of America in the Illinois Mid-West, the New York, New Jersey and Pennsylvania Atlantic East and the Virginia "Old Dominion" South. Now I had the chance to see, feel, and taste the Cajun[12] Louisiana variety of the deep South.

In that first year at LSU I focused just on my studies because the graduate courses demanded much more time and more academic interaction with my fellow graduate students and the faculty of our department. Writing reports, thought essays and term papers for the courses kept me on a constant treadmill. After attending my classes, I moved into the Main Library on a daily basis to read and write. Initially I had an open carrel where I collected my research materials and where I spent most of my time until closing time, which was usually midnight. In that time period I had few friends, since I was so focused on my studies.

During that first year my residence hall was the North Stadium, a mainly undergraduate housing unit built into the side of the stadium where the LSU Bengal Tigers met and defeated their opponents on a regular basis on Saturdays during football season. During my stay at the stadium, and even after I moved to better housing facilities, I attended only one of their games during the five years that I was physically on the campus of LSU. I'm not proud of this record, but I mention it only to document how focused I was on my studies. My two Cajun roommates thought I was particularly weird, and decided to try to shake me out of my scholarly obsession during Mardi Gras, by setting me up with a date for the festivities in New Orleans. It was my first Mardi Gras in New Orleans and a fascinating opportunity to be in a setting that provides for many an escape from their mundane existence. For me the

---

12 *Cajun* was/is the Louisianan North American subcultural variety of the French language and civilization derived from the original French colonial settlers who established New Orleans and other settlements in the southern part of the state.

date became a dead-end when I realized that she thought that Hungary and Honduras were both located somewhere in South America where they speak Spanish.

Aside from Mardi Gras, during that first year, my only escape from the library was to join Cuban and Central American students in ad hoc soccer games on the big open field next to the stadium. In my second year at LSU these opportunities continued but less frequently, because seminar presentations and preparation for my German language proficiency examination took more of my time. The presentations went well, but my German lapsed. To remedy the situation I applied for a Shell Scholarship to the Salzburg Summer German language school in Austria near Schloss Klesheim. These weeks of concentrated language study helped establish my German language proficiency. It also gave me an opportunity to re-visit Hochburg and other locations in Upper Austria where our family had spent time as D.P. refugees. The visits were made particularly enjoyable because two attractive German language teachers from Cleveland (who were Hungarian-Americans) had a sports car with which we could visit the more interesting sites between Linz, Salzburg and Munich.

My third year at LSU provided yet another opportunity to focus my interest back on East Central Europe. I took two courses from George Putnam on Russian political thought and Soviet Politics. At the same time I got involved in a study group that was planning a trip to Belgrade in Yugoslavia for a six-week language immersion program in Serbo-Croatian. This was a group Fulbright/IREX undertaking in which upper class and graduate students could participate. Nine students, four women and five men and George Putnam as group leader made up the group. We were all to fly to Munich from New York City and then continue the trip together as a group on the Orient Express via Salzburg, Llubjana, and Zagreb to Belgrade.

A bad omen for me personally was that at the end of May, I think it was Memorial week-end, I went out to the Vasvári farm for a Shooters get-together and practice session. There we organized an impromptu soccer game between target practice sessions. On the uneven field there was a depression that I did not see as I was chasing the ball toward the goal. I stepped into it and immediately I heard the splintering of glass. A large Gallo wine bottle had been stashed there by a Shooter after a drinking spree. This bottle now cut into my foot right above my ankle and almost severed my tendon. The loss of blood was minimal, but the pain was intense. Immediately what flashed through my mind was that this would keep me from leaving for Yugoslavia two weeks from now. My Shooter friends, inluding my brother Pál, picked me up and carried me to a car which they drove to the closest doctor's office in Towanda. This young doctor then gave me some chewing gum, to keep me busy while he sutured the wound above my ankle. The gum was to act as my pain reliever while he did the sewing. I could again stand and walk, but with a limp. So I did make it to Belgrade, but in slippers.

When we arrived at the Belgrade train station there was no-one waiting for us. Our advisor was to arrive later, so we had to fend for ourselves. Fortunately we had the name of the "Studenski Dom" where we were to be housed. After exchanging dollars for *dinars*, we were able to negotiate with three taxi drivers the fare for our ride and baggages to the dormitory. There we encountered our first culture shock upon arrival. Most of us needed to use a restroom, since we had been squeemish to use the facilities at the railroad station. The arrangements at the dormitory were not much better. For the men in our group the transition went smoothly, but for the women it was a traumatic experience to hover over an opening in the floor of the toilet enclosure. The next shock was to learn that warm water for showers was available only on Wednesdays and that we had to stand in line to wait for our turn to shower. (Since we had to wait in line, we American men had to act as a buffer between our women and the Serb male students who also lined up for their showers, all of us covered only with towels as we waited our turn in front of four shower stalls with plastic shower curtains.) We all survived!

The academic program was not strenuous, it was linked to a light load of four two-hour sessions of Serbo-Croation classroom language instruction weekly. There were no lab sessions to practice what we learned from our textbooks. We also had a one-hour history and culture class three times a week, that dealt with the history of the South Slavs and their neighbors. This was supplemented by two social get-togethers at the Embassy of the United States, where we met students from other American institutions that sent students to study in Yugoslavia. United States foreign policy at this time was very active in supporting Tito, because since the split with Stalin's USSR in 1948 the idea of "national communism" was seen as the way to weaken the Soviet Bloc. Our own LSU exchange to Yugoslavia was part and parcel of this policy.

Our afternoons within the program were mostly free unless we were invited to some ad hoc program at the university. Therefore I spent a great deal of time in a library that provided me with access to the publications of the Hungarian population in the Vojvodina region of the country. On weekends we could also travel to different parts of Yugoslavia. I always used this opportunity to visit Novi Sad (Újvidék) or Subotica (Szabadka) in Vojvodina. Usually I was the guide or chaperone to the women in our group in at least two of these tours. These weekends also enabled me to make contact with members of the Hungarian minority community. It also provided opportunities to interact with the Serb and Croat majority populations in the stores, restaurants and churches. On one of these trips to Novi Sad the most recent edition of *Borba* was waved by one of my fellow travelers on the bus. An excited conversation was taking place among the passengers about the breaking news that had something to do with Rankovic who was in charge of the security police in the country. The Serb widow who was my traveling companion at this time, told me that Rankovic had just been removed from office by Josip Broz Tito because Rankovic had Tito's office bugged by the security police. This was the big event in Yugoslavia during the summer of 1966. The tension was present in all parts of society, including in the University, the Studenski Dom, and in the restaurants we frequented.

Bicycle Ride Through Vojvodina

For me these contacts became important during the end of our stay in Yugoslavia. George Putnam had added ten days to our itinerary before our flight would take us back to New York City. Each of us could spend this time anywhere in Europe. I opted to spend that time in Vojvodina. This stay, these extra ten days, provided me with an ideal opportunity to do field work in Vojvodina. I had several important contacts: one for Novi Sad, one for Subotica, one for Rusko Selo (Torontáloroszi/Kis Orosz) in the Banat, one in Telecka (Telecska) in Bácska, and still another one in Feketic (Feketics) also in the Bácska. These five individuals became important points on the map, stopping places for me as I traveled on my bicycle that I purchased in Subotica. It was a strong and heavy bike, made to survive on the rugged uneven country roads that connected the Hungarian settlements in the northern sections of the Vojvodina.

Before I purchased this bike, my first visit was to my Novi Sad contact. She was the widow of a Serbian economist and consequently was able to have me introduced to the anthropology Professor at the University of Novi Sad who could get me to meet a number of people in Hungarian related studies. In fact a Hungarian Language and Literature Department had just been established here in 1959 and I was hoping to get some insider information on its role in the life of local Hungarians. However, because this took place in office settings, the conversations remained very formal and little substantive information could be collected. Still the Novi Sad visit was useful and pleasant because the following dinner and stay at the "Park Hotel" provided an opportunity to observe both the positive and negative aspects of inter-ethnic relations. The following day I took an early bus to Subotica, where I purchased my bicycle and a limited amount of food for the first section of my road trip.

From Subotica I was able to make it to Horgoš via Palić by noon, a little border town close to the Vojvodina border with Hungary. There I had a good hearty meal of *pörkölt* (stew) and potatoes with a fresh tomato and onion salad. When I got back on my bike I realized that the saddle was not at all user friendly, and would require some sort of remedy at my next stop. The remedy was a thick sponge that I purchased in a small store in the next town, Kanjiza (Magyarkanizsa). This I fastened to the bike's saddle with a strong masking tape (ducktape was not available at that time and at that store), which turned out to be only a temporary solution, which I had to refasten after every major rest stop. By late afternoon I arrived in Senta (Zenta) on the Tisza river where Eugene of Savoy defeated the Ottoman Turks in 1697. There I stayed for the night at the only hotel on the main square.

In Senta after breakfast I walked around the square and enjoyed the peaceful atmosphere of the town. While I was sitting on a park bench, a man in his early thirties approached me and started a conversation about the history of the place and introduced himself as Rózsa Sándor, the name of the famous Hungarian outlaw of the late 19th century. I asked if he was indeed related to the outlaw and he said that his family claimed such a relationship. After that we spent the time discussing my trip and my intention of getting to know how Hungarians maintained their identity and institutions in Vojvodina. While he did not offer his observations, he did ask me about how I intended to study this question. Since I had only a very limited time in the region, I would simply compile an impressionistic profile of it. In the evenings I would simply note down what I had experienced and observed on that day. Later in the course of my paper research this would add meat to the bones that the readings and formal interviews provided.

I crossed the Tisza on the Senta bridge just a little north of the plains where that fateful battle was fought in 1697. My crossing meant that now I left Backa (Bácska) and would enter the Banat (Bánság) of the historic Kingdom of Hungary. Both of these areas had the richest agricultural soil of the former Kingdom and in turn became the richest agricultual region of the Yugoslavian state established after World War I. While I crossed the bridge a police officer passed me on his motorcycle. At the time I did not think anything of it, but later on I met him and his fellow motorcycle police a number of times as I toured Vojvodina. It also flashed through my mind that the friendly conversation with Rózsa Sándor in Senta was not just coincidental.

In the Banat I had an open invitation to visit the family of Matild Lőrik who I had met after a Roman Catholic church service in Belgrade. We also had dinner together at a rooftop restaurant with a beautiful view of the Danube. I shared with her my plan to travel from settlement to settlement in the northern part of Vojvodina where most of the Hungarians (at that time 506,000) were located. She did not hesitate to invite me to her home in Rusko Selo (Torontáloroszi) located not too far from Kikinda.

Since Kikinda was on my way to Rusko Selo I peddled to the center of this important center of Serb and Hungarian culture in the Banat. There I wanted to see the extent to which the Hungarian language was accepted in public discourse. I made my way to city hall and the main post office. The "gate keeper" at city hall spoke only Serbian and after he ascertained that I was a foreign Hungarian and not a local, he called the janitor to inquire about my concerns. When I asked if there was anyone in the city administration who spoke Hungarian, he smiled wryly and informed me that there were other Hungarians, but only in the janatorial services. Next I went to check out the situation in the main post office. I stopped at the first window and inquired in Hungarian how much it would cost to mail my letter by air mail to the United States. The clerk behind the window scowled and called "Kati" to answer my question. Of the fifteen service windows only one could provide bilingual service, because in that window the clerk was the product of a mixed marriage.

After this frustrating investigation I continued my journey to Rusko Selo. There I had no problem finding the Lőrik house and Matild introduced me to her parents. After a good meal Matild brought out her own bike to give me a tour of the town. I asked her to take me to the town's administrative center so that I could ask the officials a little about the demographic development of the town. As soon as they found out that I was an American student, they asked me in Serbian, with Matild providing the translation, who sent me to collect this information? When I said I was part of a study group arranged between the American Fulbright program and Yugoslav authorities, they said they needed to check out if I had a right to this information. For them this was considered sensitive information because "Bosnyák" street was the new name for "Németh" street. After World War II the deportation of the Swabian Germans, i.e., their "ethnic cleansing" led to their replacement by Bosnian Serbs. This demographic transformation of Rusko Selo was also characteristic of the rest of Vojvodina following the war. Wherever Swabian Germans were deported, their furnished homes were taken over by Serbs who were from Bosnia or central Serbia. In this way the demographic profile of Vojvodina was changed from one-third Hungarian, one-third German and one-third Serb to one-fourth Hungarian and three-fourths South Slavs (mainly Serbs). All this ethnic re-structuring was justified by the "collective guilt" of the Germans and the Hungarians.

After supper I had the opportunity to hear some positive things about Tito and the current policies of Yugoslavia. Matild Lőrik's father said that for them conditions in the Vojvodia were like those in a "little United States." Since Tito allowed for private agriculture on plots up to seventeen hectares,[13] the family's economic existence has become bearable. He also said that on the grade school level instruction was also available in Hungarian in settlements where they constituted a significant proportion of the population.

In the morning, after a good night's rest and a good breakfast I said goodby to Matild and her family. From Rusko Selo I went south toward Bašaid (Basahíd), where I struck a conversation with another biker who was on his way to work on the local collective farm. As we arrived at the farm entrance he invited me in to the canteen located there, to continue the conversation over a beer. His view was that there was more security on the collective farm for his family and he was not going to switch to "the private sector." His Serb team leader also joined the conversation and agreed with that point of view. After finishing our drinks, they told me which roads to take to get back to the Tisza river where I would find a ferry back to Backa (Bácska).

The crossing back to Backa was near Novi Bečej (Törökbecse) via Bečej (Óbecse), where I ate lunch. From there I headed west to Srbobran (Szenttamás) and then north to Feketić (Feketics). There I went to visit the family of the bus driver who I had met when I went north to Subotica from Novi Sad. During this ride I had shared my plans with the bus driver, who on the spot invited me to stay with them for at least one day. He also guided me to the shop in Subotica where I bought my bicycle for the tour. His family (wife and eight-year-old daughter) welcomed me as if I was part of the family. Over supper they shared with me the hard life they had right after the war. "Julianna" (not her real name) avoided deportation by marrying into a Bunyevac-Hungarian family and pretending to be Hungarian rather than Swabian-German. The rest of her family, parents and grandparents, were taken to a collection point/camp near Apatin, where many of the older people perished, and those who survived where simply force-marched to Germany.

The central location of Feketić and the hospitality of my host family, plus a puncture in my front tire determined that I would stay one more day here. After the tire was fixed, I also went to the local police station with "Julianna" who had to renew a license and needed to obtain a stamp from local author-

---

13   *1 hektare* = 2.471 acres

ities to prove that she was indeed a local resident. Observing this local experience with the "bureaucracy" was worth the extra day. The self-importance and arrogance of officials in the granting of this simple stamp was a lesson in itself on how the governing agencies should not behave.

The next day, after breakfast, I thanked my host family by telling them that after I complete my tour I would like to give them my bicycle. We agreed to meet at the Subotica bus station on my last day in Yugoslavia and "Julianna" would be there to pick up the bike. Then I bade farewell to the whole family and headed north to Mali Iđoš (Kishegyes) and Bačka Topola (Topolya). Here I rested in the town square and downed a strong "Turkish coffee" before continuing my tour to Telečka (Telecska). This small town in the center of Bačka was the home of the Kormányos family. I met them in Novi Sad about four weeks earlier as the mother and her daughter Erzsébet tried to get from the daughter's dormitory to the bus station. I saw that they were overwhelmed by the large suitcases that they were carrying and offered to help them to the station. Erzsébet had just completed her studies to be a kindergarten teacher. As we walked to the station I inquired about their destination and was told it was Telečka in central Bačka. I then used this opportunity to tell them about my plans to pass by there at the end of my stay in Belgrade. Again I was fortunate to get invited, this time by the Kormányos family.

After my arrival in Telečka, I asked to be able to use their clothes washer, since the biking, the weather and the dusty roads had transformed me visibly into a homeless person. I was supplied with soap and water for my own clean-up, while my trausers and shirts went into the washing machine and then onto the clothesline. Because it was a beautiful sunny day, my wardrobe was soon ready for the next phase of my tour. However, Erzsébet's mother felt that after supper it would be a good idea if I could meet other young people in the village. Erzsébet and her boyfriend took me to the local bar where I did meet a good cross-section of young villagers. They had many questions about life in the United States, most of which I was able to answer. In the discussion one person asked about the treatment of Black Americans, now Afro-Americans. This was a good opportunity for me to raise the question of inequality among the different national communities in Vojvodina. I said that in my American experience, in New York City, the police force had a proportional representation of Black officers. As opposed to this in my travels in this province I have yet to meet a Hungarian in the uniform of a Yugoslav police officer. The interesting and revealing answer was that among Hungarians there is no interest in joining the police. In fact, a Hungarian in such a position is looked on with suspicion by fellow Hungarians.

The very next day I had some verification of these observations. I had indicated interest in local access to Hungarian cultural products. To this end Erzsébet took me to the village library. This one room establishment, had mainly Serb and Croatian books on the shelves, and mainly fluff literature represented in the Hungarian language. (At that time Telečka's population was over 90% Hungarian.) I did not have a chance to ask questions regarding this matter, because a young Serb police officer entered the building and was present while I was there. Coincidental? Perhaps.

After thanking the Kormányos family for all their help I headed west toward Sombor (Zombor). Here I did not have any personal contacts so I just biked to the center of town and treated myself to a strong Turkish coffee. After noting the lack of Hungarian language signs and not meeting any Hungarian speaking people in the main square, I continued my tour toward Bajmok. On the way, I met another biker heading in the same direction. After exchanging greetings, I realized that he spoke Hungarian fluently. Riding side by side we conversed about things in general, including the weather, which at that point was threatening rain. For some time we continued at the same casual speed, when we were passed by a motorcycle policeman, who stopped ahead of us and waited until we cought up with him. He was the first policeman whose reaction was definitely not friendly. He said I was not supposed to ride next to another biker, because that would hinder traffic. I looked both ways and there was no other vehicle on the road besides his motor bike and our two bicycles. But I followed the instructions as translated for me and got in line like a little duck following the other biker. Obviously he must have had a bad day and our Hungarian communications only added to this. So he had to show us who was boss in this part of the world.

In Bajmok we parted company and I continued my way toward Subotica. However, at the edge of Bajmok I rested my bike against a tree and sat down to rest my aching muscles. A mother and her teenage daughter were passing that way and talking in Hungarian. When I saw they were heading toward a house nearby, I asked them for water and engaged them in conversation. At first they hesitated to speak to this stranger, but my friendly American smile won them over. They did not invite me into their yard, but the daughter brought me a tin cup filled with cool water. In the meantime the mother responded to my question as to how many Hungarians were part of Bajmok's population. She said that up to the end of W.W. II, there were many more then at present. They even had some Hungarian Csángó[14] families who had been transplanted from Moldavia. But most of these fled north to Hungary after the war. I thanked them for the water and continued on my way north-east.

By the time I arrived in Subotica it was late afternoon. I went directly to the hotel where I had spent a night during the previous week when I began my tour. I had left my belongings in storage at that hotel and had reserved a room there for today. After I put my bicycle in safe storage and refreshed myself at the hotel, I walked to the Catholic Church where I could meet Father "János" (not his real name), who had been recommended to me by Matild from Rusko Selo. Father "János" had been a young ten-year-old son of the local barber in Mol (Mohol) at the time of the retribution atrocities against the Hungarians in late 1944 and early 1945. His father was given the task of shaving the heads of all the village Hungarians who had been accused of collaborating with the Hungarian occupation authorities during the war. As a young boy he had to assist his father in sweeping the hair out of the barber shop after each person was shaved. The shaved prisoners (including the former mayor, parish priest, and the prominent people in the community) with hands tied behind them, were taken by Serb Partizans to a location at the town's edge. They were never seen again. But villagers claimed that many had to dig their own graves into which they were shot. This recollection is in line with the

---

14 **Csángó** is the designation of the Hungarian subculture that has its settlements furthest East, on the other side of the Carpathian mountains, mainly on the Eastern slopes in the Moldavian region of Romania. However, as a consequence of population exchange efforts some of the Csángós were re-settled in Southern Transylvania (near Déva) preceding World War I, while the Székely Csángós from Bukovina were re-settled in Bácska during World War II. The latter became refugees in Hungary when the Serbs regained control of Bácska at the end of the war. For more details see my study: "Csángó Denationalization: Romania's Self-Fulfilling Prophecy?" in *Transylvania Today: Diversity at Risk* ed. Csaba K. Zoltáni (Budapest: Osiris, 2013), 159–175.

documented history of these massacres by Márton Matuska.[15] After this interview I promised not to reveal where I heard this information. I went back to my hotel where I had a sleepless night.

The next morning, as I had promised, I took my bicycle to the Subotica bus station. "Julianna" had already arrived with an early bus from Feketic. I apologized for not giving the bike a thorough cleaning before the hand-over. She said the bike barely looked used. "Julianna" then talked to the bus driver of the next bus to Novi Sad and he put the bike in the baggage space under the bus. There I said good-bye to my bike and wished the best for "Julianna" and her family. I waved as the bus rolled out of the station and went back to my hotel room, where I packed my own bag for the train ride to Munich, West Germany. However, since my train would be leaving only in the evening I had time to visit László Rehák, the major authority on the Hungarian community in Yugoslavia. I purposely left my visit to the Reháks for the end of my stay in the country, to draw less attention to my planned bike tour.

Meeting László Rehák was fortuitous for a number of reasons. First of all, because he did not know me and I had no documented scholarly background. Secondly, because I called him on my last day in Subotica. Thirdly, because he happened to be at home nursing a cold. My call to the Rehák residence was also a gamble because why would a well-known scholar, a Vice President of the Vojvodina governing Council, and a ranking member of the Yugoslav League of Communists waste his time on a lowly graduate student from the United States? But my telephone call—taken by his wife, the gate keeper—must have been convincing enough and I was invited into their home. László Rehák talked about his own role in representing the interests of Hungarians at the federal as well as the regional level in Vojvodina. He also mentioned his own study that I could consult on other issues that relate to Hungarians in Yugoslavia. His wife Rózsa also filled in information about their family life, including that László's first wife was Serbian and that this meant that teaching their daughter Hungarian was not an automatic process. (Being

---

15 Matuska, Márton. *A megtorlás napjai* (Days of Retribution) Novi Sad: Forum, 1991. Provided the first systematic expose of the massacres of Hungarians carried out by the Partizans during 1944–45. This was followed two years later by Tibor Cseres, *Titoist Atrocities in Vojvodina 1944–1945*. Buffalo, NY: Hunyadi Publishing, 1993.

aware that Rankovic had even bugged Tito's office, the conversation in the Rehák house skirted the more sensitive problems of inter-ethnic relations.) I thanked the Rehák's for their kind invitation and wished László a fast recovery to good health. After saying good-bye I hurried back to the hotel, picked up my luggage and went to the railroad station to catch my train.

From Subotica the first leg of my trip was to Vinkovci (Vinkovác) in Croatia where I had to change trains, getting on the Orient Express toward Zagreb. While waiting for my connecting train I struck up a conversation with a young Hungarian women who was on her way to Osijek (Eszék) a remnant Hungarian settlement in Croatia. She pointed out that the declining Hungarian population in Croatia was due to intermarriage which was more widespread in Croatia than in Serbia. As I got on my train toward Zagreb my mind was spinning with all the accumulated information that I had gathered during my Yugoslav summer. Unfortunatelly in Zagreb I did not have enough time to get off the train to do even a fast tour of the city, the center of Croatian political and cultural life.

From here, through Llubjana to Salzburg and Munich I dozed occasionally, but most of the time I re-played the events of the past seven weeks in my mind. Since darkness had already enveloped the countryside I could not enjoy the natural beauty of Slovenia, Austria and the south of Bavaria. Furthermore our train arrived in Munich at 3:00 a.m. and I had nowhere to go for the night, because the family I promised to visit in the city was still asleep. The German police at that time were very hard-nosed about loitering in public places and they refused to let anyone sleep on the benches in the railroad station. So for the next three hours until the train schedules resumed, I walked the streets as if I was a homeless person. Finally at 6:00 a.m. I called the Jenő Andreánszky family (their son Károly had given me their phone number). They welcomed me in spite of the ungodly hour. After putting myself in order, the family let me take a long nap before we began our marathon conversations. These related mainly to my experiences in Yugoslavia. It was a very welcome winding down opportunity in the company of two very informed, intelligent and caring individuals.

After twenty-four hours of relaxation I had to be at the airport to meet Professor Putnam and my fellow Belgrade student group. All of us had great stories and experiences to share with each other on our flight back to New York City. There we split up and went in different directions to spend the remainder of August with our families. In September we all went back to our studies at Louisiana State University. For all of us the Belgrade experience became transformative.

Closing the Circle in my Graduate Studies

For me the 1966–67 academic year was particularly important to gain an in-depth understanding of the American political system and its historical evolution. I was consciously in need to constantly compare the reality with the idealized image that was so much a part of my life until this point. Two professors who provided me with the best comparative opportunities were Wayne Shannon and Burl Nogge, the first for American political culture, the second for the evolution of United States foreign policy. Of course I cannot blame either one for any of my misperceptions, but both provided me with thoughtful analyses and valuable sources of information.

The following image is based on a compiled picture that I have constructed on the basis of a great deal of reading, thinking and conversation with fellow graduate students at LSU. The uniqueness of the American experience and its fine contributions to human and world civilization can overwhelm any individual and it leads to a glorification of the past and losing sight of some of its flaws. As I have indicated in the introduction to this American road trip, this essay also includes experiences collected during my ONU teaching as well as my attempts to influence United States foreign policy.

The United States of America is a political system that was born as a reaction to a colonial past, based on the experience of thirteen different colonies with a dominant English language network of communications. (The British Empire had gained control over most of North America after the French and Indian War of 1754–1763.) As I wrote in a brief study for the **Hungarian Review** (May, 2017)[16]: While most of the dominant elements of these

---

16 *See*: "Absent-Minded, Uncoerced and 'Painless': Hungarian Assimilation in the United States," *Hungarian Review*, (May, 2017), 89–99. (sec.17)

colonies spoke English and were from the British Isles, the colonies from the beginning had a very diverse mixture of peoples. It included African slaves, conquered Native Americans, as well as Dutch, French, Spanish and other peoples from the European continent, mainly from the expansionist naval powers of Europe. As the frontier moved westward, the population became ever more diverse as a consequence of the expanding pool of immigrants as well as the acquired populations of the Louisiana Purchase, the incorporation of Florida and Texas, the Southwest and the Pacific Coast and beyond to Alaska and the Hawaiian Islands.

At least two sectors of this diverse population, the African slaves and the conquered Native Americans were not considered to be Americanizable. The Civil War changed that for the Afro-Americans, but not for the Native Americans. Actually, the institution of slavery had already deprived Afro-Americans of their cultural moorings. In speech and customs as well as in their names, they adopted the dominant Anglo-Saxon culture of their slave-owners. It is not accidental that many Afro-Americans carry the last names of Washington, Jefferson, Jackson, King, Lee or Brown.

For Native Americans, or Amerindians, the process was more complicated by their defeated enemy status. Their subjugation by the white population forced them onto reservations. There the rights given to Afro-Americans by the Civil War bypassed them, because many of the "Indian wars" were fought after the North-South war. This created for the "Indian Nations," now designated "Native Americans," special autonomous regions or reservations within the USA, but not really equal citizen status.

Citizen status is important, because citizenship per se is the factor that also defines nationality in the USA. In the United States national affiliation at its core means being part of the political values bestowed by American citizenship. The Declaration of Independence, the Constitution and its values and the English common law traditions provided the foundations for this citizenship. American nationality thus became synonymous with American citizenship. Having the legal rights and obligations of citizenship were also the hallmarks of nationality which you could acquire by birth on the territory of the USA or by applying for citizenship and passing a citizenship examination (naturalization).

Initially becoming an American in nationality in cultural terms meant "Anglo-conformity." This was reflected in the "White Anglo-Saxon Protestant"(WASP) dominance to the middle of the 20th century. It also meant the acceptance of the American value system, which, however, was an evolving system, reflected in the Supreme Court decisions from *Marbury vs. Madison,* through the *Dred Scott* case to *Brown vs. the Board of Education of Topeka* and more recently the *Citizens United* case. Political change generally preceded the legal change. Thus, with the election of JFK the Protestant part of the informal formula was dropped. Then with the election of Barack Obama the White aspect was also abandoned. The only traits that have remained constant are the dominance of the American English language and the role of business corporations in American society. The latter, however, is a bloodless, valueless trait that lets money rather than humans define the future.

For both citizens and corporations, the legal and technical aspects of associational criteria provide the context of being American. Yet Hungarian-Americans, even those who are second or third generation, frequently display a sense of inferiority toward those whom they consider "real Americans." However, when they talk about the "real Americans" (*igazi amerikaiak*) they do not mean the Native Americans, but the "Yankees" or English speaking WASPs. The dominant role played by the latter in business and public life put them at the center of activity. Thus, they provided the standards for Americanization. Whenever I corrected my fellow Hungarian-Americans and stressed that they were just as American as the Irish- German- English- or Scandinavian-Americans, they looked at me incredulously. This sense of disbelief and sense of inferiority led many to mimic the composite WASP *Staatsvolk,* to become "real Americans." They wanted to be like those that constituted the ruling majority and had controlled the political process during the course of American history in the face of the multi-ethnic character of the population defined primarily by immigration.

Within the context of such diversity what was the secret success for unity in the USA? Success breeds success, but it also needs a friendly, encouraging environment. The latter was the extensive wealth in land, water and resources of the North American continent. Another characteristic of this part of the world was that it was sparcely inhabited by an indigenous population which lacked the military technology of the European powers that fought to gain control over the land, water and resources. This military defeat reduced the existence of the Native Americans to bare survival on reservations or to absorption in the large urban centers of North America.

Unlike the Native Americans and the Afro-Americans, the Hungarians and other East Central Europeans were needed to bolster not just the labor force in the growing industrial centers of the land but also to strenghten the white birth rate of the overall population. This was not a stated objective, but it was apparent in the policies toward each of these groups after the Civil War. For the Native Americans the policy was separation on reservations or acculturation to Anglo-Saxon values in Indian boarding schools such as those established in Carlisle, Pennsylvania. For Afro-Americans the "solution" after Emancipation from slavery—aside from the brief period of Northern, carpetbagger dominance—was the institutionalization of segregation from the white population until the 1950s. This was reinforced with anti-miscegenation laws and other discriminatory legislation such as the White Primary elections. As for the East Central Europeans, they faced a three-stage process of acculturation, integration and finally assimilation by the WASP-dominated socio-economic ruling class. The latter was achieved by geographic dispersal via chasing job opportunities, a selective immigration policy (1920, 1924, 1952) and an English language public education system, systematic Americanisation through military service, supplemented by subtle social and economic pressures.

This process created special environmental circumstances for the formation of American political culture. In the 19th century this was the "frontier experience." For Native Americans it had an exclusionary impact, but as historian Frederick Jackson Turner (1920) pointed out, for the rest of the population—that was based on immigration—including the Hungarians, it provided a leveling impact that guaranteed a commitment to social and political equality. It provided the opportunity to "Go West young man, go West," and thereby find a world where class differences were erased and everyone had the chance to build their own little empire, or at least find a job that enabled them to survive or provide a new beginning for themselves and their families.

This land of opportunity and abundance encouraged individualism, innovation, self-help and results. However, just about the time when Hungarian mass immigration reached American shores, these very traits that had conquered the North American continent began to be transformed by the new needs of the American industrial giant beginning with the end of the 19th century and ending with the Second World War. This became the age of the "organization man," who was no longer the strong individualist, but conformity-oriented, who became an interchangeable part, a cog in the wheel, within the corporation or organization that employed him or her. This is William Whyte's thesis in his classic *The Organization Man* (1956). Other observers of the American scene also noted this important environmental and cultural change. David Riesman in *The Lonely Crowd* (1950) was perhaps most influential in showing how these environmental changes led to changes in behavior patterns and the traits that became more acceptable in American society. Unlike the individualist "inner-directed" person, the corporatist American setting now preferred the "other-directed" person, someone who would always conform to peer group pressure or the directives of the organization. This automatically led to more conformity and the acceptance of assimilation rather than the retention of strong values linked to the inner-directed personality.

At the beginning of the 21st century we are witnessing a globalization of these American traits as an extension of the multi-national and trans-national corporations which have a dominant role in the world's economy. The interests of the latter have now become the guiding power behind American foreign policy. But let us not jump ahead of ourselves. Let us back up for a moment to the time of the late 1950s and early 1960s. As I started my college career, the Eisenhower administration was concluded by a profound farewell address. The final words of General Dwight D. Eisenhower, as President of the USA (and former commander of Allied Forces in Europe) was to warn Americans, and perhaps the world, of the potential dire consequences of the marriage between the military and the great industrial interests of the country. Back then I did not truly comprehend his warning, but neither did the law makers and policy makers of the time. Nothing was done to keep this marriage from being consummated.

Eisenhower's successor in the White House, John F. Kennedy, strenghtened this unholy union. The involvement of the United States in the Vietnam conflict continued expanding the military budget and enhanced the role of those industries that supported the war effort. The justification was stopping the expansion of communism in South-East Asia. As a student at Elmhust College and later even as a graduate student in my first few years at LSU, I accepted this line of argument and felt that we had to stop the "domino effect" from transforming all of South East Asia into an extended Red Empire. Somehow the strong ideological blinders of anti-communism did not allow me to see that the Vietnamese struggle was also a national war against Western colonialism and more and more against the interests of global corporatist Capitalism.

A Life-Changing Meeting

At the beginning of the 1966–67 academic year I was invited by the Cuban student organization on campus to give a presentation on the Hungarian 1956 Fight for Freedom. I shared the podium with a 1956-er Hungarian student, who provided some personal impressions of the fighting in the streets of Budapest while I placed it within the context of the global struggle between East and West and the Cold War. The presentations stirred a great deal of discussion, because "Gábor" (not his real name) in an emotional outburst had said that he would push the button to use a nuclear weapon to stop communism. After the presentations were finished, a graduate student who had been active in the discussion, approached me and introduced himself as Lajos Éltető (Louis Elteto). Since, there were no other Hungarians on campus—to our knowledge—he and his girlfriend Zsuzsa, invited me out for a beer to an off-campus bar called the "Cotton Club." That invitation was the beginning of a life-long friendship between all three of us.

In hindsight our meeting also had a long-term impact on our lives, careers and the way we developed intellectually. While my graduate studies were focused on politics and history, "Lou's" graduate studies were focused on the German language, linguistics and literature and Zsuzsa became a librarian at PSU. Lou already had received his M.A. in German at Kent State University in Ohio before he came down to LSU to complete his Ph.D. with Professor Schroeder who had moved from Kent to LSU. Lou and I immediately hit it off and became friends, even though our personalities were in some ways very different. He was a Leo and I was an Aquarius. He convinced me that I needed a motorcycle to get around in Baton Rouge. So I invested part of my scholarship money to buy a 125cc Riverside Motorbike from Sears. Lou came out with me to practice driving this two-wheeled "monster" in the empty parking lots of some shopping centers near LSU. He enjoyed the instruction more than I did, but I have to admit it liberated me from dependence on others. Although to pass my drivers license I took the road test in Lou's VW bug. These common activities plus our occasional trips to New Orleans and "Árpádhon"[17] near Hammond, LA, welded our friendships with Lou and Zsuzsa on a personal and not just the ethnic level.

Already at our first Cotton Club meeting we summarized our lives and discussed our future plans as college teachers. Inadvertantly we turned to the problem of Hungarian survival in the United States. Referring to my recent experiences in Yugoslavia, I stressed that survival here as a cultural community was much more difficult in spite of the great differences in state policy regarding the acceptance or tolerance toward subcultures. Lou agreed. Both of us, and also Zsuzsa (she was of Irish-American background) the adopted Hungarian, felt that the real problem was that the Hungarians in the USA and Canada lacked a sense of communal solidarity. They were fragmented by social class, religion and past and present political allegiances.

North American Hungarians

In our meetings at the Cotton Club over beer and at the Éltetős' apartment over wine, we discussed how this fragmentation came about and what was needed to overcome it. In my previously mentioned article in *Hungarian Re-*

---

17 Árpádhon is a small agrarian Hungarian-American settlement in southern Louisiana in the neighborhood of Hammond, LA, founded by a lumber company in 1904. Its workers eventually became independent strawberry farmers.

view (May, 2017), I summarized the main reasons for this fragmentation. Here I will again quote from that article: "While we know that some Hungarian adventurers were present already in the original thirteen colonies, they were few in numbers. One, Mihály de Fabricy Kováts, distinguished himself as a cavalry officer in George Washington's army. However, the first really significant wave of Hungarians to the New World came only after the defeat of the Revolution of 1848–49. They and their leader, Lajos Kossuth, arrived in the United States in the 1850s. Kossuth went back to Europe and exile in Italy, but most of his followers became active as officers in the Union Army during the Civil War. Those that did not die on the battlefield were eventually absorbed by the population at large.

The numerically largest cluster of Hungarian immigrants came to the United States from 1880 to 1914. They were mainly of peasant or landless agrarian background or first generation working class background. They were for the most part economic immigrants. Their intention was to come to the land of opportunity to earn enough funds so they could go back to Hungary and purchase land or a house and provide for their families. These plans in most instances did not materialise because the First World War and the dictate of Trianon (1920) kept them from going back to the old country. However, they entered the USA at a time when the model for assimilation was re-drawn by Israel Zangwill. This model was the "melting pot." It replaced Anglo-conformity as the model, because the massive East and South European waves of immigrants could no longer be re-moulded according to the latter's image. The new model claimed that the USA was creating a new "cosmic" American from the blend of all the different peoples that entered the country. This model made mixing and inter-marriage among the white population an important component of American "nation-building."

In spite of this more permissive integrationist model, the Hungarian immigrants of this time period held on to their own institutions and traditions. They built churches, established religious and cultural associations, and enjoyed one another's company at weekend picnics and sporting events. However, they lacked schools that would be able to perpetuate their own language. Thus the next generation was handicapped by public schools that provided instruction only in English. The few church-affiliated schools and summer camps that had Hungarian language instruction had to fight an uphill battle against the legacy of being on the "wrong side" in the First World War and the growing strident "Americanization" campaign of the Daughters of the American Revolution. At the same time support from the "old country" was held up by its post-Trianon isolation and economic weakness. However, they were also hindered in their cultural survival, by lacking an extensive network of intellectual leaders. The leadership that existed was divided between Reformed ministers and Catholic priests on the one side, and on the other the left leaning newspaper editors and union organizers who emigrated from Hungary after the revolutions of 1918–1919, linked to the names of Mihály Károlyi and Béla Kun.[18]

Finally, the second generation of this immigration was also weakened in its cultural attachments by the outbreak of the Second World War. Again Hungary was on the "wrong side" in this struggle. To escape the negative labelling of being "pro-Nazi," all Hungarian-American neighborhoods undertook loyalty campaigns. The three most obvious examples of this were the collection of war bonds, the enlistment of young men in the American military, and aquiring American citizenship if you had not yet been naturalized. Inadvertantly, another wartime process also undermined cultural solidarity. This was the employment of women, young mothers and others in the wartime industries. Thus, the home which was the last bastion for learning the "mother tongue" also lost its key instructor. This trend was reinforced by the completely Americanised veterans of the Second World War who now were less attached emotionally to their former neighborhoods. Their horizons were expanded by their wartime service. This led them to escape to the suburbs from their former "ghetto" existence in an ethnic neighborhood. The

---

18 Mihály Károlyi and Béla Kun were the opportunistic and inept leaders who filled the power vacuum that was left after the defeat of the Austro-Hungarian Monarchy in World War I. The murder of István Tisza opened the door for weak, unscrupulous and incompetent leaders. Count Mihály Károlyi declared the end of the Dual Monarchy and the establishment of the Hungarian Republic. His "leadership" after October 31, 1918 led to anarchy in Budapest as mobs took control of the streets. Károlyi's reign lasted only a few months since he could not control the chaos and had disbanded the military, the only institution that could have reestablished some sense of order. In March 1919 he stepped down and opened the door for Béla Kun's power grab and establishment of the 133 days of Communist Dictatorship. The occupation of much of historic Hungary by Czech, Romanian and Serbian troops took place in this context.

dramatic expansion of access to the automobile and the improved roadways of the land made this mobility possible.

Just as these centers of Hungarian settlement began to break up under the pressures of the post-Second World War developments, a new wave arrived. These were the wartime refugees, then called DPs (Displaced Persons). They were the military officers, public officials and bureaucrats of the Horthy era, intellectuals and middle-class or upper-class people who were escaping the Soviet occupation (1945–47). Both Lou and I were the children of this wave. They were followed by a second wave of mainly smallholder farmers and democratic politicians who realized that their efforts to create real democracy in Hungary was being sabotaged by the Soviet occupation and the Rákosi "Muscovite" Communists who consolidated their control over the country (1947–49). This double wave provided the intellectual leadership that the preceding immigrants did not have. Although the "régi amerikás" (old wave immigrants) and the new émigrés[19] did not always get along because of class differences, their leaders were committed to the survival of their churches and other ethnic institutions. In fact, the émigrés organized a new institution, the Hungarian Scouts in Exteris, which filled the void of educational institutions. This organization was perhaps the most important replacement for the declining influence of the ethnic Hungarian churches.

This émigré wave still had to contend with the last gasp of the "melting pot" assimilationist momentum. I remember an incident that took place in 1954 or 1955 which illustrates this. With about three or four Hungarian scout friends we boarded a BMT subway to go from Queens to Manhattan. In an animated way we were carrying on a conversation about some event in our latest excursion to the Catskill Mountains. At this point an elderly gentleman yelled at us, stating that he had heard enough "foreign gibberish"

---

19 Emigrants refers to individuals or groups that for one reason or another leave or move out of their home country and move to another country or state. When their numbers increase dramatically we designate it "migration" or "mass migration" which on occasion takes place after major displacements caused by wars or natural disasters. In the case of Hungarians who have migrated to North America, we can distinguish between "immigrants" who become permanent settlers motivated by the desire to improve their economic conditions and "émigrés" who had to leave Hungary for fear of political or religious persecution. The immigrants of the late 19th and early 20th century were of the first variety, while the emigrés following World War II or the crushed 1956 revolt, were of the second variety

from us, that we should speak "American," or shut up, proclaiming this loudly and proudly in his thickly accented Brooklyneze.

For the next wave of Hungarian refugees, or "Freedom Fighters" as the media and the public referred to them, the 1956–57 refugees already were not likely to face such public embarassment. By this time the Civil Rights Movement was challenging the discriminatory policies of the Deep South and the "Black Power" movement appeared on the horizon. The examples of self-assertion by leaders like Martin Luther King, Jr, Malcolm X and the Black Panthers led others to be more vocal in their assertion of identity and rights. The writings of Vine Deloria Jr led Native Americans, Chicanos as well as white ethnics to be more assertive. Hungarian-Americans also joined these ranks, and the new 1956-ers were there in the front lines of this manifestation of "cultural pluralism." In our Baton Rouge, Louisiana discussions, the above outlined profile, and this environmental challenge faced us in 1967–68. In addition, we also were aware of the pessimism of many émigré leaders. Tibor Tollas, one of their best-known writers and the editor of the newspaper *Nemzetőr* (Home Guard or National Guard), stated as an element of faith that their generation had only twenty years left to carry out their work. Then assimilation and death would take their toll. Indeed, with the constant squabbling and ideological posturing the Hungarian scene in the USA was anything but uplifting.

Our Response via *ITT-OTT* (Here-There)

What could two university students do to challenge this depressing state of affairs? They had to bring into being a network of communication that would successfully reach out to the next generation, or those who had not yet been infected by the ideological extremes and struggles of the émigrés. To this end we would have to deal with real problems that would address Hungarian survival in an assimilationist setting. We had to give up the idea that we could liberate Hungary from the Soviet yoke. Instead, how could we preserve Hungarian identity over time, how could we contribute to the cultural survival of Hungarians living scattered throughout the world, but particularly on the North American continent?

First of all we had to change the attitudes of the émigré and immigrant Hungarians to think of themselves as part of a dynamic dispersed community like the Jews, Armenians or Greeks. Already in our earliest 1967–68 issues of *ITT-OTT*, we argued against the prevailing definition that we were just all emigrants (*emigánsok*) who left their homeland for whatever reason. Instead, we pointed out that "immigrants" and "émigrés" were both part of a migration out of their homeland, but the former did so primarilly for economic reasons, while the latter left because they had to for political, cultural or religious reasons. But both categories faced the dilemma that Tibor Tollas had outlined when he said that we only had twenty years left. After that we would be dead physically or absorbed and eliminated culturally. To avoid this fate, we had to become *szétszórtsági* (Diaspora) Hungarians.

Baton Rouge, Louisiana was far from most Hungarian settlements in the United States. This was a problem in terms of developing contacts. At the same time it was an advantage because it insulated us from most of the conflicts that agitated the Hungarian cluster settlements in the United States. At the same time, it automatically forced us to think of reaching out to all our ethnic kin, without becoming captives of just one city, or just one cluster. This context made us shy away from establishing just one more newspaper or periodical, instead we established a "discussion network" before Facebook, LinkedIn, or the e-mail systems of Google, Chrome or Windows. This discussion network was based on typed articles on stencils which came from everywhere and then were compiled and shared with all addresses available to us. Its title was *ITT-OTT* (Here-There), based on an Endre Ady[20] poem with the title "Négy-öt magyar összehajol"(Four-five Hungarians unite). The first compilation was shared with thirty individuals and mailed out on October 23rd 1967, on the 11th anniversary of the 1956 Hungarian Fight for Freedom. The response was almost instantaneous! From émigré circles it was mostly negative, but from the younger generation we received letters of encouragement, monetary contributions and written material for our next issue. Our discussion group address list doubled for our next issue and we had

---

20 Endre Ady (1877–1919) one of the greatest lyric poets in the pantheon of Hungarian literature, whose poem "Négy-öt magyar összehajol" (Four-five Hungarians unite) became our organization's and community's verbal logo, providing us with solidarity in spite of our global dispersion.

to switch from our gelatin plate duplication to mimeograph so that we could keep up with the demand. By the end of the academic year we had over 700 addresses and half had become active participants and not just "readers." By the summer of 1968 the "hard core" of our participants included George Csomay, Martha Frecska and Ildikó Zoltáni, all from the Chicago area.

The rapid growth of our discussion group also produced lively debate. The issue that was most divisive, was the argument posed by a number of us, that the Diaspora conciousness of dispersed Hungarians also required a religious glue. Like the historic Diasporas of Greeks, Armenians and Jews, we too needed a belief system that could somehow transcend our present religious fragmentation. Needless to say, this on top of our rejection of the "emigrant" label, led the professional émigrés from left to right, to attack us as irresponsible radicals, who wanted to establish a Hungarian "Civic Religion" or go out in the woods to sacrifice white horses.[21] The publishing of *ITT-OTT* as the mouthpiece for our discussion group, became more and more time consuming. Our Hungarian "hobby" began to cut into the work that was to establish our careers as university professors, dentists, lawyers, architects and school teachers. Doing *ITT-OTT* became a part-time job for the remainder of our active lives.

Our Lives Beyond *ITT-OTT*

Our full-time studies at LSU required that we pay more attention to what was going on in the world around us, to write our dissertations, and to complete our studies. Fortunatelly, my studies were financially covered by an NDEA fellowship for three years, and then supplemented by a Teaching Assistantship for one year, and finally provided for with a Dissertation Fellowship in my fifth year. The latter enabled me to spend three months doing research at the Library of Congress in D.C. This research in combination with my stay in Yugoslavia during 1966, provided the foundation for my Disser-

---

21   White horses were supposedly sacrificed by the pre-Christian Magyars as part of their pagan ritual practices

tation: "Hungarians in Romania and Yugoslavia" which I defended in 1971. During my fifth year at LSU writing and researching my dissertation, I was also busy looking for a teaching position either in the mid-Atlantic states or the mid-West. I was finally successful in landing a teaching position at Ohio Northern University in Ada, Ohio. As an instructor of Political Science I remained at this institution until my retirement as Emeritus Professor in 2008. ONU was a great base for continuing my Hungarian hobby, teaching subjects I enjoyed and getting involved in Human Rights activism for the Hungarian minority populations in East Central Europe. These activities also provided me with the opportunity to learn and understand more about United States foreign policy.

While at LSU the major domestic events that affected our existence were the demonstrations against the Vietnam war, the Civil Rights movement, the assassination of President John F. Kennedy, the assassination of Martin Luther King Jr, and the Presidency of Lyndon Baines Johnson. Aside from discussions over coffee at the student union, I confess I did not become involved in activities of my age group to influence politics on the domestic front. Only in one instance did I get involved, when Afro-American students from Southern University came to our campus to have the U.S. flag lowered to half-staff on the day that Martin Luther King Jr was killed. This group of ten to fifteen Black students marched to the center of our campus where the flag was on the open field between the Student Union, the bell tower (Goodrich hall) and the Law College. They were surrounded by a large group of white students. I remember joining a small group of white graduate students that supported lowering the flag to half mast. I stood with the Black students, because I admired their courage, not because I was a supporter of Martin Luther King Jr. Still, both Lou and I were relieved when campus security arrived in force and dispersed the menacing cluster of white students, saying that the university administration had decided to follow the national example to lower the flag to half mast.

By the middle and late 1960s our main activism related to international concerns, like the "Prague Spring" of 1968. We also had some debate about participation in or opposition to the Vietnam conflict. At the same time leadership changes in most of East Central Europe continued to undermine the survival prospects of minority communities. This therefore moved to the center of our concern. In particular the educational situation of Hungarians in Romania continued to deteriorate.

Family Events

In the meantime, in my personal and family life some important changes were also taking place. My younger brother, Antal Jr and his family were involved in a horrible automobile accident on Memorial Day week-end in 1968. He, his wife Madelaine, and his mother-in-law were all killed, only their twenty-two-month old child survived. (My sister Ciszka's family adopted him, Antal III, and raised him as their own.) My older brother, Tamás, married Renate Paulo a few years befor this tragedy. My youngest brother, Pál and our mother Erzsébet, moved to Danbury, Connecticut shortly afterwards. Henceforth,

Ossining, NY 1968. Family gathering on occasion of visiting relatives from Hungary: Back row l. to r. Toni with wife Madelaine holding little Antal, uncle Palkó, András, Tamás. Front row l. to r. Pál, my Godmother Ella, our aunt Zsóka, our mother Erzsébet holding little Panni, Renate with Muffin, Howard with Leslie in front, his daughter Peta with husband Rudolfo.

Our father's grave in the Valhala cemetery, Westchester county, New York state

my visits to family were no longer to Astoria in New York City, but to Danbury, Newtown, or New Fairfield, Connecticut.

Before I went to LSU for my graduate studies I had initially thought of following my father in a military career. My brother's enlistment in the Marines also appealed to my idealized view of a *semper fi* service for our country. So before my successful application to LSU, I applied for Officer's Candidate School at Quantico, VA. This involved a physical examination. The Navy doctor who examined me, asked if my glasses were safety glasses. When I answered in the negative, he told me to take them off and tell him what I could read from the eye-chart at the end of the room. No matter how much I squinted I could not read even the top line. He instructed me to walk toward the chart and tell him when I could read the top two lines. I was arms lenght from the chart when I could accomplish this feat. The good doctor told me that I did not make the cut for officers in the Marines. He suggested the Army. I chose graduate studies instead. I even thought of the priesthood for a while, but my experiences in Yugoslavia convinced me that this would not work in the long run.

From Louisiana to Ohio

Lajos Éltető's application for a Fulbright Fellowship to Cluj/Kolozsvár in Romania was accepted the same year when I got my appointment to Ohio

Northern University. Lou already also had accepted a teaching position at Southwestern University in Lafayette, Louisiana. The university administration there was glad to give him an extension of his contract for the following academic year (1969–1970). In the meantime, his brother Áron came down to Baton Rouge to help move the Éltető possessions back to Alliance, Ohio and my possessions to Ada, Ohio. We rented a U-Haul truck into which we were able to fit everything, including my Riverside motorcycle. It was the middle of August and a long hot drive to Ohio. Our stop in Alliance to unload the Éltető possessions, was memorable because this led to meeting Lou's parents, Lajos Sr and Erzsébet. They both agreed to help me continue editing *ITT-OTT* while Lou and Zsuzsi were in Kolozsvár. This would be a challenging year for all of us.

As a footnote to our departure from LSU I must mention the small agrarian settlement of Hungarians near Hammond, Louisiana called "Árpádhon." Both Lou and I made a promise to keep their fate in the forefront of our attention. Lajos and Zsuzsi went one step further by holding their wedding in the community's small Hungarian Reformed church, with Reverend Alexander Bartus presiding. Many years later I too would return with a camera crew to record the life of this settlement. By then I was only able to interview two of Bartus' sons. This work remains to be completed.

From Alliance, Ohio Áron came with me to Ada, where I would begin teaching in Ohio Northern University's History and Political Science Department in September. We drove directly to the home of my department's Chairman. After unloading my belongings and my motorcycle in Dr. Robert Hilliard's garage, Áron said good-bye and drove back to Alliance where he dropped of the U-Haul truck. I immediatelly began looking for a place that would be my "home" for the next academic year (1968–69), my first at ONU. I found a trailer home on West Montford Street that became my first Ada residence.

Teaching Career Begins at ONU

The ONU community was welcoming and I joined a department that was committed to teaching. I found personal friends as well among the new faculty that joined the university at the same time, Peter Previte in the Pharmacy College and Dick Carpenter in the Mathematics Department. Most of the faculty already had established families. This meant that single faculty had minimal opportunities for either an active cultural or social life. ONU was located in a rich agricultural region and Ada was surrounded by corn fields and soybean fields. This meant that I had to travel to Cleveland, Toledo, Detroit or Chicago if I wanted to meet young women with whom our interests might coincide.

From Chicago a good friend of mine, who had joined the *ITT-OTT* discussion group, now was my "neighbor" at the University of Michigan in Ann Arbor. The two of us would drive to social events in the mentioned cities if we heard of social gatherings where we might be able to meet women. On one such occasion, a Tea Afternoon and Dance on the West Side in Cleveland, organized by the Hungarian girl scouts, I met Julianna Rose Nádas (Panni), the daughter of Dr. Julius and Ibolya Nádas. I would say it was love at first sight. We began dating and I stopped visiting other cities and focused just on Cleveland for my weekend social involvements. To make a long story short, we were already engaged by Easter and our wedding (Big Fat Hungarian Wedding) was held on August 23rd, 1969 at the West Side Hungarian Reformed Church. Panni already became not just Mrs. Ludányi but also an active part of our discussion group. She began teaching Mathematics at Allen East High School in Lafayette, a small town located halfway between Ada and Lima, OH.

The 1968–69 academic year became a very intense time for me both in terms of my personal life, but also in meeting my obligations to my classes and also doing the editing work for *ITT-OTT*. The pace of developments kept me from paying too much attention to international happenings. Writing my lecture notes for the first presentations, involved following mainly existing text-book materials combined with the notes I had taken in my graduate studies. For physical activities, soccer still provided an occasional escape from the enclosure of my office and the Heterick Memorial Library. At this time I did not pay too much attention to departmental politics, although it involved some problems down the road because of the competition between the History and the Political Science "half" of the staff.

ITT-OTT editing work now involved a lot of driving, three and half hours to Alliance, Ohio or a five hour drive to Chicago. In Chicago a group of activists including Martha Frecska and George Csomay collected the group in the Frecska basement or reck-room. There we discussed the format of the next issue and the writing responsibilities of each member of the discussion group. This was usually a good time for fellowship, but led to promised articles or reviews of which only a small percentage actually appeared in print. This meant that most of the issues had to be compiled by the "veterans." However, this in itself was a good learning process, since most of us had only limited formal education in the writing of Hungarian. Indeed, this "ön-képzés" (self-development) was one of the primary objectives of the *ITT-OTT* circle of friends.

The sessions in Alliance, Ohio with Lou's father did pick up the slack. Lajos Sr helped with the correction of style and grammar of our amateur writing staff. He also contributed his own poems and essays which definitely raised the quality of our publication. He was not the only "elder" who helped raise our standards. My father's former adjutant on the Russian front, László De Simon, also designed one of our covers, as did Martha Frecska's elder brother, Tamás. (I had stayed at the De Simon family's home in Silver Spring, MD while I was doing my Library of Congress research in 1968.)

Although most of my dissertation research was completed before I began my teaching at ONU, the written text still needed a lot of work. This became more difficult with my full-time teaching load. Fortunatelly Panni helped type most of the second half of the dissertation. As I noted above, this made it possible for me to defend the finalized text in the Spring of 1971. The Ph.D. also meant an automatic promotion from Instructor to Assistant Professor. What was even more important, Lou and Zsuzsi returned from Kolozsvár and became engaged in the editing work of our discussion group. In fact, we can say that from this point on *ITT-OTT* was no longer just a publication of a discussion group, but had become a periodical that began to receive the grudging recognition even from émigré and other publications. Furthermore, we began to hold meetings in Chicago and Ada, to plan an organized conference that would involve many more North American Hungarian communities. In this undertaking, Tibor Cseh, who had recently joined our discussions, became an important catalyst on the East Coast. Tibor convinced

Group photo of our gathering at Lake Hope, sometime before 1989

us to bring into being a conference in Amish country not far from Philadelphia, near Hereford, PA (at the *Magyar tanya/Hungarian homestead*) over the Labor Day week-end in 1972.

Hereford Pennsylvania: Discussion Group to Movement

The Hereford Conference was the first public appearance of our "Discussion Circle." It brought together people from all parts of the United States and even the László and Mária Soltay couple from Toronto, Ontario. Lou Éltető came to the conference all the way from Portland, Oregon. He had in the meantime left his teaching position at Southwestern University in Louisiana for a position at Portland State University. Others who came from far away were Ferenc Béres from Hungary and Panni Bart from California. Altogether about one hundred people attended this meeting, from all walks of life, and mostly young people at the beginning of their careers, but some in their forties and fifties and a few above sixty. The one thing that united all of them was their desire to be more effective in representing the rights of Hungari-

l. to r. Panni Nádas Ludányi, András Ludányi, Péter Kovalszki and László Bőjtös discussing the significance of the 1972 Hereford, PA meeting for MBK (Lake Hope, 2018).

ans left behind the Iron Curtain. By 1972 this was particularly the case in relation to Romania where the neo-Stalinist Ceauşescu regime was more and more openly turning its policies in the direction of a red fascism that wanted to solve the Hungarian minority question via total absorption, through policies of forced denationalization.

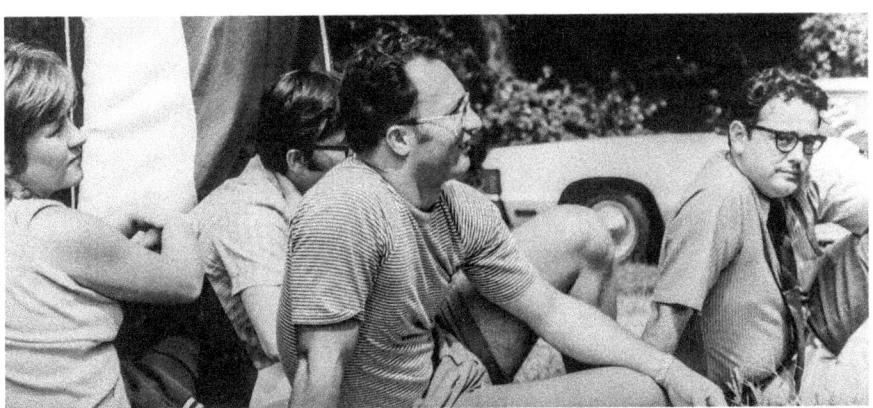

Hereford, PA conference in 1972: l. to r. Martha Frecska, my brother Paul Ludányi and myself, and Louis Éltető

At Hereford our concern was to make our discussion group into an effective agency for mobilizing Hungarians on this and other issues. To achieve this we invited speakers from all groups that seemed, at that time, to be seeking ways of sustaining Hungarian cultural and social activism in the United States and Canada. The Scouts were represented by Edward Chászár and Viktor Fischer, the American Hungarian Foundation by August Molnár, the Alumni Association by Károly Nagy, Reformed ministers by András Hamza, the Student Associations by Csaba Tóth, historians Miklós Érdy and Ferenc Veres, Károly Andreánszky from ABN and some new faces which included Géza Madarász from the media world and from a variety of local organizations Tibor Lukács and Károly Endre Nagy (Ohio) István Kun Szabó (NJ) and the Shooters, Pál Ludányi (CT). From our own core editorial group, besides Lajos Éltető, Tibor Cseh and myself and Panni, and Tamás Frecska as well as Márton and Magda Sass came from Chicago, and the Soltays from Toronto. The ideas and plans shared at this meeting provided a good summary and synthesis of the thoughts that had been discussed and debated on the pages of *ITT-OTT* until this time. At any rate, the publication of these discussions in a special issue of our journal provided new visibility and greater recognition in the Hungarian-American world.

U.S. Policy and Human Rights

Of course Ceauşescu's abuses, which motivated us to organize, were to some extent hidden to Western observers. In 1972 the Ceauşescu[22] regime was set on proving its "liberal" credentials in the West by letting a group of Hungarian Transylvanian writers and poets visit some Hungarian communities in the West. Sándor Püski organized their tour in the United States. The group included András Sütő, Géza Domokos, Sándor Kányádi, Árpád Farkas and Győző Hajdú. The last named was the party loyalist who was sent on the tour

---

22 Nicolae Ceauşescu was Party and Government leader of Communist Romania from 1965 to 1989. His rule was a neo-Stalinist dictatorship which he consolidated with an appeal to Romanian chauvinism, victimizing the country's minority nationalities, particularly the Hungarians of Transylvania.

to keep his eyes on the others. (At the time he was the editor of *Igaz Szó*/True Word, a literary journal totally under party control.) At that time, Hajdú became acquainted with a number of Hungarian-Americans who dealt with art collectors. One such "friend" found out that we were driving from our family in CT to Ohio and asked us to give Hajdú and his girlfriend Böbe a ride to Detroit, MI, to visit his elderly uncle there. This ride proved to be very useful for me, because during that long drive we learned a great deal about the inner workings of the Ceaușescu regime. They were our guests in Ada, Ohio for one night and the next day we dropped them off at their relatives in Detroit. For our help Győző Hajdú promised to help us in turn if we ever travelled to Transylvania.

The very next summer, Panni and I took up his offer as we knapsacked our way through Transylvania from Oradea/Nagyvárad, through Cluj/Kolozsvár to Târgu Mureș /Marosvásárhely and the Székely region to Brasov/Brassó, Timișoara/Temesvár and Arad. Hajdú joined us in Marosvásárhely, up till then we had used the Romanian railway and bus system exclusively. After giving us a guided tour of Marosvásárhely and an exclusive meal in the Mureș Hotel, he had us chouffered in a party sedan through small villages in the Székely region, including a visit to his "Grandmother" (he was an orphaned child raised by her and later the Romanian state), who cooked up a great puliszka/polenta meal for us, while she lambasted her influential grandchild for all the ills of the Romanian state. After this meal he took me aside and asked us to say only nice things about him and Romania after he drops us off at our hotel in Szováta. The implication was that our room is certainly bugged. As we turned in for the night we followed his advice, and said only neutral or positive things about our experiences.

The next day we travelled by bus to Mircurea Ciuc/Csíkszereda where we visited a great artist friend of ours, László Imets. He immediately took us to see the modest museum, but beautiful art collection of Imre Nagy, the region's best-known painter. After a long and rewarding conversation we went to our own residence which was a reserved room (by Hajdú) at the local Party Hotel. As we picked up our keys to the room, we overheard the concierge tell three just arrived members of a TV crew that unfortunately the last room had been taken by the "American comrades." Ohhh great, what will the people in Ada say when they find out about this. Better yet, what will the people say in Cleveland among our Hungarian kin??

After a good night's rest, we left Csíkszereda by bus and arrived in Brassó to catch our train to Budapest via Southern Transylvania. The train followed the magnificent scenic valley of the Olt and Maros rivers, hemmed in by the grandeur of the Transylvanian Alps. The only downside to this scenic ride was that we had to share our compartment with two employees of the Romanian Securitate, and one spoke Hungarian fluently! On the one hand we were surrounded by the beauty of the outside natural world, while in our train compartment our conversations were constrained by the narrow-minded, petty world of Ceaușescu's dictatorship.

Lobbying for Human and Minority Rights

Nicolai Ceaușescu was able to get away with this pretense of being a maverick because he inherited the mantle of his predecessor as a "striver for independence" within the Soviet bloc. I wrote an article about this in *Hungarian Studies* (January, 1990).[23] Here I will quote from that source: Ceaușescu's "role had been laid by Romania's rebellion against COMECON's tighter economic integration in 1964 and, more importantly, Ceaușescu's refusal to break off relations with Israel in 1967 or to participate in the August 1968 Warsaw Pact invasion of Czechoslovakia. The latter two commitments assured Romania of American sympathies, which in concrete terms meant that President Johnson warned the Soviet Union "not to unleash the dogs of war" in Eastern Europe by expanding the interventionism of the Brezhnev doctrine to Yugoslavia and Romania. This was followed by the Kissinger years of the Nixon and Ford administrations, which tried to expand the trend toward greater independence in the bloc. Romania's Ceaușescu was a direct beneficiary of these commitments. In 1968 Nixon selected Romania to be the first Communist country to be visited by a U.S. president af-

---

23 "Hungarian Lobbying Efforts for the Human Rights of Minorities in Rumania: The CHRR/HHRF as a Case Study," *Hungarian Studies,* Vol. VI, No. 1 (1990), 77–90.

ter World War II. In 1975 President Ford was also given an enthusiastic reception in Bucharest on his state visit. In the meantime Ceaușescu visited the United States on three separate occasions in 1970, 1973, and 1975. All this meant that Romania had become the darling of Kissinger's own version of *Ostpolitik*. In concrete terms this meant trade benefits, finally including most-favored-nation status.

Against this kind of background Hungarian-American groups had very little impact on the State Department in defending the human rights of Hungarians in Romania. The lack of influence can best be explained by two other factors. One was internal to the Hungarian-American subculture, the other was the strength of competing interests that favored continued good relations with Romania. The latter were mainly a limited number of business interests and some of the American Jewish groups affiliated with the American Israel Public Affairs Committee (AIPAC). The former saw advantages for gaining some untapped markets in Eastern Europe, while the latter wanted to maintain contacts with the only East European bloc country that had not severed its diplomatic relations with Israel following the 1967 war. Also of more immediate concern, was the desire to maintain contact with an East European country–besides the USSR–from which some of the Jewish population wanted to emigrate to Israel, to replenish its population in the face of a higher birth rate among the Palestinian Arabs.

On the other hand, the Hungarian-American subculture was not capable of fielding an effectively organized human rights lobby until the early 1970's. Although the Hungarian-American community included about one million seven hundred thousand people according to the 1980 census, it lacked effective lobbying organizations. Their church and fraternal organizations were well established, but avoided politics because they associated it with the fratricidal struggles that the post-World War II and post-1956 new political émigrés brought with them. Thus, those who had the most established roots were the least willing to participate in efforts to influence American foreign policy. The new émigrés, on the other hand, had all the desire to participate, but they initially lacked citizenship and for a long time did not acquire the know-how that would make them politically effective in their new environment. It was not until the second generation came of age that the "week-end" old country politics of the 1945-ers and 1956-ers was replaced by the political pragmatism of a new, Americanized, younger generation.

This younger generation became the backbone for the human rights activism of the 1970's and 1980's. They became involved with lobbying not as an *ad hoc* endeavor to salve their conscience, but as an activity that was supposed to achieve concrete results. This was a totally novel approach, and required that Hungarian-American society undergo a process of re-education. Henceforth they would no longer be pacified by purely symbolic payoffs, the days of the verbose election-day speaker or the wordy memorandum "promising liberation" were now numbered.

The *ITT-OTT* discussion group and periodical supported this new posture whole-heartedly. It also mirrored the activism present at the end of the 1960's in the USA. Furthermore, it came to a head at the same time as Romania's new international prominence, from 1968 to about 1975. This time period also witnessed the opportunity of prominent Hungarian artists and writers from Romania to travel in the West, while more and more Hungarians from the West had the opportunity to visit their relatives in Transylvania. The intersection of these two developments convinced the younger generation, that the stillborn politics of their forefathers must be replaced with the kind of political involvement that actually changes or challenges adverse government policies.

Two other specific events also set the stage for Hungarian-American human rights activism. One was the passage of the Trade Act of 1974, while the other was the signing of the Helsinki Final Act in 1975. The first provided the framework within which Romania acquired access to American markets following President Ford's granting (in 1975) of MFN status to it. The second provided a means of monitoring compliance with the human rights requirements of Basket III of the Helsinki Final Act. The latter offered a standard of behavior for all 35 "Helsinki" signatory states and follow-up conferences which could check up on the progress for keeping the promised guarantees. These two policy commitments of the USA and Romania, established the mechanisms by which human rights activists might bring pressure to bear on Romania.

One other important change was the Carter administration making human rights the centerpiece of its foreign policy. Although the State Department did not immediately abandon its commitments to the "realism" of the Kissinger era, it began to pay lip-service to human rights. This verbal commitment provided an in for human rights activists trying to influence American foreign policy. Already during the spring, summer and fall of 1976 a newly formed organization called the Committee for Human Rights in Romania (CHRR) took advantage of this opening. It challenged the renewal of Romania's MFN status just one year after the status had been granted.

This Committee, representing the younger generation of Hungarian-Americans was able to mobilize a significant number of U.S. Representatives to speak against renewal of MFN status. While in this first challenge to MFN status renewal the CHRR allied itself with many more traditional and long-established organizations (i.e., the American Hungarian Federation), it already played the most important role in mobilizing opposition. Although this first challenge to the State Department professionals and the Executive Office was unsuccessful, it brought together the core support for an enthusiastic and talented organization. These second-generation college-age activists were effective because of their familiarity with the American political landscape, their English fluency in both writing and speech, and their willingness to be workhorses rather than showhorses. From 1976 to 1987 the CHRR (after 1984-HHRF) utilized the annual review of MFN status as a means to focus attention on Romanian human rights violations, and the Helsinki follow-up conferences (Belgrade, Madrid, Ottawa, Budapest, Vienna) to keep world attention on this issue.

Both Lajos Éltető and myself, because of our research on Transylvania for our dissertations, and others like Tibor Cseh, Balázs Somogyi and Zsolt Szekeres, were from the beginning very supportive of CHRR/HHRF activities. In numerous fundraising events, in demonstrations, letter writing campaigns, and direct pressure on Senators and Congressional representatives we helped to mobilize our support groups. One example stands out in my memory when we targeted Senator Howard Metzenbaum (D-OH) to withdraw his support of Romania's MFN status. The Senator was finally willing to meet with us at the Cleveland Hopkins Airport at his VIP lounge before his flight to Washington, D.C. We invited representatives from all major Ohio cities to show the Senator the wide-spread support for the withdrawal of MFN status for Romania. Present at this meeting were two university professors, two architects, one retirement home administrator, one Democratic party secretary, one Calvinist Minister and László Hámos of CHRR/HHRF, who flew in from New York City. The Ohio cities represented were Cleveland, Akron, Dayton, Toledo, Cincinnati, Columbus and Ada. The effective presentation by László Hámos, backed up by supporting comments from Ohio constituents must have had their effect. The votes in both the House and the Senate ended the MFN status of Romania in the summer of 1987.

Teaching, Writing and Model UN Activities

Before getting involved in this lobbying work, I did have to establish my reputation as a teacher at ONU. Because I was the only full-time Political Scientist in the department, with two other faculty members teaching politics on a half-time basis, the History "half" of the staff, was actually 80% in a department wherein the student history and political science majors were divided about 50-50%. Soon after my arrival, Dr. Hilliard retired in 1971 as Chair and was replaced by Dr. Robert Davis, also a historian. Bob Davis realized that this departmental ratio was untenable if we were to provide an attractive program in Political Science. To overcome the course deficit, the Department hired Tony Salmone, a specialist in American politics and bureaucratic behavior. This was a good supplement for my Comparative Politics and International Relations focus. Still, it was not enough, we really needed someone in Political Theory and also Constitutional Law. The latter was particularly important for our students who were to go on to continue their studies in our Law College. At any rate, the stresses and strains continued on this issue. However, I was not able to exert more pressure until I received my Ph.D. in 1971, even if my student evaluations were good and my classes were popular.

Parallel to my teaching responsibilities I continued my research interests and also became the Godfather of the soccer club at ONU. Because the established varsity sports were not willing to share the athletic budget with us, we did everything on a shoe-string budget. This meant that we provided for our own uniforms and used our own cars to travel to away games, since university vehicles were reserved for varsity teams. Of course enthusiasm is not enough if you are playing against teams that have regular coaches and institutional support. Since I was a "player-coach" I was also on the soccer field with the team. In fact, in my last year as "player-coach" I scored 50% of the goals for our team. (However, two goals out of four is nothing to brag about.) So after three years Amar Bhattacharya (from the Pharmacy College) became their coach and his diplomatic skills as well as his soccer know-how transformed the club into a real varsity team.

The activity which replaced soccer as the center of my focus was ONU's adoption of the Model UN program. From 1974 every Easter break I took a group of students to New York City and represented a different country at the National Model United Nations. Our first country was Iceland, then Costa Rica, Algeria, Libya, Botswana, and the list goes on. In each instance the students had to learn how to be "in character." In other words, they were not representing the USA, but had to get into the shoes of a different people, with a different culture and different national interests. When possible we tried to apply for a maverick state, so that we could be controversial and still be in character. Syria and Libya were a pleasure to represent. India was also a real challenge. In most instances we were able to get a mission briefing from the real representatives of "our country" and both the opening session and the closing sessions were held at the General Assembly of the real United Nations. It was always a great learning experience for students and teachers alike. (In the 35 years that I participated in the NMUN we were even able to represent Hungary on two occasions!) Until 2008 I was the adviser to this group each year, except during the year when I had a Fulbright teaching Fellowship at Debrecen University in Hungary.

For me personally this experience of "political simulation" was a great supplement to my courses in International Law and Organization, International Politics, and Comparative Politics. It was also a great experience because only highly motivated students were drawn to it. At the same time it gave me almost a week in New York City, where I could relive through my memories my teenage years and high school adventures. Even more important on a practical level, I could make personal contact with members of the CHRR/HHRF network of human rights activists. On occasion I visited them in their offices at the upper East Side or they would send me the latest briefing papers in unmarked brown envelopes to my hotel room. In one instance I remember that Bulcsu Veress biked up to my student group just as we were leaving the Metropolitan Museum of Art on 5th Avenue near 84th street, and "dropped" the unmarked envelope for me. This impressed and mystified my students. They were sure I was someone's double agent.

These trips to New York, at least during the first twenty years, were always via ONU marked university vans that could fit 12–15 passengers. However, because the parking in New York City was exorbitant for a week at any of the hotels we stayed at, after dropping off the students at the hotel (Sheraton near Penn Station, until the fire, and then the Hyatt on 42nd Street near Grand Central) I would drive out to Midland Park in New Jersey and leave the van in the drive of my friend, Tibor Cseh, who was one of our main organizers for *ITT-OTT* on the East Coast. This too was a great opportunity for networking and catching up on the latest developments in the New York City area organization. On the bus ride back to Port Authority terminal I always slept off the exhausting long drive from Ada, OH to the Big Apple. I had to be wide awake for the roller coaster series of events that were always part of the NMUN. (True, I always found time for one brief visit to my family in New Fairfield, CT where my mother, later my sister, would provide me with a good home-cooked Hungarian meal.)

One other activity which I developed for my students was field work on the East Side in Toledo, OH. In this part of the city the Birmingham neighborhood was one of the most diverse East Central European "ethnic" enclaves. It included end of the 19th century settlers who were drawn to the area by jobs provided by the Maleable Steel Corporation. They were Hungarians, Slovaks, Moravians, Italians and Ruthenians. In the 1930's they were joined by Afro-Americans and in the 1970's by refugees from Vietnam. Of the roughly 4000 inhabitants, the Hungarians constituted the largest cluster and their three churches provided the backbone for the neighborhood. Since Toledo was only seventy miles from Ada, it was within reach for an oral history project for those of my students that were interested in ethnic studies. For about three years on a bi-weekly basis I arranged for students to visit Birmingham with cameras and voice-recorders. Our local contact person was Peter Ujvagi, Toledo Councilman (later also Lucas County Democratic Party Secretary, and State Senator). Ujvagi set up appointments for us with all the key people in the community. This resulted in more than thirty hours of recordings about the history of the neighborhood. Later, these recordings provided the foundations for a documentary film about the area.

In the meantime, at the University a major leadership change took place. Dr. Samuel Meyer, the President of the university since the retirement of President McIntosh, in his turn was now ready to retire. For the selection of the next chief executive a search committee was to be appointed. The selection of committee members came up on the agenda of the next meeting of the Executive Policy Council. Since I had been elected by the faculty to this decision-making body, I felt it was my responsibility to offer the faculty's perspective on this selection process. I did just that, and at the next meeting of the E.P.C. I circulated a proposal for the inclusion of at least three faculty members on the search committee beside the two administrators and the two Board of Trustee members. The audacity of this democratic proposal from a young, inexperienced, untenured and junior member sent shock waves through all who were present. Dr. Meyer got red in the face, and suggested that I withdraw my proposal. I did so, but indicated that I saw nothing wrong with the inclusion of faculty members in a search that dealt with the selection of a leader who was to determine academic policy. After this I resigned from E.P.C.

Perhaps the selection of the next president for ONU bore out my concerns. The next president selected was Raymond Loeschner, whose main concern was the bottom line. He had a business background and he paid less attention to the mission of the university than its economic viability. For example, the violin section of the Music Department could be eliminated because it drew too few students. In its place the marching band should be beefed up and its director hired to replace the instructor of the string instruments. Of course this was not the only problem with his vision for the University. The new president also set out to change our academic calendar from the quarter system to the semester system. This change could probably have been carried out if the president had really attempted to win over the faculty, rather than rush through the change without consulting those who would be most directly affected. The "bull in the chinashop" approach of this new president also led to the attempted firing of a number of tenured faculty members and a string of lawsuits against the university. This in turn led to some very lively faculty meetings, the collection of signatures on faculty petitions, and ultimately to the organization of a faculty union on campus. (But more of this later!)

MBK and Hungarian Summer Studies

The middle of the 1970's also was a very busy time for our work on supporting the work of CHRR and the regularization of our *ITT-OTT* meetings. For the latter we had to find a new location farther to the West, since more of our active members were from the mid-West rather than the East Coast. At our meeting in Ada, OH one year after our first public conference at Hereford, PA we selected Lake Chautauqua in Western New York state as an ideal location. Many Hungarian-Americans from Cleveland had summer homes on the shores of the lake which they would be willing to rent out for our conference. This meeting brought many new people to Chautauqua, for the reasons that our address list had grown and the Hereford conference increased interest for the friends of *ITT-OTT*. Important additions for our long-term development were the Bőjtös family from Cleveland, the Somogyi family from Connecticut, the Ertavy family from Buffalo and Béla and Melinda Kovács, and József Megyeri and Erika Bokor from Chicago. For our continuous religious debates the presence of Bishop Sándor Szent-Iványi (Unitarian) and Rev. András Hamza (Hungarian Reformed) were particularly welcome. At this time Sándor and Ilus Püski (Budapest and NYC) also contributed to our debates and our access to Hungarian reading materials. Furthermore, this first (1974) meeting at Lake Chautauqua committed us to establish a formal organization to replace the loose "discussion group" structure of the Friends of *ITT-OTT*.

Our second conference at Lake Chautauqua in 1975 brought into being the Magyar Baráti Közösség (Hungarian Communion of Friends). This organization adopted its constitution and by-laws at this meeting, stressing its commitment to its Hungarian religious roots, which included the pro-

Louis Éltető and myself addressing the participants at Lake Hope

The participants behind the Lake Hope Lodge, Márton Sass on the left, Tibor Cseh seated in the front row

At our Lake Hope Conference: Nárcissza, Erzsébet and Pál

motion of "non-denominational religious life in the Hungarian tradition, charitable work by and among people of Hungarian extraction, and cultural-educational endeavors that further Hungarian values." To achieve this commitment, those present and voting at this conference, who also accept-

Gáspár Nagy presenting and Márton Sass seated

L. to r. part of the audience, János Tokay, József Takács and András Hamza

L. to r. taking a break, Árpád Kovács, László Fülöp and Márton Sass

ed these goals, then elected Lajos J. Éltető as the interim "Gondnok" (Care-Taker/ President) for the organization until regular elections could be held for the officers of this Communion of Friends. In the meantime, it was Lajos J. Éltető's responsibility to charter us in the state of Oregon as a non-profit organization under the Oregon Revised Statutes, Chapter 61 and as an organization exempt from Federal Income Tax under section 501(c)(3) of the U.S. Internal Revenue Code. As our "Care-Taker" he duly carried out this responsibility.

Shortly after our conference we had to change the location of our future meetings. The house with the largest room for presentations, burned to the ground due to an electrical fire. For the next few months we (Panni and I) carried out a detailed search for possible alternative sites. Our active friend, Károly Endre Nagy and his wife, Emmi, suggested we drive down to Lake Hope State Park near Athens, OH and do a personal tour of the cabins and conference facilities. All four of us immediately fell in love with the lake, the park and the conference and housing facilities. It was not overcome with the touristy gadgets of golf, tennis and TV reception. At that time it did not even have air conditioned conference rooms or housing cabins. But it was in an unspoiled natural setting, with a beautiful lake surrounded by scenic hills and wonderful nature trails. Furthermore its name "Lake Hope" (Reménység tó), had particularly important meaning for Hungarians, it could resonate with their inner being after the Soviet crushing of the Hungarian fight for freedom and independence in 1956.

It was not difficult to "sell" this site to the Council and Care-Taker of the Hungarian Communion of Friends. We were also lucky that no-one had yet reserved the park for the middle of August when Saint Stephen, the Hungarian Christianizing king had his day of commemoration, that is August 20th. Since 1976 we have held every one of our annual conferences on the shores of Lake Hope, including the 50th anniversary of the founding of the Friends of *ITT-OTT* in 2018. Since 1976 Lake Hope has been transformed into *Reménység tava*, for one whole week, with Hungarian language, song and dance, making it into a cultural island mirroring the life of the Carpathian basin and the life of Hungarians in the Diaspora. For the latter, it has become one of the most important centers for cultural survival on the North American continent.

Lake Hope also became the organizational source for the Hungarian Studies Program at Portland State University from 1974 to 1979 as a site for planning and recruitment. After the Mount St. Helens volcano eruption near Portland we switched the Hungarian Summer Studies Program to Ohio Northern University from 1980 to 1985. In both instances we provided Hungarian language instruction at three levels, as well as History, Political Science, Literature and Folk culture courses. These courses were provided with college credit by Portland State University. (The instructional staff included besides Lajos Éltető, myself and my wife Panni, two guest language and literature instructors: Gyöngyi Köteles and Csilla Prileszky from Hungary, and Tibor Cseh, János Tokay and Louis Szathmáry in the area of folklore, and András and Mary Boros-Kazai, also in the area of language and literature.) These summer programs provided great immersion opportunities in Hungarian Studies for Diaspora youth. By the second half of the 1980's, however, our program could not compete with programs in Hungary. The opening of the borders made immersion in a Central European setting more attractive than that which we could provide them with on the other side of the Atlantic Ocean. Still, while they lasted, both the PSU and the ONU sites performed a very important role in fostering Hungarian studies.

Our Growing Family

When Panni (Julie for our English reading friends) and I were married on August 23, 1969, both of us wanted a large family with many children. Our efforts in this direction were not successful and many fertility related examinations later, we began to look into the possibility of adopting a child. We took steps in this direction in Hungary, because at that time it was bureaucratically less cumbersome and many orphan children were available for adoption. In the midst of our PSU summer program in 1977, just before we planned to finalize the paper work for adoption, Panni became pregnant. That was the year when Csilla Prileszky came to teach with us in the PSU Summer Program and became our daughter's namesake. On May 24th 1978, Csilla Anna arrived after making us wait for nine years instead of nine months. She was born at Lima, Ohio's Saint Rita's Hospital delivered by our family doctor, Dr. Gene Wright. The long wait was well worth it, she has enriched our lives in every way. Just one month after her arrival we took her in a "Moses basket" to

Portland, OR to be a star witness in our 1978 PSU Hungarian Summer Program.

Csilla Anna's younger sister, Anikó Ilona, did not make us wait another nine years. She appeared promptly on September 17th, 1980, also delivered by Dr. Gene Wright in the same hospital in Lima. She too has been a gift and an enrichment of our lives. For their love and affection and the challenges they have provided us with in their upbringing we have attempted to reciprocate with an existence that provided them with exposure to Hungarian culture and values parallel to the world view they acquired in growing up in Ada, OH, the heart of the American mid-West. To this end, we exiled TV from our home until they began to attend Ada public school.

Our family in Ada, OH: grandmother Erzsébet, András, Anikó, Csilla and Panni (1984)

The objective was to provide them with a Hungarian language setting, that would make them truly bi-lingual by the time they joined the educational world of the USA. (One sad side-effect of Anikó's arrival, was that Panni was not able to attempt to become pregnant again. Anikó's birth was surrounded with complications caused by blood-clots that required an extended hospital stay for Panni. So reluctantly we gave up on the idea of raising a soccer team.) But God gave us two beautiful, versatile and talented daughters who were healthy and self-assertive from the beginning. We were also fortunate that until both girls began school, Panni could be a full-time mother. In addition to all this, as a family we had the good fortune to spend a half year in Budapest on an IREX/Fulbright research grant in 1982–83, and a Fulbright Teaching grant in Debrecen during the 1992–93 academic year. This gave the girls an opportunity to be immersed in Hungarian culture and education for extended periods. Just what the doctor ordered for the perfection of the Hungarian language skills of the entire family.

My 1982–83 Research in Hungary

In line with some new opportunities I also applied for a research study grant in Hungary. I received such study support for six months starting in August 1982 and ending in February 1983. My IREX/Fulbright fellowship to do research in Hungary at the Gorky Library in Budapest also provided me with the opportunity to fulfill a promise I had made to Béla Lipták just before we left for Hungary in August. The promise was that I would visit the section of the Kerepesi cemetary where the martyrs of the 1956 retributions were buried, mostly in unmarked graves. To keep this promise I had to go outside my regular routine of visiting scholars and specialists of the national minority question in the Soviet bloc. (Most of this research was done at the Gorky library on Molnár street, where a fragment of the former Pál Teleki Research collection was disguised and protected by a few patriotic researchers like Rudolf Joó and Lajos Arday.) However, the state security apparatus still kept me in their sights, and whenever I departed from my daily routine, I felt the presence of these watchful eyes. In fact, as our landlord pointed out, at the apartment where we stayed, at given intervals a black sedan was parked near our residence with a youngish driver reading the latest news, hours on end.

Keeping my promise to Béla, when I realized the observer car was not present I headed toward Molnár street on the regular bus #102, which I always took to get to the Pest side of the Danube. But this time I cut through the city and boarded the Metro that took me to the Keleti railroad station, all the while checking, that I was not being followed. From there I backtracked a few blocks to Mező Imre street which runs along the outer edge of the cemetary. At the entrance I obtained a cemetary map and went directly to plot 21 in which about 400 graves were located. I then took photos of some of the graves and of the neglected, weed covered plot. After checking that I was not being observed, I went to the announcement nailed to a post, which declared that this plot would be emptied of graves and that those affected, should evacuate their own dead before December 31, 1982. (The announcement was dated July 9th, 1982.) This was twenty years after the general amnesty was supposedly issued to all who had been involved in the 1956 Fight for Freedom. Apparently the amnesty was not extended to the dead. I took one more look around before I tore the announcement off the post and tucked it under my shirt. I left the cemetary without being spotted. The next day I went to the American Embassy where the Cultural Charge D'Affaires promised to get the announcement into the Embassy's mailing and to my address in Ada, Ohio. This arrived and was forwarded to Béla Lipták, who used it to document the continued two-faced policies of the Kádár regime. We also published a facsimile copy in *ITT-OTT*.

These study opportunities in Hungary also enabled me to carry out important long-term networking with future leaders of the post-Soviet society. An example of this was the trip to Transylvania which was offered to me by Rudolf Joó at the Gorky library. His research contact was János Szász, a Sociologist, who was in the process of planning a trip to Cluj/Kolozsvár with a Hungarian from Sweden who was the fiancé of the younger sister of Sándor Kányádi's wife. While this trip involved meeting Kányádi and his family again (he and his wife had been our guests at Lake Hope in 1979), it also involved meeting Edgár Balogh [24] and András Sütő [25] two important writers of the Hungarian community in Romania. While we missed Sütő, we did have the opportunity to have a long two-hour interview with Edgár Balogh and also long conversations with Sándor Kányádi.

On the way to Transylvania all three of my fellow passengers were chain smokers and we were traveling in a small three-wheeled vehicle. The cramped space transformed me into a smoker although I did not light up even once.

---

24 Edgár Balogh (1906–1996) began his political and writing career as a member of the Sickle (Sarlós) Movement in Slovakia during the interwar period. In 1935 he moved to Romania where he continued his career in Kolozsvár/Cluj in Transylvania as a staff member of *Korunk*, at that time a leftist periodical. He was an important source for understanding inter-ethnic relations in Romania from the middle of the 1930's to the Ceaușescu era.

25 András Sütő (1927–2006) was the most significant Hungarian prose and drama writer of post-World War II Romania. One of his most significant works is *Anyám könnyű álmot ígér* [My mother promised me sweet dreams]. He was among the writers who first were allowed to visit Hungarians in the Diaspora in 1973. He also was our guest at Lake Hope in 1993.

However, because in Romania at that time gasoline was rationed and long lines formed in front of every gas station, we had to take a spare large ten liter gasoline can with us. This can was my seat in the back, covered by a makeshift pillow which made the five-hour trip bearable from a comfort perspective. But comfort was not my main worry, my silent prayers related more to the flamable content of my seat. Fortunately, on the trip back to Budapest—in a snow storm—the storage can was already empty.

General Transmission of Mission

From the very beginning our Hungarian Communion of Friends assumed that the transmission of our values, language and identity is a desirable and possible goal. In raising our own children this was always part of our "gameplan." Exiling English language television from our home was motivated by this quest. This also required a great deal of commitment on our part to read Hungarian fairy tales or folk tales, to read poems, sing songs or tell stories that served the purpose of cultural transmission. This required a lot of energy after a long day at the office or in the classroom. Both Panni and I were com-

Father & daughter trip along the Ohio River: Csilla and myself (Anikó's snapshot)

General Transmission of Mission

Father & daughter trip along the Ohio River: Anikó and Csilla (my snapshot)

mitted to providing Csilla and Anikó with a solid bi-lingual capability and an emotional attachment to their ethnic roots. This meant we had to spend quality time with them even when we had to do other things, like preparing for our next lecture. I remember well the moment when my four-year-old Anikó took my face in both her little hands and turned it toward herself, saying that she wanted my complete attention. Sharing our language and values always required that kind of attention. The hope is that the next generation in turn will retain and transmit these values to their children and will become the organizers of Human Rights workshops.

Successful sharing also requires institutional support. Although we lived in a small town that had no other Hungarian speakers, we were able to send the girls to summer girl scout camps where their peers reinforced their language skills. Their emotional attachments to things Hungarian was also reflected in their work and play habits. For example Csilla helped me compose the index for my book on Transylvania in 1983 while I was on a research summer grant at Ohio State University. (At the time she was five years old!) Both girls also learned the poems of Sándor Kányádi which they presented at Lake Hope in the context of the program at the end of the week. Otherwise, their lives were part and parcel of Ada, OH. They were Ada Bulldogs, involved in 4-H, involved in ballet and gymnastics, and all-around "A" students. Anikó was also a member of the girl's soccer team. When they went away to college, Csilla to Butler University and Anikó to Valparaiso University, both in the neighboring state of Indiana, we could only hope that the Hungarian connection would also remain a part of their formal educational interests.

With our daughters both Panni and I were always tuned in to their educational and cultural development. Our busy organizational life, on the other hand, hurt our relationship with each other. Both the academic conference schedule, particularly the annual pilgrimage to the Columbia University ASN[26] conferences, the annual cycle of the NMUN conferences also to New York City that I mentioned before, my own conferences and workshops, plus my share of the editing of *ITT-OTT*, became too much after I also began working on the Birmingham documentary film and the filming of the Árpádhon Hungarians in Louisiana. At the time I did not realize that each of these activities incrementally deprived us of time that we should have been spending together. There was also another issue under the surface, it was the problem that Panni and I were drifting apart because we had strong religious preferences that were in conflict. To bridge the differences we attended meetings with marriage counselors, but our efforts were by then too little, too late. At a certain point we realized that a great gulf separated us, which made it impossible to compromise. However, we agreed to stop short of divorce until Csilla and Anikó completed high school. When our divorce was finalized it was based on mutual consent, but led to a great deal of psychological pain for both of us. Remaining friends and respecting each other, did not help us to mend our own relations, it just made separation and divorce later somewhat more civilized. In the interim, I moved to Bluffton, a nearby college town, from which I commuted to teach my classes at ONU.

Documenting the Hungarian Community in Toledo

The oral history projects of my ONU ethnic studies seminar students were in large part possible because we had excellent support from ethnic community leaders like Peter Ujvagi in East Toledo, particularly regarding the Bir-

---

26 ASN stands for Association for the Study of Nationalities which publishes *Nationality Papers* and holds its annual conferences at the Harriman Center of Columbia University.

mingham neighborhood. Ujvagi had already helped to put together a film on the Mummers play tradition in the neighborhood. In our conversations we began to talk about doing a documentary on the Hungarian past and present in Toledo. Ed Jurevicz, a documentary film maker from Kent State also worked with us to put together such a proposal for the support of the Ohio Humanities Council.

We began working on such a proposal in 1981 and were finally able to get grant support for the filming in 1985. However, the OHC did not approve our cinematographer, so we had to find someone else. Fortunately, our MBK network came through with flying colors. One of our friends, Ignatius Kazella, sat next to a Hungarian cinematographer, László Mihályfy, flying from Budapest to Newark Airport. His discovery, led to connections to a friend in Cleveland who knew about our efforts, who in turn informed us that this person would be willing to join our project. We began the filming of the Mummers (Bethlehemes) Play in Birmingham, during Christmas week. In a whirlwind schedule of interviews, of folkdance sessions, neighborhood barroom conversations at the VFW, and the reflections of multiple generations on the survival of the community, provided close to 70 hours of interesting material for our documentary. Mihályfy also returned during August, and with the help of Steve Bognar, filmed the Birmingham Ethnic Festival, the neighborhood's celebration of defeating City Hall's efforts to build a four-lane highway through the geographic center of the community. After this came the long hours of editing the film, with the assistance of Rosemary Kurek, which was finally completed in the winter of 1986. With the title of "Urban Turf and Ethnic Soul," it was finally broadcast by Toledo Public Television in the Spring of 1987.

To take advantage of László Mihályfy's talents, I got the University to underwrite a one-week filming trip to Hammond, Louisiana and the Hungarian strawberry farmers of the Árpádhon settlement. Our team was composed of a former resident of the settlement, Judy Balogh, who was our contact to the local residents. I was the driver of the ONU van and László Mihályfy, plus a young technician from our media services, traveled to do the filming. This too was a whirlwind operation and we were able to record about thirty-five hours of interviews and community activities. Unfortunately we were not able to get the funding for additional recordings and the editing time to produce a pilot film. This remains to be a project that a future member of the younger generation may be able to complete.

Departmental Transformations

As I noted earlier, the retirement of President Samual Meyer brought many changes to ONU, including to our Department. For a few years, the atmosphere on campus was filled with turmoil. In this decade we also witnessed some turnover in the personnel of the Department. David Saffell joined the faculty from Baldwin Wallace as a dual replacement for Tony Salomone and Steve Bennet, both on the Political Science side. On the History side we had the retirement of Oscar Darlington and the hiring of David Sefton and Ellen Wilson. These changes were taking place in the midst of the faculty's unionization to challenge the arbitrariness of the Loeschner presidency. Personally I was very much involved in the organization of the union, because I realized that unless we were considered eligible for "collective bargaining" we did not exist. To gain claut we also affiliated with the Ohio Education Association (OEA). This finally got the attention of the University administration, when the vote on campus got the two largest colleges (Arts & Sciences and Engineering) to be part of the bargaining unit. Members of the Pharmacy and Law College did not join us, for obvious reasons: the lawyers already had

ONU: My home base and employer from 1968 to 2008

Departmental Transformations

Faculty and staff of the Department of History, Political Science & Criminal Justice in 2003: front row l. to r. Andrew Ludányi, JoAnn Scott, Patricia Badertscher, Ellen Wilson, John Lomax, back row l. to r. Steve Moore, Keith Durkin, David Smith, Raymond Schuck, Robert Cupp, Michael Loughlin, Robert Alexander

Hill Building which housed both the History and Politics and the Sociology and Psychology departments during my tenure at ONU

a union, while the pharmacists were the overpaid beneficieries of the existing system. At any rate the NLRB recognized us as a bargaining unit, which meant many hours after classes, sitting across the table from the top administrators (George Hassell, Financial V.P.; James Moore, the University Registrar; and the University's lawyer), on our side we generally had Anne Lippert, President of our Unit, myself as V.P. of the organization, and Terry Kaiser or Phillip Compton, plus our OEA lawyer. The bargaining involved almost constant eye-ball to eye-ball confrontations, but generally carried to a conclusion in a civilized context. At any rate all faculty members gained from our efforts, even those who voted against the union. Finally, the Board of Trustees also realized that Ray Loeschner was hurting the future of ONU and they bought out his contract and initiated a search for a new President. The new selection fell on DeBow Freed a graduate of West Point and a leader who paid attention to our academic reputation as well as the bottom line.

In the early years of the Freed Presidency our Department also underwent a renewal. Bob Davis stepped down in 1978 as Chair and David Saffell became his successor. Under David's leadership we had four important new hires and two retirements. The retirees were Boyd Sobers in American and Ohio History and Anthony Milnar in European History. They were replaced by Terry Gilbreth in Public Administration and JoAnn Scott in Constitutional Law and Criminal Justice. We also hired a European Historian in the person of Michael Loughlin and a Medieval and Ancient Historian in the person of John Lomax. In the 1980s and 1990s this department was the academic powerhouse of the College of Arts and Sciences.

Canadian Studies at ONU

At the urging of Ellen Wilson, our Chair David Saffell, considered adding Canada as a component of our offerings in Comparative Political Systems. Ellen had joined our Department at the height of the crisis with the Loeschner administration. She was our specialist in American Colonial History and also on American Frontier History. Therefore when she became a member of our Department as a change in our perspective she wanted to increase our offerings and our interest in our neighbor to the North. I must admit that I knew very little about Canadian politics and began to attend some seminars and special lectures on Canada at Bowling Green State University. These peaked my interest and I applied for a Canadian Studies Faculty Enrichment Grant, which enabled me to spend almost two months in Ottawa, Ontario in 1990. These weeks of focused attention on Canadian politics led to the development of a syllabus for a new course in Canadian studies. It was team taught by colleagues in true interdisciplinary fashion. Those weeks also added to my own comparative political enrichment.

At the same time Panni and both Csilla and Anikó came to visit me with their best friends, Elizabeth and Kirsten. This visit saw us take in all the significant sights in the city, including the Canadian Parliament. We also had the chance to drive out to visually take into account the Canadian "wall" north of the Ottawa river which has concentrated the population to hug the U.S. border throughout most of this beautiful and untamed land. It was great having the family together in this way even for a brief week, but for some reason the Ada solidarity of flying a kite together or participating in the graduation parades as cheer leaders just failed to bring us closer to each other even in this ideal setting. In this sense, on the personal level, the Canadian promise was not fulfilled.

1992–93 Fulbright Professorship in Debrecen

In 1992–93 I again received a Fulbright Fellowship, this time for teaching at the University of Debrecen (at that time still called Kossuth Lajos University). This was a wonderful teaching opportunity since it came only two years after the regime change in Hungary. It gave me a sense of mission, since I was attached to a department that had previously been responsible for the instruction of "Socialist Realism" a highly politicized section of the "Sociology Department" which was back then completely controlled by the Hungarian Socialist Worker's Party. Most of the members of this Department were left-overs of the pre-regime change years. I'm sure many of them thought of me as a "hatchet man" who threatened their teaching careers. Actually, on a personal level I got along well with most of them and I did not influence personnel decisions. My main concern was to share with them a syllabus and teaching method that involved greater give-and-take, more participation by the students. In my own classes I found it much more difficult to lecture in Hungarian, but in most of my classes I could lecture in English. For me it was a great teaching experience, although I never really got used to testing my students verbally without written paper tests. Our year in Debrecen also gave Csilla and Anikó the opportunity to be enrolled in the Teacher-training "Kis Kossuth" (Small Kossuth) grade school affiliated with the University. This enabled them to participate in all the activities, field trips, of their classmates. This provided them with life-long friendships as well as total immersion in their culture and language. For Panni and me this provided similar opportunities. We could act as a bridge between American Fulbrighters throughout Hungary and the University of Debrecen. Huba Brückner, the Director of the Hungarian Fulbright Commission, asked me to plan an excursion for all Fulbrighters to the Hortobágy[27] National Park. This was a full day of activities, but a great mixer between the American and the Hungarian academic communities.

Two other side trips for faculty were trips to Transcarpathia and Transylvania, both significant regions of historical Hungary, but then a part of the Ukrainian S.S.R. and Romania respectively. For the Transcarpathian trip we will forever be grateful to András Görömbei of the Hungarian Literature section of Debrecen University, while for my excursion to Transylvania I can thank my niece Paulette Layton who was teaching English at this time in Cluj/Kolozsvár. Both trips were memorable for the excitement and the lessons we learned about Hungary's neighbors to the East.

In my own classes on occasion I was able to bring in a guest lecturer from the outside, who had some insight into the American political or economic world. One of the most interesting such lectures was presented by Magda Sass, the special representative of the State of Illinois in Budapest. (She was the former wife of Márton Sass, second Care-Taker/President of MBK, and she was also the future wife of Nobel Laureate Imre Kertész.) Magda gave a lecture to my class on American Civilization regarding the issue of "corruption." This was a very popular issue with our State Department, since many

---

27 Hortobágy is a region of Hungary near Debrecen, which is today a major tourist attraction, but used to be the locale for traditional animal husbandry, the romanticized "Hungarian West" where outlaws (betyárok) and horsemen (csíkós) culture dominated until the end of the 19th century.

American investors hesitated when they encountered lower level payoffs and other such abuses. In the building where she worked opposite the "Astoria Hotel," the Arthur Anderson Corporation shared offices with her operation on the fifth floor. I also felt that her lecture would serve my mission of holding up the shining American example of uncorruptability. Magda used her contact with Arthur Anderson to reflect on the impeccable character of the American business world. It was an impressive lecture. Unfortunatelly, within a few years came the revelations of the vast accounting abuses of this firm. This came as a major shock not just to Magda and myself, but also all the students who had attended her lecture. Unfortunatelly this was not the only case that year, the ENRON abuses followed soon in its wake.

Academic Conferences

As a supplement to the annual Model UN Spring excursions to New York City, I became a regular participant in conferences at the Harriman Institute at Columbia University, at the Duquesne History Forum in Pittsburgh and at meetings of the AAASS[28] and the AHEA.[29] But more important was the development that led me to organize conferences on my own. The catalyst for this was the organization of a history conference held at Kent State University by scholars from that institution jointly with scholars from Romania to celebrate the 60th anniversary of Romania's unification with Transylvania in 1918. When I found out about the upcoming conference, I immediately helped mobilize a demonstration on the Kent State University campus against this event because it was anything but scholarly. Its main objective was simply to propagandize and legitimize Romania's right to Transylvania.

We were able to bring demonstrators to the campus of KSU in front of its library and then moved many demonstrators into the building to fill the con-

---

28   AAASS stands for American Association for the Advancement of Slavic Studies (later renamed ASEEES: Association of Slavic, East European and Eurasian Studies), one of the largest multidisciplinary scholarly organizations devoted to the study of Eastern Europe, the Soviet Bloc and the publication of *Slavic Review*.

29   AHEA stands for American Hungarian Educators Association, founded in the early 1970's in Cleveland, Ohio.

ference room. Needless to say, the tension in the room was very high and the organizers realized that they had to let some of the demonstrators to the rostrum to question the Romanian presenters. From the protest speakers, the message to the KSU conference organizers was that the one-sided nature of the presentations, necessitated the organization of a second conference to put things right. In the end, the KSU organizers agreed to host a second conference in the Spring of 1979 to rectify the inbalance of the presentations. They asked me to work with Professor John F. Cadzow of KSU to put together such a conference. He left most of the planning to me and focused mainly on the local arrangements.

This was a great opportunity because Kent State had a high visibility profile as a consequence of the National Guard shootings on campus which had targeted demonstraters against the Vietnam War. Thus, the university administration was very sensitive to public pressure and I was given a free hand to come up with the focus of the conference and the list of participants. With this responsibility on my shoulders I approached as many big name scholars as possible. Fortunately many such scholars were willing to be on the program including such well known scholars as Stephen Kertész of Notre Dame University, István Deák of Columbia University and Joseph Held of Rutgers University. These "big names" were supplemented by young scholars whose work was already known in the area, including Louis J. Éltető, Stephen B. Vardy, Peter Pastor, László Domonkos and myself. For chairs of the panels we recruited mainly KSU professors, while as commentators we were able to get people like Karl Roider and Gerald J. Bobango. The conference was a success and the papers that provided its content were ultimately included in a book edited by Cadzow, Éltető and myself and published under the title: *Transylvania: The Roots of Ethnic Conflict* by KSU Press in 1983.

For me the KSU conference was a watershed event because it demonstrated to me that even on a shoe-string budget it is possible to organize significant events. Furthermore, that these conferences can lead to publishable results which will be available to future generations on library shelves or as materials incorporated into the lectures or syllabi of courses on East Central Europe. It also provided me with an academic network that would be available for future similar activities. Just two years later, based on my KSU contacts and the support of the American Hungarian Educators' Association I organized a symposium in 1981 at Kent State commemorating the 25th anniversary of the 1956 Hungarian Revolution. Again, among the presenters there were many big names including Denis Sinor of Indiana University, János Horváth of Butler University, Béla Király of Brooklyn College, and Paul Jónás of the University of New Mexico, as well as many younger scholars. Again it produced studies that were later published in collections about the revolution.

This was followed by five other conferences, one in 1985, two in 1990, one in 1992 and one in 2004. The first was a conference devoted to the role of Oszkár Jászi and Nationalism, held at Oberlin College where death had ended his teaching career in 1957. What was interesting and different in the organization of this conference was that it included scholars from Hungary whom I had the chance to meet while I was doing research in Budapest at the Gorky Library on my IREX/Fulbright grant in 1982–83. Among them were Rudolf Joó, Lajos Für, Attila Pók, György Litván, Péter Hanák and Géza Jeszenszky. They were joined by American and Canadian scholars like Thomas Spira, Nándor Dreisziger, Béla Várdy, Stephen Borsody, Lajos Éltető and myself. This conference also led to published results, including a special issue of *Hungarian Studies Review* edited by Nándor Dreisziger.

The remaining three conferences already took place after the collapse of the Soviet Union and the satellite states of this empire. The first was a brief one-day conference that dealt with the process of Soviet collapse as a consequence of re-emerging nationalism in East Central Europe. It was held at my home institution of ONU in the Spring of 1990, and involved my own colleagues as presiding chairs and commentators. The participants included Michael Loughlin, David Saffell, Ellen Wilson, John Lomax, Károly Jokay, Bulcsú Veress and myself among others.

In that same academic year I also had the chance to organize a conference in October on Religious Freedom in Transylvania at the University of Toledo. This was a three-day conference and had the support of the Ohio Humanities Council, the First Unitarian Church of Toledo, the Meadville/Lombard Theological School of Chicago and our own Hungarian Communion of Friends. At the same time, the local Birmingham neighborhood provided its support and UT was the host at its Canaday Library and by providing design and secretarial assistance in the person of Bernadett Ujvagi. Chef Louis Szathmáry loaned the University a special Transylvanian book, art and history exhibit for the conference. The Unitarians of Toledo allowed the play written by András Sütős *Star at the Stake*,[30] to be performed in their church by the New York City Threshold Theatre group of Pamela Billig and Jenő Brogyányi.

This conference focused on the importance of the Diet of Torda (1568) in Transylvania which was the first on the European continent (perhaps in the world) to declare religious toleration. It declared that the Roman Catholic, the Calvinist Reformed, the Lutheran and the Unitarian religious denominations were accepted and the others tolerated. For its time this was the most far-reaching expression of religious freedom. It would take the rest of Europe almost a century before it caught up with the Declaration of Torda. The presenters at the conference included among others Donald Harrington of New York, Alexander S. Unghváry of Buena Vista, Colorado, Klára Hegyi of the Hungarian Academy of Sciences, Judit Gellérd of Chico, California, Raphael Vago of the University of Tel Aviv, Walker Connor of Trinity College, George M. Williams of California State University, Stephen Fischer-Galati of the University of Colorado at Boulder, as well as Thomas Szendrey, Lajos J. Éltető, Charles Z. Jokay, Rudolf Joó and myself.

The 1992 conference was also held at the University of Toledo. Its focus was on Urban Communities, Ethnicity and American Civilization. This conference was co-sponsored by UT, the AHEA and the Hungarian Community of Friends. Peter Ujvagi, Bernadett Ujvagi, Enikő Basa-Molnár, and Jack Ahern were involved in making the program a success. In addition to faculty members from UT, Bowling Green State University and ONU it included some researchers from Hungary, among them Zoltán Fejős. Presentations and discussions by Peter Ujvagi and Congresswoman Marcy Kaptur were

---

30 *Star at the Stake* was one of the plays written by András Sütő which dramatized the conflict in the early history of the Reformation between John Calvin and Michael Servetius, the conflict between a rigid and dogmatic interpretation versus a different one. In the play Servetius becomes the "Star" at the stake. Before its performance in Toledo, OH the play had already been performed in NYC by the Threshold Theatre company. Its first performance was at the Madách Theatre in Budapest in 1975, followed by performances in Kaposvár, Kolozsvár/Cluj, Zagreb and Marosvásárhely/Târgu Mureș.

linked to opportunities to visit the Birmingham neighborhood as well as the Muslim Mosque south of the city in the suburb of Oregon. At this conference there was also an opportunity to showcase our documentary film "Urban Turf and Ethnic Soul" which deals with the Birmingham community.

Finally the last conference I organized before my retirement from ONU was a two-day "Symposium on Chechnya and Russia" in 2004. The objective of this conference was to reflect on the conflict in the Caucasus region both under the Boris Yeltsin and the Vladimir Putin administrations. Official American policy under the George W. Bush administration was to make a dirty deal with Russia's Putin concerning the latter's dirty war in Chechnya. The "deal" was simple, the USA would not criticize Putin's war against "Chechen terrorists" if Putin would keep out of Bush's "war on terrorism" in Iraq and Afghanistan. In fact, with the help of the complicit American media "Chechen terrorists" were always encountered even in Iraq and Afghanistan. At any rate, our conference with presentations from B. Williams and Thomas Goltz as well as commentary by Michael Loughlin and James Satterwhite as well as myself, we were able to present the Chechen perspective in a more objective context. The voices of Anna Politkovskaya, Alexander Litvinenko and John Russell were present at the conference without their physical presence.

Human Rights Workshops

Almost as a continuation of the Hungarian Summer Studies programs the Hungarian Communion of Friends and the newly created Hungarian American Coalition began to sponsor Human Rights Workshops. We arrived at this decision because we began to worry that HHRF was so overwhelmed by its day-to-day responsibilities of defending Hungarian minority rights, that it did not have time to think about training future human rights activists in the American art of lobbying. We held our first "workshop" at Wellsburg, WV in 1989. Our host was the William Penn Fraternal organization, which owned the scenic property on the WV shore of the Ohio River. Steve Danko, a former classmate of mine at Elmhurst College, had become the President of the William Penn Association. He attended the first day of our workshop and provided the welcoming words and overview for the next day's activities. Peter Ujvagi, Beáta Kovács and myself provided the details for effective letter writing to Congessional representatives. In the midst of our workshop we heard the news that in Tiananmen Square in Beijing the military was used to break up the demonstration of pro-democratic forces. It led to a massacre of many demonstrators. This was a dramatic signal to all of us that the workshops were our link to world events and struggles for democracy.

Contacting political leaders via phone calls and visits were also discussed. By late afternoon Emese Latkóczy and László Hámos also arrived to present their know-how on mobilizing local support groups and the writing of effective position papers. We also discussed the development of contacts with the mass media.

Before I turn to our 1990, or next workshop, I must mention my participation in the establishment of the Hungarian American Coalition. In 1989 not only the Soviet Union collapsed, but there was a crisis in the representation of American-Hungarian interests in Washington, D.C. The major umbrella organization of our interests was the American Hungarian Federation which had been established by the economic emigration in 1906. In the 1980's it was torn asunder by factional struggles between the 1945, 1948, and 1956 émigrés who wanted to wrest control of the organization out of the hands of the "old timers." The organization fragmented into at least three parts and lawsuits began to dissipate its financial foundations and the credibility of its leaders. This convinced many of the younger generation, including the non-ideological leaders, that a totally new start was necessary. Rev. Imre Bertalan, Frank Koszorus and representatives of the large fraternal organizations called for such a new start in the summer of 1989. Many from MBK joined this effort of renewal. Initially HHRF was reluctant to join because it did not want to share its successful influence in lobbying activities. My role was simply to be the recording secretary for this organization, named Hungarian American Coalition (HAC). This role, plus friendship with key leaders like Edith Lauer and Zsolt Szekeres, enabled me to obtain the support of the organization for future Human Rights Workshops.

A Model Human Rights Workshop

We organized the 1990 workshop at Catholic University in Washington D.C. June 9–12. HHRF was well represented by Edith Lauer and her daughter Andrea, William Penn Association was represented by Gay Banes, HAHRC[31] was represented by Ildikó Bodoni and MBK was represented by Beáta and László Kovács and myself. We also had NJ, NY, CT, PA, VA and OH represented among the participants. What made this workshop "different" was that we could set up meetings with our representatives or their administrative assistants directly in their offices and inform them about the deteriorating conditions of the Hungarians in Romania.

This workshop deserves a little more detailed attention since it set the standard for all the subsequent workshops. It was attended by a good cross-section of Hungarian-Americans and affiliated human rights activists from the region East of the Mississippi. In total the workshop doubled the number of participants of the first such workshop held at Wellsburg, West Virginia. Of the twenty-five participants (not counting the briefings attended by many others) the majority were of college age, but also a handful of veterans who added a wealth of personal experience to the group.

The workshop was made possible through the cooperative efforts of seven Hungarian-American organizations, including the Hungarian Communion of Friends, The Hungarian Human Rights Foundation, the Hungarian American Coalition, the William Penn Association, the Hungarian Reformed Federation of America, the Young Hungarians' Political Action Committee, and the Hungarian-American Human Rights Council. The financial support of three of these organizations covered the housing and other rental expenses at the Catholic University of America. These organizations also provided most of the instructors who directed the workshop.

The unique feature of this CUA workshop—as opposed to Wellsburg the previous summer—was that it combined the instructional opportunities and group discussions with direct exposure to the political process via briefings

---

31 HAHRC stands for Hungarian American Human Rights Council, established by Ildikó Bodoni to supplement the work of HHRF in the Chicago area.

Participants of the 1990 Human Rights Workshop in Washington, DC, including 2nd from left Edith Lauer, 4th from left Andrea Lauer, 7th from left Zsolt Balla, 11th from left Gay Banes, 13th from left László Hámos, and 16th from left András Ludányi

at the Executive Office of the White House, the Capitol, and the Hungarian Embassy. The theoretical was combined with meetings with actual policy-makers.

Dr. Kay Scrimger of the U.S.Conference of Mayors set the tone for the workshop with her presentation on the characteristics of the American political scene and the role of pressure politics. Next, Bernard Hanley, Public Affairs Manager from Chicago, discussed "The Care and Feeding of the Mass Media," combined with a series of worksheets that the participants received. After lunch, the next discussion dealt with organizing an effective phonathon network. This was presented by Bernard Tamas on the basis of the New Jersey experience of the Young Hungarian Political Action Comitee. Edith Lauer, the Director for Special Events of the HHRF, outlined the considerations that must guide an effective fundraising campaign. She focused on the winning psychology of such campaigns. Finally, I discussed the choice of words, the use of concepts in public discourse. What is meant by ethnicity or nationality, and how can their use lead to effective or ineffective communication with public officials or the media? I shared some sample publications with the group. After supper Stephen Benko of the NSC staff shared his insights about the executive side of the decision-making process.

Monday morning I outlined the do's and dont's when writing letters to the editor or public officials. László Hámos (President, HHRF) then discussed the meetings we were to attend during the next two days and distributed profiles of representatives who play key roles in the human rights areas of concern.

After a fast lunch at the U.S. Conference of Mayors, the participants hurried to the Hill, for a briefing with the staff of Senator Lautenberg of NJ. Diana Rubin provided a summary of the Senator's role in the human rights struggle. From here we went to a meeting at the White House for a meeting with Robert Hutchings on the staff of the NSC responsible for Eastern European policy. This was followed by a tour of the Old Executive Office Building led by Stephen Benko and Marika Gulden.

Tuesday, June 12 was the concluding day of the workshop. A wrap-up session was held, discussing future plans and the organization of similar workshops. I suggested that for the coordination of the work an advisory committee should be established including at least one representative from each sponsoring organization. This was followed by László Hámos' run-down of the activities of the Congressional Human Rights Caucus and the role of representatives Gibbons, Atkins and Lantos.

The highlight of the briefings was the testimony of András Sütő before the Caucus, with Congressman Lantos and László Hámos providing the background for the testimony. It was followed by a videotape of the pogrom of March 19th, as a result of which Sütő lost his eyesight. This was followed by meetings with representatives Gibbons and Atkins. This provided the opportunity to confront both an unfriendly and a friendly official regarding the rights of Hungarians in Transylvania. All in all, the learning experience was many-sided, practical, and hopefully successful in strengthening the network of those who will continue the truggle for human rights in the future.

The Subsequent Workshops

After the Washington DC experience, we also felt that it was necesary to have more outreach to Hungarian-American communities beyond the "beltway." To this end we began to turn to other population centers. The 1991 workshop was held in Bannockburn, Illinois just outside of Chicago. It was organized by Ildikó Bodoni and HAHRC and Márton Sass and his son Marci Jr., for the social get-together with the Chicago Hungarian-American community. Two special features of this workshop were our meetings with Illinois representatives in their home offices and a visit to the headquarters of the Polish-American Congress where we received a guided tour through their operations. Also important components of this workshop were the methods to influence the electronic media. This was highlighted for us by Bernard Hanley a specialist in this field.

In 1992 we organized our workshop in Cleveland, OH at John Carroll University. The local organizers included Márta Pereszlényi (AHEA), Edith Lauer (HAC and MBK) and representatives of the Hungarian Scout troops of Cleveland, including Gabriella Nádas. This workshop also had the input of three active political leaders, including Kay Randle Scrimger of the U.S. Conference of Mayors, János Horváth of Republicans from Indiana, and Peter Ujvagi of Democrats from Ohio. It had a very strong group of participants from OH, but there were some people present also from IL, IN, PA, NJ and CT. One interesting spin-off from this workshop was that Paulette Layton from CT was inspired to spend a year in Kolozsvár/Cluj to observe Hungarian community existence in that city while teaching English to Seminary students.

In 1993 we did not organize a workshop, since during that academic year I was on a teaching Fulbright grant in Debrecen. However, in 1994 we picked Hartford, CT for our next workshop and brought together a good group of participants from the East Coast, including NJ, NY, CT, MA and Washington D.C. At this time we also involved Árpád Nemes who was an intern for HHRF and Réka Szemerkényi, who was in the midst of graduate studies in DC. Balázs, Csilla and Ilona Somogyi and Narcissza Layton helped with local arrangements.

The 1995 workshop was organized in Shepherdstown, WV close to Washington D.C. For local organization Dr. Katalin Vörner Almay set up arrangements. This included an exhibition of Hungarian folk art from different parts of the Carpathian basin. It also included a discussion of Yugoslavia's collapse and the effects on the Hungarians of Vojvodina. The discussion became quite lively as my interpretations were not shared by Tibor Purger and some of the faculty at Shepherds College. (Of course their observations were not based on a bike ride through Vojvodina!) Because of Shepherdstown's proximity to Washington, DC. we were able to drive into DC for special meetings with our representatives. I took a group of Ohio participants to the Office of Senator John Glenn. At the last minute he could not meet with us, but his administrative assistant spent an hour listening to our concerns. Besides the OH, WV, MD, VA and DC participants we had two people from NJ and PA. For all of them we emphasized that it is very important to have some sort of written record and follow-up with the representatives that we visited.

This workshop was in the midst of the next presidential election campaign. Almost as a follow-up in one memorable event we attempted to focus the attention of American policy-makers on Hungarian problems during the 1996 Presidential campaign in Milwaukee, Wisconsin. The Democrats were always more pro-active when it involved mobilizing ethnic voters. They invited the representatives of Polish, Czech, Hungarian and Slovak voters,

Between Al Gore and Bill Clinton during the 1996 national campaign

through their most active organizations to come to Milwaukee, where they could meet with incumbent President Clinton, for a briefing and discussion of common concerns, including NATO expansion. The Hungarians at this meeting were represented by the Hungarian American Coalition, the Hungarian Communion of Friends, the Hungarian Human Rights Foundation and the American Hungarian Federation. All of us arrived in the city in the midst of a major early snow storm. The President, however, could not join us because his mother had just passed away a day earlier. Vice President Albert Gore came to the meeting with the President's foreign policy advisors. We sat in a semi-circle facing Albert Gore and the advisers, but the Hungarian-American delegates were in the more dimmly lit quarter of the room. Thus, most of the questions were fielded from the Polish-, Slovak- and Czech organizations who sat in the middle under the lights. We began to feel left out of the conversation and realized that time was running out. The moderator in fact made the point that we had time for only one more question. At this juncture I elbowed László Hámos, who sat next to me, to raise his hand while I knocked over the water glass that was in front of me. The clattering glass turned all eyes toward us and Al Gore saw Hámos' waving hand. Hámos could then unload the issue we had all wanted to put on the table, the linking of the rights of Hungarian minorities to the question of NATO expansion. Hámos then let loose with both barrels, his usually well formulated statement on this question. I would say this was one small glass sacrificed for a moment's attention. Sometimes a well placed water glass can have a greater impact than innumerable waving hands!

After a great deal of soul-searching, we decided that the next workshop would be organized on the West Coast in 1996. Edith and John Lauer (HAC) Géza Kádár (HAC) and the Unitarian-Universalists of Berkeley, CA helped with local arrangements. The first day's meetings were held on the Berkeley campus, the second day was held at the former Haraszthy winery, with the final day and housing also on the Berkeley campus. Most of the participants were from California, but Helen Szablya's family and a few others also represented Washington state and Oregon. My colleague Michael Loughlin also attended and participated in the lively discussions related to minority and religious rights in Transylvania.

The 1997 workshop moved back to the mid-West, to Ypsilanti, Michigan. Local organization was in the hands of Krisztina Ujvagi at Eastern Michigan University. Peter and Bernadett Ujvagi also assisted with local arrangements as did Sándor and Piroska Zoltán. An interesting part of the workshop was the presence of a Tibetan human rights activist who shared their experiences with our group. Most of the participants were from the Great Lakes area, from MI, IL, IN and OH. Drs. Péter Kovalszki and Mária Repolszki and their daughters participated in the campus discussions, as did Csilla Ludányi from Butler University. Congresswoman Marcy Kaptur contributed her experience to the discussions during the conclusion of the workshop.

The final workshop was organized three years later in Washington D.C. in 2000. It was held at SAIS, but poorly publicized and sparcely attended. Because the Albanian crisis in Kosovo was at center stage, we wanted to co-ordinate our workshop with their human rights activists. Although we put together an interesting program including Julie Mertus from the ONU Law College, Béla Lipták of the electronic Hungarian Lobby, Emese Latkóczy and László Hámos of HHRF, and Frank Koszorus (HAC and AMSz), the last minute withdrawal of the Kosovo participants, left only a handful of PA, NJ, NY participants. The local arrangements were all in place, the presentations were excellent, but the mobilization was inadequate. I must bear the blame for the latter. With this I stepped out of workshop organizing, but I have the hope that younger activists will pick up the slack!

My Meeting with Márika

In the meantime, a number of important events also took place in my personal life. When our friends and extended family found out that Panni and I had separated, they could not believe it. In their eyes we were the perfect couple, but appearances sometimes mislead even those who are closest. After the first shock, they tried in various ways to get us back together, but by then both of us had crossed the Rubicon. Then some of our friends actually tried to get us to meet other separated or divorced singles who were in the same unhappy boat as we were. I remember one such effort quite well at the Labor Day week-end Scout festival in Cleveland. But these encounters were somewhat strained and in our minds, at least in mine, I was always comparing the new with the idealized Panni whom I married. At the same time there was also the fear that things just could not possibly turn out in a way that my daughters would accept anyone else as a "substitute" for Panni.

Then an opportunity arose for me to visit Kossuth Lajos University in the Fall of 1995. This is the institution where I had taught three semesters as a Fulbright lecturer from September 1992 to December 1993. Now I set up meetings with their university administration to establish a student exchange program with Ohio Northern University. When our good friends in Chicago, Márton Sass and Rozál (his second wife), got wind of my planned trip to Hungary over the Thanksgiving break, they asked me to deliver a gift to Rozál's friend, Anna Mária. Of course I agreed to deliver the gift. However, since my time was limited by my scheduled meetings at Kossuth Lajos University, I took the gift to Anna Mária on the run, at her work place where she was the manager, the Gourmand café near Erzsébet bridge. We sat down and had a good strong espresso with a fine pastry. I do not remember too much

Márika and András

more, because I had the same enchanted feeling that I had when I first met Panni. So after I handed over the gift, I just asked if we could meet again after I returned from Debrecen. She agreed and invited me to have a relaxed "home cooked" meal, "rác ponty." The trap was set and András fell right into it. From this time onward, she became "Márika, " not the formal Anna Mária.

After a successful meeting with the people at the Kossuth Lajos University and obtaining the contracts for the exchange program, I rushed back to Budapest where we had a long marathon conversation over a magnificent dinner. I learned that Márika was born on May 29th 1944 in Kisújszállás, about half way between Szolnok and Debrecen on the Hungarian lowlands. But very soon thereafter her mother and father decided to move further west to Budapest to avoid the advancing Soviet armed forces. Unfortunately, the Red Army cought up with them six months later, and they were trapped in the besieged capital. The encirlement and siege of Budapest lasted for over sixty brutal days, after Stalingrad it was the most destructive siege of the war. The house in which they lived on Böszörményi street received a direct bomb hit, and became uninhabitable. They moved into the basement of the home of some elderly relatives on Nyúl street, but the latter could not take Márika's constant crying for fear that it would attract the attention of marauding Soviet soldiers. So Márika's whole family left the shelter to find a new refuge some place else. The timing of this departure was unfortunate, it took place on February 11th, just as the defenders of Buda castle tried to break out of the Soviet encirclement. The break-out was in the direction of Márika's family's new refuge search. The family stumbled into Soviet soldiers who were advancing in the direction of the break-out. They immediately took away Márika's father for a "labor detail." He was never seen again. Márika at eight months became an orphan, together with her mother and grandmother. By the time she told me all this, both her grandmother and mother had also passed away. I too told her my life story and we promised each other to keep in touch via the postal system and by telephone. After our divorce with Panni was finalized in 1998 Márika and I were able to hold our wedding in Budapest on May 22nd 1999 and she moved to our new home in Ada, Ohio in October of that year.

"Bácsi Bandi"[32] Our Chauffer with a Mission

From our meeting in the Fall of 1995, I made a point to visit Márika every occasion when I could schedule a conference or some assignment in Hungary. On one occasion it was the 50th anniversary of the Fulbright Program celebrated in Budapest, while on another occasion it was the global Harvard Model UN organized at the Economics (formerly Karl Marx) University on the Pest side of the Danube. Then after the Second "Hope Ball" organized by the younger generation of Lake Hope activists in New Jersey, in the raffel I won two New York to Budapest airline tickets. On this occasion I took Anikó, my younger daughter, with me to see Budapest and Transylvania. Márika arranged the trip for us through the Knights of Malta, in which her uncle was a major organizer of the Hungarian branch. This is when we met "Bácsi Bandi"! Endre Atzél, his real name, was the driver of the Knights of Malta van that took regular trips to Transylvania and beyond, delivering aid packages to the needy. He also took passengers if they covered his gasoline expenses for the trip. His nickname was given to him by the Easternmost Hungarians, the Csángó inhabitants of Moldavia. It is this most forgotten cluster of Hungarians that he took under his wings and provided with aid and support at every turn, both in Moldavia and in Budapest. On four occasions Bácsi Bandi was our driver and guide. The first occasion was when he took us to Bözödújfalu, the town that Ceauşescu destroyed by flooding it. Only the church steeple was left reaching toward the sky out of the murky waters that covered everything except the small hillside cemetery of the town. Anikó wanted to take a photo of the memorial plaque that Hungarians had erected above the flooded town. I could not lift her high enough to take the photo. Bácsi Bandi, five years older than I, took her on his shoulders so she could take the picture. This tall, but gaunt man, had more strength in his arms and legs then I, who prided himself of being a former boxer and wrestler.

The rest of the trip with Anikó in Transylvania flew by in a flash. We stayed in Kolozsvár /Cluj for the night and visited the sights in the main

---

32   Bácsi Bandi (in this sequence), was the nickname of Dr. Endre Atzél among his beloved Csángó fans.

Brother Csaba Bőjte and András discussing common concerns at the Déva orphanage

square of this historically significant city which had a Hungarian majority population until 1956. (Currently the Hungarian share is only 17% as a consequence of Romanian colonization settlement policies.) On our way back to Hungary we made two stops, one in a small village where some old friends of Bácsi Bandi were in the midst of milking their water buffaloes. A taste of their fresh unhomogenized buttery milk was a treat for all of us. We also purchased some of their pottery before we continued our drive toward the Romanian-Hungarian border. Before crossing the border we stopped in Nagyvárad /Oradea to visit Bishop László Tökés the 1989 hero of the Revolution that overthrew the Ceauşescu dictatorship. He was not at home, but his sister welcomed us with tea. Unfortunatelly, while we were sipping tea, someone broke into the van and took Aniko's camera and knapsack with her medications. Since Bishop Tökés' house was under constant surveillance, the likely thief was a member of the Securitate. The regime may have changed, but the habits did not!

The next trip with Bácsi Bandi took place later in the summer (1999) and this time we took my older daughter Csilla with us. Since this was already during school vacation time, we were able to take four days into Romania and this meant we could go deep into Moldavia, to towns like Pustina and Trunk inhabited by Csángó Hungarians. There we were welcomed and Csilla was given an opportunity to wear the colorful clothes of a Csángó lass. Some of these settlements were so far off the beaten track, that Bácsi Bandi was able to get to them only by following the creek bed or driving through the common grazing territory of the local livestock. His driving skill and great reflexes were a constant wonder for all of us. Of course on the open highway his speeding and passing skills did leave us under constant stress, and I found that I had sore muscles in my right leg from the constant breaking after each ride in the Knights of Malta van under Bácsi Bandi's command.

While our physical survival was frequently on the line, the ride was always an adventure and Bácsi Bandi was a great tour guide. He took us to places we would never have seen on our own and provided us with a constant flow of information about what we saw. Furthermore his network of contacts enabled us to find lodging by the time it was dark after each day on the road. At the same time, he never neglected his role as a Knight of Malta, who had to deliver necessary equipment, medicine, clothing or foodstuff to the needy. I remember well his delivery of a cement mixer to the Csángó youth organization in Iași /Jászvásár during that second trip. The mixer was under a plain canvas tent cover, but the border guards just waved him on. His priestly collar that he added to his black shirt at our last stop before the border and his commanding demeanor did the rest. The next two trips continued providing us with a thorough knowledge of the geography, history and peoples of both Moldavia and Transylvania. His strenuous life, his exhausting marathon driving on endless winding roads, kept awake by thick sugary espressos, was bound to undermine his health. After one of these long drives he returned to Budapest, parked his van just in time before a massive heart attack killed him at the wheel on December 7th, 2005.

Whenever we have the opportunity to travel in Moldavia or Transylvania, we always think of Bácsi Bandi. His advice and his network of friends and contacts have provided us with concrete objectives and an emotional attachment to the region's cities, villages, churches, mountains, rivers and peoples. It has enabled us to become informed and interesting tour guides for our own friends and extended family. We have made this pilgrimage with friends or family almost every second year. These have always included Torockó/ Rimetea, Borbátvíz/Barbat, Déva, Kolozsvár/Cluj, Petrozsény/Petrosani, Marosvásárhely/ Târgu Mureș, Torda, Nagyvárad/Oradea, Székelyudvarhely/Odorheiul Secuesc, Csíkszereda/Mircurea Ciuc, and numerous small settlements like Lozsád, Csíksomlyó and Fehérvíz. These tours have also provided us with opportunities to re-connect with some of our Lake Hope guests and friends, as with Hajnal and Lajos Dávid from Nagybánya/Baia Mare, Árpád Kovács from Szatmárnémeti/Satu Mare, and Péter Cseke and Irénke from Kolozsvár.

2000 A.D. Human Rights Conference in Bucharest

As with our lobbying to have the NATO expansion into East Central Europe we also had some success in making the State Department become more aware of the fate of minorities in Romania. Almost as a follow-up to the 1998 briefings by James C. Rosapepe (U.S. Ambassador in Bucharest, Romania) for members of the Hungarian American Coalition in Cleveland, OH, he helped to orchestrate a conference in Bucharest, Romania to look into concerns regarding the treatment of minorities in that country. Edith Lauer, President of HAC, asked me to attend this conference from July 6-9, 2000. This followed closely on the less than successful Washington DC workshop, but Márika and I flew to Bucharest from Budapest. For both of us this was a new adventure, since we had not ever been to this city. Our accomodations at the hotel were first class, but just a few blocks from our hotel, many of the problems of post-Ceauşescu Romania were evident and pervasive. Just two examples are the uncleaned streets and the packs of stray dogs on the streets looking for something to eat. The conference itself was well planned by Rosapepe's staff, representation from most of the significant Romanian political parties were present, as also those NGOs that followed the fate of religious and ethnic minorities. Although there was no representation from the Teleki László Foundation's Budapest research center, György Csepeli was present from Hungary, George Schöpflin from the United Kingdom and myself from the United States representing outside perspectives on the issue of minority rights in Romania. All three of our presentations stressed that the reputation of Romania was at stake in this area. Furthermore, I also pointed out that at least in the United States we have the capacity to influence our representatives through the effective lobbying activities of a number of our NGOs, including HAC, HHRF, MBK, AHF, and others which are the watchdogs of the rights of Hungarian minorities. At the time some of the Romanian party activists viewed this as a "threat." Whereas we pointed out that we are just sharing a fact of life. This did not get into the published summary of the conference.

Meanwhile Back in Ada and ONU

In addition to my organization of academic conferences, my two research and teaching trips to Hungary in 1981–82 and 1991–92 supported by the Fulbright program, gave me opportunities to share information and know-how with my ONU home base. After every one of my longer excursions to East Central Europe, I attempted to provide my colleagues and my students with a picture of what was taking place in that corner of the world. The first such summary in 1982 was about the time that the Soviet Empire was gasping for air in its effort to pacify Afghanistan. Bob Davis had stepped down by that time as the Chair of our Department and David Saffell replaced him. My next major summary was after 1993 when David Saffell concluded his stint as chair. This summary was already after the Soviet collapse and tried to bring our perceptions up-to-date. Then in 2001, after 9/11 our new ONU President Baker asked me to be part of a panel discussion that would answer "why they hate us so much?" My analysis was subsequently published in the ONU Alumni publication of that year, and republished in the *Methodist Newsletter* (April, 2002) in Northern Ireland. The conclusions I reached were the following:

9/11 and Terrorism

Before the terror and the panic of 9/11 had a chance to subside, the drumbeat for immediate retaliation began to be heard throughout the land. Riding on this crest of popular revulsion President George W. Bush addressed the public on television and formulated the nation's response. Unfortunately, in his haste to calm the nation and steel our nerves, he became a victim of the mass media's propensity for sound bytes. In other words, he responded to the public outrage by simplistic formulations driven by patriotic fervour rather than measured statesmanship. In this atmosphere he declared war on terrorism!

This declaration was against a new and undefined enemy, although linked to the person of Osama bin Laden.

The immediate consequence of this declaration of war was that our foreign policy objectives suddenly were narrowed to one track: finding those who were guilty and punishing them. The President talked about 'unleashing a crusade' in a region wherein 'crusades' have always had a bad press. Furthermore, he wanted Osama bin Laden 'dead or alive,' even before the posters for his arrest had been nailed down by credible proof of his involvement. Finally, the President said, 'if you are not with us, you are with the terrorists.'

After the definition of this struggle, he began to construct a coalition to assist him in his efforts to get bin Laden and other terrorists, as well as the governments that provide them with shelter and support. All this pointed to punitive military action in one of the most hapless, helpless and devastated countries of the world, the Taliban-controlled state of Afghanistan.

Why was this response flawed? First and foremost because 'terrorism' is left undefined. Perhaps President Bush felt that no further definition was necessary after the events of September 11th. This tragedy spoke for itself, it was clearly the work of terrorists on a grand scale. But the failure to go beyond this act means that Chechen, Tibetan, Tamil, Kurdish, Palestinian, Uigur or Albanian freedom fighters can also be labelled as terrorists. Such a broad definition of terrorism makes George W. Bush and Tony Blair into the strange political bedfellows of Vladimir Putin, Ziang Zemin, or even Ariel Sharon. This will not improve the USA's standing in the front line states which it needs to capture or kill bin Laden.

What then is terrorism? Cindy Combs in her study on *Terrorism in the 21st Century* contends it is an act comprised of at least four crucial elements: (1) It is an act of violence, (2) it has a political motive or goal, (3) it is perpetrated against innocent persons, and (4) it is staged to be played before an audience whose reaction of fear and terror causes anxiety, uncertainty and disorientation in the targeted population. I would add that terrorism has become the weapon of the weak to counter the power of the states that control the existing distribution of power in the world.

To paraphrase the great German strategist of the early 19th century, Karl Maria von Klausewitz: 'Terrorism in the 21st century is becoming a form of struggle carried on by other means beyond diplomacy and beyond war.' This form of struggle is based on relatively low-cost methods of violence, the advantage of surprise and the ability to pick the time and place of your next attack. The forces who defend the status quo are always at a disadvantage, always forced to be on the defensive, even when they seem to take an offensive posture as presently in Afghanistan.

This vulnerability is a consequence of the difficulty to define the terrorist. But this difficuly should not lead us to make the mistake of defining all who challenge the existing distribution of power as terrorists. Most acts of terror were in themseves born as a response to state terrorism. As Combs points out, the victims of state terrorism are generally much more numerous than those of revolutionary, guerrilla or insurgent terrorism.

The word terrorism was itself coined initially to describe the "reign of terror" in France, perpetrated by the new people's power of the state after the overthrow of the French monarchy in 1789. In his analysis of the 9/11 crisis ("Bush is Walking Into a Trap," *Independent*, Sept. 16, 2001), Robert Fisk points out that the most devastating example of state terror in recent years was the Israeli invasion of Lebanon in 1982. Beirut, the Paris of the Middle East, was devastated. In front of a global audience, 17,500 innocent bystanders were killed. The international community did not move a finger to stop the carnage of the Shatila and Sabra refugee camps. Ariel Sharon was in charge of this overall campaign, under the watchful eye of former Irgun terrorist Menahem Begin, then Prime Minister of Israel.

This brings us to the root causes of the terror that hit us on September 11th, the confrontation that is ever present in the Middle East between client states/dependencies of the West and the Islamic world that does not want any of this subservience. President George W. Bush seemed unaware of this as the source of the area's discontent. In his immediate response to the events he stood incredulous and blamed blind hatred of democracy and our system of values as the reason. Here again he resorted to defining the world as good and evil, we being the good and our opponents the evil.

There are at least three more immediate causes for terrorism. The world, particularly the Middle East, includes many states in which injustices fester and continue to produce a steady stream of helpless victims who can become terrorists. For good or ill, the victims associate the USA and the West with the problems, the unbearable status quo, the oppression and the persecution. We inherited the Western colonial legacy. Finally, modern technology makes the USA vulnerable to such attack and not necessarily by sophisticated intercontinental ballistic missiles. This time the weapons of choice were box-cutters, knives, and hijacked airliners loaded with jet fuel.

How did we get to be associated with this negative legacy? While the Cold War was with us, this was not apparent. We were immersed in a no-holds-barred struggle, with mutually-assured destruction hanging over our heads, with the evil empire of the USSR. Until that was resolved between 1989–1991, all other struggles were put on the back burner, including the legacy of colonialism in the Third World, our dependence and exploitation of oil resources in the Middle East, and the hazards of our close alliance with Israel.

When the Cold War ended, and the problems mentioned above were not addressed, the kettle boiled over. We became the targets of the forces of discontent who had previously been our allies against the USSR in the Afghanistan war of 1980–88. With the Soviets down and out—and no changes in sight—we became the focus of Mujahadeen rage, including Osama bin Laden, Al Qaeda, and other terrorist organizations in the Middle East, Central and South Asia. Until we address the roots of this rage, killing off one or two generations of terrorists will do nothing to re-establish American security.

We have to adopt a strategy that is both persistent and patient. It must be based on the needs not just of ourselves but of the rest of the world. On the one hand, we must find and punish the criminals responsible for the devastation of September 11th. We must be sure we get the guilty party and have them put on trial before an international court of justice. (We do not want to be accused of being judge, jury and executioner.) In hindsight we know we became all three, as the Barack Obama administration, rather than the George W. Bush administration, located and executed bin Laden in Pakistan and then dumped his body somewhere in the Arabian Sea. This was the kind of law enforcement characteristic of our frontier experience!

But our credibility also depends on two other factors, one significant in the short run, the other important for the long haul. The short run credibility factor relates to the coalition that we have created. Many of these new found friends are potential liabilities. We must be wary of "friends bearing false gifts," particularly the Russians, Chinese and Israelis who have all enthusiastically jumped onto the anti-terrorist bandwagon with their own hidden agendas. They will want us to ignore their transgressions when they apply a re-invigorated "anti-terrorism" against Chechens, Uigurs, Tibetans and Palestinians respectively. These old and new friends have extensive experience imposing state terrorism within their own jurisdictions. They contribute to the cycle of violence and the rise of counter-terrorist activity among the weak and the oppressed inhabitants of their occupied or conquered territories. We do not want to do other people's dirty work or even to give them an approving nod. This will only discredit us in the eyes of our Muslim allies and the rest of the world.

Finally, if September 11th has changed everything, lets hope it has also made us more aware of the need to reassess our role in the world as a great power. President Bush's statement that September 11th was inspired by those who hate our freedom and democracy may help whip up enthusiasm for the present war. It does not get us closer to understanding why they attacked us. The real reasons relate to our exploitation of the oil resources of the region, and our sponsorship of Israel at the expense of all others. Add to that our attachment and continuation of the former colonial legacies of the British and the French and their old policies of divide and rule, and the support of corrupt and undemocratic political systems in Saudi Arabia, Egypt and elsewhere, and all this adds up to a rich recipe for hatred. For long-term co-existence we must map out a strategy that will not be exploitative or provocative. We must protect our national interests, with due consideration of the cultural values and legitimate interests of other peoples. We can do this best by being true to our own ideals of justice and respect for human rights. If we become this model for the world, terrorists will have no reason to target us.

As an afterthought we should not use our war against terrorism as a cover for our above mentioned hidden agendas. Not just because a "war on terrorism" can become an excuse for an endless involvement in the region, but because it squanders our wealth and strength on a threat, that is much less significant than global warming, environmental degradation, and world hunger and poverty. (Furthermore, we kill more people on our national highways anually then the terrorists kill globally!)

Lobbying for Chechen Independence

Soon after I organized my last conference at ONU to provide a better, more objective perspective on the Russian-Chechen conflict in 2004, I also tried to export my commitments to Hungary. Along this line I began to organize a lobby group that would support the Chechen independence movement. My first ally in this effort was Hajnalka Babirak who had been to the Caucasus during the break-up of the Soviet Union and had established close relations with the leaders of the Georgian independence movement. She also wrote a book about her experiences and Georgian Literature. Having the American experience of MBK, HAC and HHRF behind me, I assumed we could build a similar lobby organization in Budapest. We were able to get the support of János Horváth, senior FIDESZ Representative in Parliament to join our group (he was also an ex-patriate who became re-engaged in Hungarian politics). He had actually visited the Caucasus region (Georgia and Azerbaijan) a number of times officialy and felt that our efforts were worthy of his support. Besides my wife, Márika, I also recruited Márton Sass (former MBK president, who in the meantime had moved back to Hungary) and Zoltán Koller, the son of a good friend from New Jersey.

The six of us actually met twice at a Georgian restaurant, to adopt an organizational Charter. However, efforts to recruit additional members and to engage in any meaningful lobbying activity was met with passive resistance even in the media. I remember writing a letter to the editor of *Magyar Nemzet* (Hungarian Nation) challenging the anti-Chechen position of an article. Instead of publishing my well documented letter, the reporter of the article called me up and argued his case again over the telephone, thereby avoiding the possible public airing of the other side. This perspective also dominated the official line in the Ministry of Foreign Affairs, where I was rebuffed by a higher official when I mentioned the name of a representative of Chechen interests. Of course I have not given up on this issue, but it disappoints me that members of the younger generation do not see the parallels between our 1956 and the Chechen struggles for independence. Instead, for many contemporary activists such issues involving national destiny seem very remote, but many can actually be mobilized by the mass media or internet bloggers to sabotage the holding of the Olympics in Hungary! For which action the Momentum[33] successors of SZDSZ, were ready to provide the grist.

The 2004 Gyurcsány Betrayal and the Öszöd Confession

Similar problems of fuzzy thinking can be encountered on the other side of the Atlantic as well. American blindsightedness regarding Hungarian political life has been demonstrated time after time. In retrospect, however, I have concluded that it was not blindness, but a very self-centered concern to maintain stability and the status quo. Thus, toward Hungary and its leadership the American posture was directed by a pragmatism that favored those Hungarian leaders who tended to be more submissive to the interests of corporatist expansion into the former satellite states of the USSR. The leaders who fit this submissive characteristic were primarily the children of the former communist ruling-class, who wanted to compensate for their parents' "anti-Capitalist" legacy. Perhaps the best example of this cluster is Ferenc Gyurcsány. A former activist and leader of KISZ (Communist Youth Federation), who saw the handwriting on the wall, and became an aggressive robber Capitalist with regime change in 1989–1990. In the transformation of "collective state properties" to "private property" he became an overnight millionaire. This new status transformed him into a groveling servant of global multinational corporations and their World Bank and their IMF instruments of control.

To prove his status quo credentials Gyurcsány continued the subservience of Hungary to the credit dispensing globalist financial power centers. On the symbolic level he even went one step further and undercut Hungary's attempt to assert support for kin-nationals living in neighboring states. When a referendum was started in 2004 to provide Hungarians in these states with dual citizenship, as the leader of the Left coalition (MSZP and SZDSZ) con-

---

33 Momentum is a movement that came into being to oppose the application of Hungary's organization of the Olympic games. In the process it mobilized existing anti-Orbán forces in the country. At the time it was under the leadership of András Fekete-Győr, but also includes the support of some disenchanted members, old left-leaning members of the former Hungarian Democratic Forum and seems to be a successor to the collapsed SZDSZ, although made up of a younger generation of supporters.

trolling the government in Budapest, he did everything to sabotage the referendum. The Left was discouraged from voting, thus the low turnout (less than 50%) assured the defeat of the referendum even when a majority supported dual citizenship. This anti-national posturing had the support of his globalist handlers, but finally contributed to his loss of support in Hungary. It took only his "Öszöd confession" to put the nail into his political coffin. At Öszöd, where he owned property, a Party meeting took place at which he told his party loyalists "that we have screwed up everything" since being in power, and we have covered our tracks by "lying to the people of this screwed-up country from sunrise to sunset." This confession was too much even for one of his party loyalists, who had taped the talk and leaked it to the press.

Waves of demonstrations swept the country and calls for Gyurcsány's resignation followed. However, he held on with tooth and nail. The opposition did not relent and the demonstrations continued. These came to a head in 2006 on the 50th anniversary of the 1956 Hungarian Revolution. At that time my teaching responsibilities did not enable me to be on the scene in Budapest. But Béla Bognár of Wright State University and his son Steve went to record the memories of Béla by filming the places where he had been active during those memorable days. They witnessed more than they had bargained for. The paranoia of the Gyurcsány administration led to police brutality on the streets of Budapest reminiscent of some Samoza-like Central American dictatorship. Peaceful demonstrators, including entire families with children and strollers, became the targets of teargas grenades and rubber bullets fired at close range. Demonstrators lost their eyesight, others were clubbed and dragged away in police vans to city jails for disturbing the peace. The American mass media and the elite media (Washington Post and New York Times) reported on the demonstrations but ignored the over-reaction and brutality of the police. I remember even one of my colleagues at ONU remarked "what is wrong with those Hungarians (the demonstrators, not the police!)?"

What was "wrong" with them was that they had enough of the abuse of power and corruption of the Gyurcsány cabal. Not one peep of criticism emerged from either the State Department, the American Ambassador at the time, or the American media. As opposed to this, when Viktor Orbán came to power, he became the butt of constant criticism in the face of the population's overwhelming popular support (four consecutive two-thirds majorities in Parliament in 2010, 2014, 2018. 2022). Why the double-standard? This in the face of an administration that has ended the rule of the Gyurcsány cabal and has reigned in the power of the multi-nationals and had the courage to tax even the energy companies and the international banks. Ahaa, there is the rub!!!

The Béla Bognár and Steve Bognar witnessing of the 50th Anniversary, deserves a footnote about both of them. This father and son combination had contributed their talent and know-how to assist a number of Hungarian-American related causes. Béla brought his son to attend our Hungarian Studies program at ONU in 1980. Prior to that the whole Bognár family also attended one of our earliest *ITT-OTT* programs at Lake Hope State Park. Béla and his second wife April, also came to our meetings almost every summer to raise scholarship funds for Hungarian students in the Carpathian basin. Steve Bognar devoted many days and hours filming and editing our documentary film on "Urban Turf and Ethnic Soul" about the Birmingham Toledo Hungarian-American community. Steve also did a documentary of his own father with the title of "Personal Belongings." But Steve did not stop there, joined by his partner Julia Reichert, they developed a very outstanding cinematography program at Wright State University. The two film producers topped this off with their documentary "A Lion in the House" for which they got an Emmy Award in 2007, and then an Oscar in 2020 for their "American Factory" documentary! What an extraordinary and beautiful American and Hungarian family achievement!

Re-Visiting Vojvodina after Milosevic

At the 2004 Szeged Conference of AHEA I presented a paper on the differences between the American and Hungarian perceptions on minority issues. Margit Nagy from Serbia heard my presentation and invited me to Novi Sad/Újvidék to be part of the program she was organizing for Hungarian teachers in Vojvodina. Márika and I both attended that meeting and had a chance to witness a revival/or self-assertion among the Hungarian teachers of Vojvodina. After my presentation to the teachers, one young teacher approached me and asked me to follow her to the near-by law office of her father, Antal Bozoki. This was an opportunity to meet one of the most prominent human rights lawyers in the country.

As a follow-up to this meeting I was able to recommend Antal Bozoki to our MBK Council to invite him to be our main speaker at our 2007 Lake Hope conference. There he outlined for us the problems related to the protection of Hungarian minorities in present-day Serbia. This included the fate of the Temerin Five teenagers who were imprisoned for long jail terms (14 years each) for their assault of a Serbian drug dealer, and the double standard that prevailed when Hungarians were assaulted by Serbian youth gangs and received merely a slap on the wrist.

After his presentation, I told him that I would like to again go to Vojvodina to witness and taste minority existence there. He suggested that I take part in one of the summer youth camps organized in that region. During the summer of 2008 I was able to join the adult staff of such a summer camp for one week as an instructor of English. The experience was eye-opening. During the week I was instructor in a small class of six to ten students. Most of them were enthusiastic learners, but at very different levels in their language skills. As intense as the schedule was, the time was too short to judge what they had learned. However, I learned that both the organizers and the youngsters did not assert their ethnic identity in this camp. There was nothing Hungarian either about the cultural content or the camp's overall theme. The camp was organized on the property of the local public school in Pacsér/Pacir, a little town just north of Telecska where I had been on my bike tour in 1966. From dawn until dusk only the globalized heavy metal music reverberated in the campground. We were housed in tents, whose canvas did not provide protection against this travesty. For my first two days in the camp I really considered throwing in the towel and going back to Budapest. But I persevered, because I could not believe that parents would impose this form of baby-sitting on their kids during summer vacation time without expecting more!

In the halls and classrooms of the school, the walls were plastered with the artwork of students and organizers celebrating the theme that "We are Vikings." The story-line that the camp inmates followed, was that a Viking Prince sets out to find a bride somewhere in the world at large. He and his crew set out to find such a lucky girl in England, France, Italy, Egypt and China. In the process they learn about each of these cultures/civilizations. But they learn nothing about themselves! On the last evening an immense bonfire was lit, now they will sing and dance I thought! Nothing of the kind happened, they just sat around and waited for the fire to burn itself into embers. Ooh how I wished I could have transported my old #7 Erős Gusztáv New York Scout Troop to Pacsér to show these youngsters what a real campfire can and should be like! You need such a fire in your memory bank, in your soul, to survive as a people, to survive even when the majority Serbs force you to name the street in front of your school, Tomas Masaryk[34] street.

Showing America to Our Lake Hope Guests

Péter Cseke was one of our most recent guests at Lake Hope. After our 2014 conference at Lake Hope, Márika and I took him and Irénke on a guided tour and book presentations from Chicago to Detroit and finally to Toronto and Niagra Falls. This trip around the Great Lakes had as one of its objectives the presentation of Tibor Cseh's Collected Writings with the title *Csernátontól a Reménység taváig* /From Csernáton to Lake Hope (2014). I had worked on this book for four years as its editor and fundraiser. With Péter Cseke as the introducer of the book to both USA and Canadian audiences, I had the good fortune of having one of the most prolific writers of the periodical *Korunk* /Our Age/, published in Kolozsvár/Cluj, act as the Transylvanian interpreter of the book. This followed not only our Lake Hope conference, but also a book presentation in Kolozsvár and Csernaton, Tibor's birthplace, in late June and early July.

Other visitors at Lake Hope who received such a tour of North-West Ohio and the region around Lake Erie included Ildikó Orosz and László and Zsóka Brenzovics from Transcarpathia, László Vetési, Szilárd Tussay and Timea Virág from Kolozsvár, Rozália Kóka from Érd, András Görömbei from Deb-

---

34 Tomas Masaryk was the founder of the Czechoslovak state following World War I. Together with Eduard Benes he was mainly responsible for undermining the credibility of historic Hungary among the Entente powers prior to and during World War I.

MBK Council meeting in Chicago at the home of József Megyeri and Erika Bokor (2016)

On March 24, 2012, MBK receives the "Magyar Örökség" (Hungarian Heritage) Award in the grand hall of the Hungarian Academy of Sciences (András seated second from the r. represents MBK at the ceremony)

recen, and many others whose names escape me at present. But they had the opportunity to see not only ONU, but the Neil Armstrong Space Museum in Wapakoneta, the Amish settlement south of Kenton, OH and the Birmingham ethnic neighborhood in East Toledo, OH.

The Ludányi András Wine Celler in Gyöngyöstarján

In the meantime on the other side of the Atlantic in 2009 we settled in for our new life of spending nine months in Hungary and three months in the United States, mainly in Ada, Ohio. Our daughter, Csilla came to Budapest with a Hungarian heritage family that wanted to visit the settlements in present-day Slovakia from which their ancestors had emigrated to the United States. Csilla came with them as their Hungarian interpreter, since they no longer spoke the language. Their stay at the Mercure Hotel on Calvin square in Budapest, increased their thirst for Hungarian wine. They sent Csilla out to purchase a bottle of this heavenly drink. Csilla went to the nearest CBA grocery store near the square and made a beeline to the wine section. As she began looking for the kind of wine she liked, all of a sudden she saw her father's name on bottle-after-bottle of fine white Muscatel, Zinfandel-like Rose wines, and even "Kékfrankos" deep reds. Sure enough, the label on the bottles read from the "Ludányi András Winery." After purchasing some of her father's wines and delivering them to the thirsty family at the hotel, she immediately called me. "Dad you did not tell us about what you have been doing in Hungary. I had to accidently stumble on your wines in a grocery store to find out about your activities here!" After my surprise wore off, I confessed that I had not been the one who slaved away on the Mátra hills to harvest the grapes. I can only imagine that there is another person with my name who is responsible for these fine wines.

Csilla immediately went on the internet and located the "other" András Ludányi. His winery is located in a small town called Gyöngyöstarján, about six miles west of Gyöngyös, the major city in the county of Heves. Not a day passed and I contacted the "other" András. With our good friends Rozál and Márton Sass we drove out to the winery and had a wine tasting afternoon. The following year, in 2010, we celebrated my 70th birthday at his winery and ever since I have always purchased all my wine at his establishment. Whenever we are invited to dinner or a party (the Hungarian custom is to take flowers to the hostess and wine to the host) we always take wine from the "Ludányi András Winery."

Transferring American Experience to Hungary

The Orbán government initiated an outreach program to Diaspora Hungarian communities in 2013 named after the famous explorer and linguist, Sándor Kőrösi Csoma. In its first year 50 young Hungarian interns spread out to all corners of the world with the mission to strengthen the Hungarian cultural ties of all their fellow nationals who had been dispersed by the traumatic events of the 20th century. The program proved to be so successful that during the next year the government doubled their number and continued the program with increased participants in subsequent years. The focus of this mission included the teaching of the Hungarian language, folk dance and folk song, scouting lore and the building of ethnic community solidarity. An interesting side-effect of this program was that the interns went back to Hungary with a new awareness of their own identity.

I had the good fortune to observe the work and the enthusiasm of these young interns within the context of our own organization (MBK) as well as their activities in a number of other organizations and institutions in Chicago, Cleveland, Detroit and Ann Arbor. This was a magnificent pool of talent that also acquired a conciousness and collective solidarity, that was missing in the greater consumer and materialistic American and Hungarian societies. I felt that this cluster of positive individuals should be sustained together into the future. To this end, with a good friend, József Komlóssy, we began to think of a way to bring them together after their return to their everyday existence in Hungary. I provided the idea of bringing them together in a "mini-ITT-OTT" conclave, where they could discuss the possibility of creating an "alumni association" type of organization. József Komlóssy provided the setting for this get-together on his magnificent property in Szigliget on Lake Balaton. The natural beauty of this locale plus its isolation from the outside world made it ideal for brain-storming and planning.

Just as MBK is an NGO, it would be great to create such an organization for the returned interns of the Kőrösi Csoma Program. As I pointed out on June 4th 2016, there is no guarantee that a future Hungarian government will continue this program. Thus, the talent, enthusiasm and commitment of the KCSP interns would continue as a civic organization serving Hungarian national interests. (Why the governmental originators of this program have not yet brought into being such an "alumni association" is a mystery.) Perhaps, it is not part of the national culture, to plan ahead. In the USA we learned that survival demands that you think in terms of alternative scenarios. At any rate, we had a great time together in fellowship, with fine food,

Get-together with the Kőrösi Csoma Sándor veterans and their friends on the Balaton/Szigliget estate of József Komlóssy (back row, fifth from the left)

drink and conversation. The invited interns then spent most of the next day discussing the steps necessary to establish such a civic organization. To this day it has not come into being.

Why? This was a very select group of young Hungarians, yet they were unable to join together. In my opinion two factors kept them from establishing such a civic organization: the lack of governmental approval and support (via salaries or other financial commitment); second, that they lacked the volunteerism of civic culture that is wide-spread in the United States context. Until this changes in Hungarian culture and "big brother" is not expected to provide guidance and budget control, such a civic spirited independent organization is not likely to come into being on its own!

Tamás and Renate Visit Saxon-German Transylvania

We took many trips to Transylvania, but taking members of my own family to the region was most rewarding, because we could touch the roots of our family's origins. In early June, 2018 my older brother Tamás and his wife Renate made the trip with us. For years after we moved to Hungary on a permanent basis I tried to convince my older brother Tamás and his wife Renate to come visit us in Budapest. The last time they were in Hungary was in 1965 when I was in Salzburg improving my German so I could satisfy my foreign language requirement for graduate studies. Now finally I had the feeling that Tamás would convince Renate that it would be a good trip for both of them. The issue was not that they did not travel, they just did not travel to Hungary. Renate was a German-through-and-through, and both her family and professional interests tied her to Germany. But as we talked about Transylvania and our mother's roots, I also said that they should consider a visit to South-Eastern Transylvania with its strong Saxon-German traditions. This peaked Renate's interests and she started planning to visit our family jointly with the former German cities of Transylvania.

Their trip was complicated by flying to Budapest separately, since Renate still had some German language school related business in Berlin. Tamás was supposed to arrive June 4th, 2014. I went out to the Budapest airport, but he did not arrive with the scheduled flight. Since I could not contact Renate in Berlin, I called their daughter Réka in Connecticut, to find out if he had missed his flight. After innumerable phone calls Réka was able to contact her mother to try and locate Tamás. He had become confused on his arrival in Berlin and missed his connection to Budapest. Renate was finally able to locate him at the airport and put him on an early flight the next day. After a hearty breakfast Tamás and I spent some time sight-seeing in Budapest and the next day

András and Tamás at their grandmother's grave in Borbátvíz (2018)

we went to Kaposvár to do the same in the city that was our father's last command post in Hungary. On Sunday, June 8th Renate also arrived in Budapest. After supper we went over our plans and our maps for the trip to Transylvania.

The next morning, very early, we left Budapest and travelled via Nagyvárad/Oradea to Kolozsvár/Cluj/ Klausenburg, where we found housing for the night at the Hungarian Reformed High School's dormitory. We took in the sights in the center of Kolozsvár before we drove to Torda to see the church which had been the site of the Diet where the famous Torda Edict of Toleration was declared in 1568. Our second night in Transylvania was spent in Torockó, which was our favorite residence, with the magnificent view of Székelykő mountain. From there we turned toward Segesvár/Sigişoara a beautiful former Saxon-German city that has been almost completely Romanianized during the course of the past forty years. (It should be remembered that Hitler's *Drag nach Osten* involved the exploitation of German minorities in all of the regions where the German military forces were present. Thus, many young Saxon-German and Swabian-German men were taken into the SS Units. Many never returned from the Russian front. Those that returned were rounded up by the Romanian government together with the Saxon-German women for "labor duty" in the Soviet Union. This brutal system reduced the Saxon-German population to about 250,000 from the close to 800,000 preceding World War II.) This was followed by further reductions under Ceauşescu, who "sold" the remaining German and Jewish populations to West Germany and Israel respectively. The subterfuge for these business transactions was that the Germans or Jews who were allowed to leave, had to pay the Romanian government for the education they received in the country. Thus the going price for an M.D. or Ph.D. was ca. $25,000. while a university graduate might be able to leave for $15.000. or a high school graduate for $8,000.[35] The result of

---

35 The Sale of Saxon-Germans and Jews was known to specialists as a secret operation carried out by the Ceauşescu government to fill Romania's hard currency needs. The cover for this operation was blown by Ion Pacepa, former member of Ceauşescu' inner circle and deputy chief of the Romanian Intelligence Service, after his defection to the West. In his expose *Red Horizons,* Pacepa quoted Ceauşescu as saying: "We've...got to up the price Tel Aviv and Bonn are paying for Jews and Germans... Oil, Jews and Germans are our most important export commodities." According to Pacepa the "basic price for emigres was $2,000 to $50,000, depending on the individual's education and other criteria... Yitzhak Yesahanu, the deputy director of intelligence for Israeli Immigration, was asked to pay $250,000 in some cases. See: "Emigres reported 'sold': Governments paid Romania in secret, defector says," *The Columbus Dispatch* (Oct. 25, 1987)

this business was to reduce the German population of the former German cities to elderly mini-minorities. Their homes were taken over in most instances by the colonizing Romanian populations transferred from Oltenia or Moldavia to Transylvania. Thus, as we visited these cities, the old medieval architecture reflecting about 800 years of German care and industry, now witnessed a new demographic profile of mainly Romanian or Roma (Gypsy) inhabitants.

From Segesvár we drove southward toward Brassó/ Braşov/Kronstadt, but stopped for the night at Ilyefalva a small settlement on the very edge of the line separating Hungarian and Romanian (formerly German) settlements. The Reformed minister in this town, Béla Kató, had done wonders to create a conference center in this small town, including camping facilities for young people on religious retreats. (He had been one of our invited guests at Lake Hope in 2003.)

In Kronstadt we spent an entire day. This beautiful city, one of the most important former trading centers of the Saxon-Germans, includes the "black Church" an imposing gothic architectural marvel. It acquired its name from the sooth that covered its outer walls after a major fire. It survived, but most of its worshippers, or their descendents, come now to visit as tourists from some part of Germany. Klaus Iohannis, the current President of Romania, is an exception, he is a remnant of a Saxon-German family, but completely Romanianized. He was for a time the mayor of the other Saxon-German center, Hermannstadt/Sibiu/ Nagyszeben. He utilized his "German" roots to bring significant investment to his city, including the renovation of the splendid Brückenthal Museum. The German tourists were everywhere in evidence in both Kronstadt and Hermannstadt.

We travelled the long southern road back toward Hungary and checked in for the night at the Franciscan orphanage in Déva. This is a great institution which takes care and educates the children from broken families or orphaned children. We reserved two nights at one of the guest houses and left a generous donation for the orphans from our Hungarian Communion of Friends. We drove south to visit family graves in Borbátvíz and visited with the Ernő and Márta Mara family in Fehérvíz. From there we drove north to

---

p. 3A. The sale of Jews and Germans also served a more sinister purpose to reduce Romania's ethnic diversity, isolate the Hungarian population and make the country more homogeneous.

Vajdahunyad/Huneodora castle which had been build by the great Renaissance Hungarian monarch Matthias Rex in the second half of the 15th century. On the north side of the town as we were leaving toward Déva, we inadvertantly drove past a "new rich" Roma (Gypsy) settlement. The extremely ornate towers of the houses and their gleeming copper and tin roofs attracted Renate's attention for some photos. However, as soon as she got out of the car to snap pictures, a self-appointed guardian of Romanian culture, yelled at us not to take pictures. "This is not real Romanian culture," he seemed to assert. So we got back in our car and drove away with only two photos. From Déva we drove home to Budapest. The next day we organized a family get-together before Tamás and Renate flew back to New York City.

From Torockó to Graz with Pál, Theresa, Lizy and Lona

The summer of 2018 promised to be a really challenging time for my family and for me personally. For my family, the decision of Pál, Theresa, Lizy and Lona to visit Hungary was timed for the end of June and the beginning of July. Márika and I were really thrilled by the prospect of this visit, since Paul had not been in Hungary for about twenty years and Theresa and Lona had never seen the country. However, the timing of the visit created some logistical problems, since I was scheduled to present a paper at the Center of Southeast European Studies in Graz, Austria on July 5th.

My commitment to this conference was also more serious than to other conferences, for two reasons: First, because I had mobilized a lot of my colleagues at the Budapest research center (where I did some gratis work in English translations) to submit paper proposals to this conference; Second, because I had been working on a study about Viktor Orbán that I wanted to present to a Western audience. So, I had to figure out how I could "ride two horses with one ass" (Hungarian folk saying). At any rate, family comes first, so we planned a good two weeks of sight-seeing in Transylvania, Eger and Transdanubia. All locations that had some connection to our family. For this time period we rented a car, because otherwise we do not own one in Hungary. (Here public transportation is excellent and also free if you are of retirement age.)

Upon their arrival, we let Pál and his family overcome jet-lag, before we began to see the sights. I took them on my practised Budapest tour, starting with St. Gellért Hill for an overview of the city, then a Metro ride out to Hősök tere (Hero's square) where I gave them a thumbnail review of Hungary's 1,100-year history. I also took them to the Parliament building and to Castle hill. On the third day of their stay, we woke early, to leave Budapest before rush hour so that we could get to Transylvania still during daylight hours.

Our first stop was in Déva, where we had reserved rooms for the family at Franciscan Father Csaba Bőjte's orphanage. From there we travelled south to Hátszeg, Borbátvíz and Fehérvíz within view of the imposing Retyezát and Páreng ránges of the Transylvanian Alps. It is here that our mother was born and where she spent her teenage years. We visited both the Prileszky and the Balázs graves in Borbátviz. We also had the opportunity to have a wonderful meal and conversation with Márta and Ernő Mara before we went back to Déva. This city is under the watchful eye of Déva castle, where Ferenc Dávid, the founder of the Unitarian faith was imprisoned and where he died. We too went up to it via the service-hoist lift on the mountainside and enjoyed the view in all directions, something poor Ferenc Dávid was not allowed.

The next day we took the long drive to Torockó by way of Gyulafehérvár/Alba Iulia and Nagyenyed/Aiud. From there we drove through Torda and visited the Church where the historic convention took place in 1568, declaring religious toleration for the first time in Europe. Next we visited the Reformed Church and its high school in Kolozsvár/Cluj, followed by our visit to the grand gothic Catholic Church with the equestrian statue of Matthias Rex. On our way back to Torockó we viewed the Gorge of Torda from the distance, because of the rain and road conditions we did not descend into it by foot. After a fine evening meal we went to bed early to wake up to a double sunrise over the twin-peaked Székelykő mountain which provided the backdrop for our stay in this exceptional settlement.

The next day, after an early breakfast we began our long treck back to Hungary. It was already July 4th, and I had to be in Graz, Austria the next day at 9:00am to present my paper: "Is Orbán a Populist?" We reached the Hungarian-Romanian border by 6:00pm and Igal in Transdanubia (Somogy county) at 8:30pm. This is where we left Paul and his family at a small hotel near a health spa. We were to meet up with an old friend, who had been one of the active members of the Shooters in Pennsylvania. Apparently, our timing was off, because he left for Budapest just before we reached Igal. Márika and I drove on to the Austrian-Hungarian border, where we found a motel room for the night at 12:00am. We slept until 4:00am and got on the road by 5:00am. We reached Graz at 7:30am but ran into the morning rush hour and barely made it to the University of Graz for the starting time of my panel. In fact, my colleague from Budapest already began to read my paper, saying apologetically that the opinions expressed therein are mine and not hers, just as I burst into the room. I finished the paper without apologies, and was glad to see that I added some paprika to the discussions of the panel papers.

After the panel ended we began the drive back to Hungary. I was very tired, so we stopped to eat in Austria close to the border. Both of us also drank a lot of coffee so we could make it back to Igal to pick up Pál and his family. From there we drove to Kaposvár where the Ludányi family lived during most of World War II. Our father's role as commander of the Somogyi brigade meant that we had to do a fast tour of the town where Pál was born and the house where we lived. We also drove past the barracks where the troops had been stationed during the early part of the war. Then we drove north to Lake Balaton, where we met our cousin Gyöngy Prileszky in Balatonboglár with whom we went to the lake shore where her daughter Anna runs a fast-food fish-fry enterprise. We had our supper there and got back to Budapest that evening around 9:00pm.

After returning our rent-a-car we all rested for a day. On the 9th we went to Eger by bus to see our father's birthplace, the Bazilika and the fortifications of the city. After our return to Budapest, Mária Korossy (the daughter of my Godmother) hosted a good-by supper for the entire family.

While Back at ONU

After David Saffell's retirement as Chair, Ellen Wilson replaced him in that position. David's publications in American Politics with Prentice Hall provided him with an additional income so that he could retire before he reached retirement age. During Ellen Wilson's tenure as Chair our department also began a process of bringing in younger faculty members. Under her leadership we gained the services of two Geographers, Jimmy Wilson and David Smith as well as Russ Crawford in Sports History and our own former student, Robert Alexander in Political Science. We also gained the services of Raymond Schuck in Public History and Archeology. A surprise addition to the department was Robert Waters in African and Afro-American history who was driven to us by the Katrina Hurricane that swept through New Orleans and most of Louisiana in August of 2005. In addition to all this, because of our Criminal Justice program under JoAnn Scott's direction we received 25-30 Saudi Arabian police and security agent students per year who were supposed to learn about American Law Enforcement practices.

Why was Ohio Northern University selected for this program? Probably because of ONU's relative isolation from the rest of American society. Presumably because of its distance from sinful Western urban influences it was less likely to "corrupt" the Saudi students and they could be kept together in ghetto-like isolation while they received their law-enforcement instructions. This program also provided ONU with a great source of revenue. But it led to jelousy from other departments and the Law College. This jelousy resulted in the Administration's decision (when the Law Dean became the Academic Vice President) to reduce the number of our student majors by one-third by taking away our criminal justice program and attaching it to the Sociology and Psychology department. I had already retired after forty years of teaching when this castration occurred. However, this in combination with other petty matters, and the Administration's mishandling of the funds of the Saudi program led to the protest resignations and retirements of both Ellen Wilson and JoAnn Scott. Fortunatelly, Robert Alexander became the next Chair in the department, and his leadership has led to a new revival rather than collapse. (My replacement was Professor Kofi Nsia-Pepra a specialist in International Organization and the role of Blue Helmet operations. He also took over the direction of our Model UN program.)

The American Macro Political Scene

This tempest in a teapot at ONU, reflects at the micro-level some of the problems of American politics at the macro-level. As I had already outlined in my presentation after the 9/11 panel discussion, the animosity toward the USA in the Greater Middle East was due more and more to the nature of our interventionism in that region. Since the end of World War II, when my own life became intertwined with the destiny of the United States, the global reach of American power was not only all important in occupied Europe, but also in the Far East with the occupation of defeated Japan and the onset of the Korean War. At the same time the retreat of the British Empire from imperial status in South Asia and the Greater Middle East and the retreat of France from Syria and Algeria as well as Indochina, opened the door to American involvement in these areas also. We filled the power vacuums that were left after the French and British retreats. This was to forstall a Soviet move into these areas, but it also transformed us into the imperial successors of the British and the French. At first this was not apparent because of Cold War fears and because during the Suez crisis of 1956 the U.S. put pressure on the British, French and Israelis to cease and desist their aggression against Egypt. The latter move actually made the USA seem to be a friend of the de-colonizing Third World. At the time, this reflected historical American anti-colonialism, rather than a new form of empire building replacing the old fashioned British and French imperialism.

What drove this new form of empire building was the emergence and dominance of global corporatist interests. Private interests and corporations had been involved in the quest for control of global markets before this time, but the ingredient of competition now became energy, particularly oil and natural gas, this focused the imperial quest more and more on the Greater Middle East. The role of oil in this region received new emphasis when the British navy, the largest global navy at the time, switched from steam/coal to oil in 1906. This in combination with the mechanization of warfare made control of the Persian Gulf for the British inevitable. German attempts to challenge this control via the construction of the Berlin to Baghdad railroad also was driven by this quest. The Second German Empire was the dominant power on the losing side of the Central Powers in World War I. This enabled the Entente powers to divide among themselves the oil rich territories of Germany's ally, the Ottoman Turkish Empire. The French moved into the region that was later to become Lebanon and Syria, while the British consolidated their control over Palestine, Transjordan and Iraq. This Western consolidation of the oil rich Middle East was securely nailed into place with the establishment of Israel as a permanent military beachhead in the Eastern Mediterranean in 1948. True, American oil interests already had their foot in the door on the Arabian Peninsula with the Saudi ruling family. But this was not yet the United States government. The latter became seriously embroiled in the region with the establishment of Israel and "the need" to protect oil interests in Iran, when Mossadegh tried to nationalize the oil production in Iran. The CIA was directly involved in overthrowing Mossadegh and putting Reza Mohammad Pahlavi Shah in as the ruler of the country. If we are looking for root causes of "why they hate us?" we must bear this in mind. It was not always this way, for many years America was the shining example atop the mountain of hope! For a long time this latter idealized version also dominated my understanding of our place in world history. This shining image finally was shattered for me by the Bush wars against Iraq. Both Bush wars! I marched in anti-war demonstrations both in Washington DC and locally in both Lima and Findlay, Ohio. (Some ONU students and faculty also participated in these symbolic rejections of this brainless American imperialism.) However, I and many others, were naive enough, that we thought that Barack Obama could and would take us out of this dead-end.

Kossuth-Lincoln-Obama

"Government of, for and by the people." This phrase from the Gettysburg address was Abraham Lincoln's succint definition of democracy. Barack Obama used this key phrase also after accepting the Democratic Party's nomination for the Presidency of the United States in 2008. In the campaign that followed, Hungarian-Americans of the Democratic persuasion, quoted both Obama and Lincoln together with Louis Kossuth in their electoral brochure. The design and the quotes were selected for mobilizing Hungarian-American voters, and to educate the public and policy-makers about the linkage between Hungarian and American democratic values. Lily Érdy deserves most of the credit for this attractive brochure. Although our organization and Péter Ujvagi's Toledo Democratic Party did most of the legwork for the Obama "Hungarian" campaign, in the long-run it was the "Hungarian" (Gati, Bajnai, Simonyi) cabal around Hillary Clinton that got most of the credit. This hurt Hungarian interests in the long run, because the "cabal" undermined the positive relations between the two countries for more than a decade.

On the other hand, in Ohio, we made the most out of the Kossuth connection. State representative, Peter Ujvagi located Louis Kossuth's speech in the state archives which Kossuth had delivered at the statehouse in 1852. The key phrase in this speech was: "The spirit of our age is democracy – All for the people, and all by the people. Nothing about the people without the people. That is democracy. And that is the ruling tendency of the spirit of our age." Around this quote and around this speech we developed a chautauqua-like historical presentation and submitted it to the Ohio Humanities Council for funding. The submission was through Ohio Northern University with the co-sponsorship of the Hungarian Communion of Friends, the Hungarian American Coalition, the Hungarian Reformed Church of Columbus, the Toledo Magyar Club and the Cleveland Hungarian Association. The community support and the merits of the ONU proposal convinced the Ohio Humanities Council to support the project with a $2,000. mini-grant. With matching funds coming from the community organizations we were able to take "Kossuth's Message" to seven locations in Ohio. First to the ITT-OTT/MBK conference at Lake Hope State Park in Zaleski, Ohio; then to the Hungarian Reformed Church in Columbus; then to Saint Stephens Roman Catholic Church in Dayton; then to the Magyar Club of Toledo; then to Bluffton College; then to John Carroll University in Cleveland; and finally to Ohio Northern University, my home institution.

The presentation had as its center piece the Louis Kossuth speech at the Ohio statehouse in 1852. It was imbedded between two presentations on the European historical setting, presented by Professor Michael Loughlin and the American reception of Kossuth in 1852, presented by Professor Ellen Wilson. I linked together the elements of the performances of Louis Kossuth (by Tamás Csajka and Endre Szentkirályi) as his secretary Károly László. The background was provided by a power point presentation of historical images and Kossuth songs performed by Katica Szabó. The Zaleski performance required last minute substitutions for two missing professors by my daughters Anikó and Csilla. For the editing and preparation of the script Katalin Juhász and I worked together for most of the Spring of 2012. The chautauqua-like tour had a limited impact on American historical consciousness, but it was a rewarding experience for all of us who were direct participants. Furthermore, the audience reactions were a good indication that we were able to communicate the significance of the Kossuth message. However, this message was not reflected in the continued American interventionism in the Greater Middle East, now labelled "Arab Spring."

21st Century Profile of the USA

When I retired from ONU and looked back on my teaching career at the university, I was at times embarassed by my performance. In most instances I followed the standard textbook interpretations and my own idealized version of Washington DC's role in the world. In the last ten years of my teaching career, particularly after 9/11, I became more critical of our global behavior. 9/11 was a cold shower for me as well as for most Americans. But most Americans did not study political relations for their careers, they worked at other careers to feed their families and most of them were not members of the "attentive public" (less then 10% of the population) and in their spare time they attended baseball games, played cards or took their kids to T-ball or soccer practice. They had an excuse, I did not!

This backward glance forced me to re-asses some of my conclusions about the benevolence of US policy in the international setting. Since the Korean War and the Vietnam imbroglio (and defeat!) we have become a Global Empire that keeps itself afloat by constant interventionism, voluntaristic militarism and corporatist imperialism. The global presence of our major corporations has been followed by our global military footprint. Building this kind of empire is hard, nay impossible, to reconcile with the American democratic ideals that made the USA great! The same ideals that were present in both the Kossuth and Lincoln speeches that I quoted above. So how did we get here?

The roots of this empire building are the extension of the American expansionist tradition which was linked to the Westward movement of the population from the original thirteen colonies to the West Coast. One could argue that the momentum for this original continental expansion was mainly motivated by security concerns, the vast natural wealth of the continent and the relative weakness and fragmentation of the native American population. The Louisiana Purchase removed French power from the continental USA. Aquisition of Florida removed Spain as a contender for North American turf, while USA incorporation of Texas and the South West, including California, pushed Mexico out of the way in our drive to the Pacific. In the North, the War of 1812, and agreements with the British Empire consolidated USA control all the way to Washington State facing Canada's Vancouver Island. Finally, the purchase of Alaska from the Russian Empire removed the last outside power that could threaten our continental hegemony. After this the interests of corporations rather than national interests drove the expansionism of the USA. (Unless of course you agree with Eisenhower's Secretary of Defense Wilson: "That what is good for General Motors is good for the United States!")

American corporations, major economic interests, took over in the drive to compete with other empires in areas beyond our shores. The "island hopping" in the Carribean, in the Pacific Ocean and in the construction of the Panama Canal all reflect the interests of major corporations and not solely that of the United States. United Fruit Company, Chiquita and Dole had a dramatic impact on our involvement and control of the "Banana and Coffee Republics" in Latin America and our conquest of the Hawaii pineapple kingdom in the Pacific. Of course for the former we already formulated the Monroe Doctrine at the beginning of the 19th Century. But while these efforts were in part justified as consolidation of our backyard, the 20th and 21st centuries witnessed an even more aggressive and global process as "Big Oil" corporatist power asserted itself both in the Greater Middle East and in Venezuela, Ecuador and Mexico! In fact its tentacles streched into Indonesia in South Asia as well as Nigeria in sub-Saharan Africa.

The Coalition (HAC) and White House Briefings: Shades of the Indian Treaty Room

As I had already intimated when I related the water glass episode, the Coalition (HAC) had a more welcoming reception in the White House when it was occupied by a Democratic President, rather than a Republican President. Democrats just played the ethnic card more successfully than the Republicans. As a consequence, we had more access to the National Security Council under President Bill Clinton than under either of the Bush presidencies. We tried to perpetuate this access also under President Obama, but were less successful. This was the case even though we had played a very active role in trying to mobilize the Hungarian ethnic vote for his election. The probable reason for this was the emerging influence of George Soros and his generous campaign support for the Democratic ticket. The Soros plan for Hungary was dominated by the influence of Charles Gati, Gordon Bajnai and András Simonyi, all opponents of the Orbán vision for the country. During the Clinton era we were invited to a number of meetings independently of our annual White House briefings preceding our St. Nicholas[36] HAC conventions, such was not the case with the Bush administrations. But our meetings were always in the Indian Treaty Room. Considering the legacy of treaties with defeated Indian tribal communities, I could never really be sure that our voices were important in helping to define policy. I cannot imagine that either George Soros, or one of his cabal would be consulted in the Indian Treaty Room.

This raises the question what is real democracy? The number of votes generated or the number of dollars that are contributed by George Soros and associates or other corporate power centers? The campaign to elect Barack Obama, more than any other before this time, opened my eyes to some of the limits of American democracy. Since Ohio was a key state in determining national elections for President, a number of us who worked for the Democratic party's success developed a grand strategy that helped to win the state for

---

36 St. Nicholas Day falls on the first Friday of December for the Annual Convention of the Hungarian American Coalition. As a day of Christian celebration it is always December 6th. However, for the Coalition it means the Friday closest to that date

Meeting President Bill Clinton in the "Indian Treaty" room (1993).
l. to r.: Rev. Imre Bertalan, Edith Lauer, András, László Hámos

Obama by also mobilizing the ethnic Hungarian voters. In the end, Obama's foreign policy was at least as disasterous as George W. Bush's had been in both the Greater Middle East and in Hungarian-American relations. In the first instance, it destabilized Libya, Egypt, and Syria. In Egypt the overthrow of a democratically elected government, after the pro-American dictatorship of Hosni Mubarak was overthrown. The successful overthrow of the Khaddafi dictatorship in Libya has resulted in constant bloodshed, chaos and a migration explosion across the Mediterranean. The intervention in Syria has failed to topple Bashar al-Assad, but the attempt has produced a brutal civil war and a refugee crisis that has spread across the borders of Lebanon, Jordan, Iraq, Turkey and beyond. All of these have impacted on the European continent in waves of migrants and refugees. By 2010 the cost of our military interventionism just in the Iraqi theatre was 1,455,590 Iraqis killed as opposed to the 4,801 USA servicemen killed and the 3,487 international personnel of allied forces killed. Is it really surprising that ISIS could recruit young Muslims to fight those who are responsible for this boodshed? Also from the same 2010 source we learn that the total cost of all our wars since 2001 neared the

5 trillion mark. To be a little more precise for both the Iraq and Afghanistan wars the American taxpayer provide $4,730,513,493,140. according to www.informationclearinghouse.

Of course 90% of the mass media (CBS, Time Warner, Viacom, Disney, etc.) have not found this important enough to share with the American public! Since then another decade has passed of our endless military engagements (direct or indirect) with Syria, Libya and Yemen joining the list of our victims.

Decision After Retirement

When I married Márika in 1999 I promised her that after my retirement from ONU I would move "back" to Hungary with her. After my retirement in the 2007–08 academic year, I told Márika that my promise needed to be amended, because I did not want to move across the Atlantic while my 101 year old mother was still alive and well under my sister Narcissza's care in New Fairfield, CT. She agreed with my amendment, and we visited my mother a number of times during the course of the following year, when she passed away a little less than two months before she reached 102 on November 1, 2009. Since that time, we have alternated our time in the USA and Hungary by spending August-September-October in Ada, Ohio and November to July in Budapest, Hungary. This dual existence, with nine months in Budapest and three months in Ada, has given me a special insight into the domestic politics and the foreign relations of both countries, particularly concerning American-Hungarian relations. This visceral connection to both, has made me particularly sensitive to misrepresentations in the mass media, whether of American or Hungarian origin.

The treatment of Hungary in the American Media has been primarilly negative since the Viktor Orbán government has been in power (2010). This is particularly the case in the so-called elite media outlets like the *New York Times* and the *Washington Post,* two sources for information (and disinformation) that are most influential for both policy makers and members of the "attentive public" in the USA.

Why this has become the case since 2010 is probably a consequence of Hungary's desire to assert its independence from both "Soviet tanks" and "Western banks." The mega-financial power centers, the multi-national corporations and the IMF and World Bank are miffed by this national self-assertion and they have exerted pressure on Hungary from every conceivable direction. The mood setting agenda of the elite media is only one of these constant pressure centers.

These trend setting media outlets receive their information about Hungary and the Orbán administration from mainly two sources: the discredited opposition parties (followers of Gyurcsány, Bajnai, Kóka, Kuncze, etc.) who dragged Hungary into the abyss of corruption and economic collapse prior to 2010. (Interestingly, prior to 2010, at the height of the discredited opposition's power, not one peep of criticism came from the American elite media!) The second source of such double standard criticism comes from the professional bloggers of the North American internet set. Perhaps the most active are the "Hungarian Free Press" bloggers Christopher Adam, György Lázár and András Göllner. They grind out their anti-Hungarian and anti-Orbán fare on a weekly basis. Their well financed operation is truly admirable from the quantity perspective. From a qualitative perspective, however, they provide a grossly distorted picture of present-day Hungary.

Unfortunatelly this grossly distorted image is unquestioningly adopted by the American elite media and disseminated for all to see. The content of this negative image is that Hungary and the Hungarians are anti-Semites, anti-Roma, narrow nationalists, bigoted foreign haters, anti-liberal ideologues and populist anti-EU fanatics. Parallel to this, the Orbán government is presented as autocratic, even dictatorial – tending toward "Putinism." It is responsible for facilitating the worst features of Hungarian society to perpetuate itself in power. To this end it has adopted a constitution that is homophobic, intolerant toward minority religions, Islamophobic and does not exercise the values of separation of church and state. At the same time this "new" constitutional structure does not provide for separation of power and allows for the intimidation of the democratic opposition, muzzles the press and limits the restraining power of the judiciary. In leveling these charges, neither the discredited opposition or the "Hungarian Free Press" bloggers provide concrete cases of intimidation, abuse of power or suppression of freedom of press or expression!

Anyone who has actually lived in Hungary, and understands and reads in Hungarian, knows that the discrediting campaign is based on falsehoods and distortions. However, the "free press" in the West or on the pages of the *New York Times* and the *Washington Post* does not allow for challenges. We know that this is the case because even "Letters to the Editor" do not get published if they contradict the "established negative image." My numerous pro-Orban letters have never seen the light of day in either one of these newspapers. (My efforts to challenge this negative image manufacturing led to my study "Is Orban a Populist?" which I presented in Graz on July 5th, 2018. I have added this study as an appendix to my present reflections!)

Under Secretary of State Hillary Clinton, the Obama administration also attempted to undermine the position of Viktor Orbán in Hungary. This interventionism sponsored by the Soros cabal, pushed American-Hungarian relations to a new low. The irony of all this is that recently the Donald Trump administration tried to overcome this Soros manipulated conflict. (His appointment of Ambassador Cornstein reflected this.) But the Joseph Biden administration and the new American Ambassador (David Pressman) has reverted to the policy of demonization. While Trump was able to improve American-Hungarian relations temporarily, it is highly unlikely that he altered established American practice in the rest of the world. As we saw this fatal flaw was continued in relation to Iran, where President Trump had actually ordered the murder of a high-ranking Iranian military leader. Why?

My Revised Perspective of Our Global Role

To answer this question for myself and the present readers of this essay, I have developed a revised readings list for both myself and all those who desire to better understand our present role in a globalized world. For background I still depend on such classics as Hans Morgenthau's *Power Politics* and E.H. Carr's *Twenty Years Crisis,* but my supplemental reading list now also includes Andrew J. Bacevich's *Breach of Trust* and *The Limits of Power,*

Anatol Lieven's *America: Right or Wrong*, the writings of Udo Ulfcotte on the role of the media and the asylum industry relative to the migration crisis in Europe, Benjamin R. Barber's *Consumed*, F. William Engdahl's *A Century of War: Anglo-American Oil Politics and the New World Order* and John Perkins' *Confessions of an Economic Hit Man* and *The Secret History of the American Empire*, Noam Chomsky's *Profit Over People*, Patrick J. Buchanan's *Suicide of a Superpower*, Ron Formisano's *American Oligarchy: The Permanent Political Class* and for those friends who also read Hungarian, Tibor Purger's *A Birodalom Odavág (The Empire Strikes First)*.

What is the picture we can distill from all these sources as well as many others, plus our own observations of the world around us? First, that the main players or actors in the international setting have dramatically changed since the conclusion of World War I. Up to that time period the state system inherited from the Westphalian Peace[37] determined the recognized actors in the international setting. Actually the Westphalian system determined the trait of "sovereignty" for states in the modern world, but it was the Congress of Vienna and the Congress of Berlin that determined the number of recognized state actors in the international setting by the end of the 19th century.

Until World War I the number of such states ranged between thirty and thirty-five. This number doubled to about 54 states in the inter-war period and then tripled to close to 200 such entities between World War II and the end of the 20th century. This proliferation of state actors did not enhance their status as centers of decision-making. In fact most of these states were the former colonies of the British, French and other European empires. Within the United Nations they now constitute the majority of states, which represent the underdeveloped ("Developing") poverty stricken part of the world, geographically located mainly in Southern Asia, the Greater Middle East, Africa, and most of Central and South America. These states have shaken off their former imperial exploiters since the end of World War II, but they are now controlled and exploited by major multi-national or transnational corporations controlled in turn by the major North Ameri-

---

[37] Westphalian Peace ended the Thirty Years War in 1648 and established the theoretical foundations of the modern state system. The effective exercise of sovereignty became the basis of the modern state system.

can, European, Australian, or East Asian states. Economically they are in a dependent neo-colonial status. The vast majority of these corporations are owned by stock-holders in the United States, but a significant number have their home base in the United Kingdom, France, Germany, Japan, China and/or the "Asian Tigers."[38]

The Global Corporate Power Structure

These major corporations are more powerful than most of the ca. 200 states in the world. In fact, the twenty largest such corporations have more employees and larger budgets than 80% of the states. Only the largest states are able to limit or contain the influence of these economic conglomerates. However, even the largest states now reflect the interests and needs of these corporate giants. A good example of this state of affairs is the influence of major oil companies like Gulf Oil or EXXON-Mobil Oil. Since the 1930's these companies in alliance with car manufacturers like Ford, and General Motors, have helped to determine not only our foreign policy in the Persian/Arab Gulf but also domestically in relation to such policy questions as the expansion or restriction of urban public transportation systems. The consequence of this, in combination with fast food giants like Coca-Cola, McDonalds, Burger King and KFC along our highways, has been to pollute and devastate our physical environment and destroy our health. The dramatic spread of "civilizational deseases" like obesity, heart desease, diabetes and cancer has been the result. These in turn have bloated our health care industries and produced giant pharmaceutical concerns that continue this out of control spiral that has become part of our American existence, but not our American dream! Add to this the GMO, pesticide and fertilizer abuses of Monsanto, and the limitless selfishness of the food processing and packaging industries, and you have to really wonder where the nightmare ends.

---

38 *"Asian Tigers"* refers to the emerging dynamic economic smaller states such as South Korea, Taiwan and Singapor.

This consumer and profit driven existence has now been globalized and we are exporting this self-destructive spiral to the rest of the world. However, in the "Developing" countries the consequences of this export threatens their very existence. This is quite clear in the case of Iraq, Libya, Yemen and Syria, but it also threatens Iran as our military footprint becomes ever more assertive in the Greater Middle East. I hope by putting all this in my life story, I have contributed to the construction of a mirror which all Americans can look into! If we realize what we have become, perhaps we can find our way out of this consumer driven morass!

At the End of my American Roadtrip

When my Father and Mother brought us to "Amerika" in 1949 they were filled with optimism regarding the future of their five children. From the two dairy farms in Virginia through the factory work at Swingline staples in

Visit to Éltető family in 2018: standing l. to r. András, Bandi, Tas and Jónás, seated Lajos

Last meeting of three founding members of MBK in Portland, Oregon (2018): Panni Nádas Ludányi, András Ludányi and Lajos Éltető

NYC, they put us on an upward trajectory. In one way or another, each one of us found a nitch in American life. In my case, the forty years of teaching at ONU enabled me to follow my own interests in the scholarly world as well as in Hungarian-American politics. Furthermore, this teaching position provided me with a modest but stable income that allowed both our daughters to complete college and continue on in developing their own careers. Both in my career and in my personal life I have been a satisfied and happy person. Both my first wife, Panni, and my second wife, Márika, have provided the love, caring and affection that leads to human happiness. This experience and the growth of our family with three grandchildren has added to our quest to be together as often as physically possible.

Csilla and Anikó and the Vastness of the USA

One of the greatest challenges that people face in the United States is the physical distance that can separate members of a family from each other. Both our daughters left the family nest in Ada, Ohio when they finished their college studies and soon thereafter got married. Csilla and Ryan moved to Houston, Texas where Ryan found work with BP Oil Company, while An-

Together at Lake Hope, the third generation, Leó, Jace (Öcsi) and Katalin

ikó settled in the Chicagoland area where her husband, Brett, found employment with the Panduit computer company. From Ada, Ohio it was only a five hour drive West to Chicago, but to Houston it would have been a seventeen to twenty hour drive south. And as I noted earlier, my brothers and sister lived in the other direction, in the Danbury, CT area, which was a good twelve hour drive East. Thus, after we moved to Budapest, our August to October stay in the USA always required a lot of logistical planning and constant traveling. From Budapest we initially always flew to Chicago, where we had left our car with Anikó and Brett. Later, when they too moved to Houston, we left our car with my brother Pál in Danbury, CT and flew to Hungary from JFK airport in NYC. (Our house in Ada, OH remained our stable base of operations, which was either under the watchful eyes of our kind neighbor Eddie Grimes, or the effective administration of Patricia Badertscher, our former departmental secretary at ONU.) Furthermore, as a fallback for family unification we had our annual get-together at Lake Hope State Park near Zaleski, OH during the first week of August.

Adjusting to Budapest

After my retirement from ONU, the next ten years of my life became immersed in the challenges that faced me in adjusting to life and work in Budapest. Márika made this re-adjustment easy. Her apartment near Széll Kálmán tér/square (formerly called Moszkva tér) is located on the Buda side of the city, close to everything, because it is a major hub for the Metro, major city busses, and street cars, including the famous 4-6 line and the 56A line. As I mentioned previously, for people over sixty-five, public transportation is free. This means that we do not own a car, and do not have to worry about finding parking spots or fighting city traffic. We have been liberated from the scourge (and questionable blessing) of the internal-combustion engine, at least as this relates to our everyday existence in Budapest. For the occasional trips to neighboring countries, we resort to rent-a-cars. Otherwise, our favorite means of transportation for long-distances is the railroad, which for retired people is also very cheap in Hungary.

The mobility of our environment opens the door to travel and tourism. But much of our traveling is actually linked to conferences and additional study opportunities. Most of the latter are directly linked to my interests with researching the fate of Hungarian minorities in the region. Since my "return" to Hungary I have been kept busy by both my scholarly interests and our residence near Széll Kálmán square. Our home is located in an apartment house including six other apartments. It is managed by a committee composed of all the owners of the seven apartments. Almost all the residents are retired people living on a limited and fixed income. Because I had an American income based on my university retirement fund plus Social Security, the other residents assumed that I had more "sunk cost" in the building and should therefore be the "Communal Representative" (Közös Képviselő). In fact this assignment should be designated care-taker of the house! After my election to this "honor" I became responsible for every burst plumbing in the house, for every rodent that invaded our storage areas in the basement, for every tree limb that almost fell on a neighbor's car from our yard, and the reconciliation of every personal conflict among the residents. On top of all this I was the go-between for the problems of the house and the local government administration. My training and career as a university professor never prepared me for the challeges of this "honor" to serve the house.

In my role as "Communal Representative," I encountered Hungarian bureaucracy in all its glory. My election to this post in 2013, occurred after my predecessor resigned when a roofing accident led to the collapse of the terrace over the house's front entrance as well as the ornamental elements under the eves. In order to bring our house back to its former attractive status, the owners of the apartments decided to sell our attic space to a developer for the construction of two additional apartments. This plan had to be approved by the local government and its engineering staff. I had to wade my way through a bureaucratic labyrinth for the next five years to obtain this approval. I can hardly wait until the construction is completed and I can in good conscience resign as "Communal Representative." At any rate, from this frustrating experience I learned that American bureaucracy is incomparable to the legacy of Ottoman-Habsburg-Soviet practices which have been imbedded in the Hungarian administrative world. On this score Americans can consider themselves very lucky.

Fortunatelly, I continued my scholarly activities which provided an occasional escape from the problems of the house. Initially I took advantage of the minority research facilities called the Teleki László Reseach Center near the Budagyöngye shopping center at the end of the Szilágyi Erzsébet Avenue. This had been established right after regime change with the moral and financial assistance of Diaspora Hungarian institutions. When the MSZP (Hungarian Socialist Party) and SZDSZ (Free Democrats) established their left-leaning coalition, one of their first acts was to eliminate the Teleki László research center at the end of December, 2006. For me personally this was a major set-back, since it was an ideal location for research and for building contacts with scholars interested in similar issues. I even wrote about this loss in a bitter article ("Öncsonkítás,"/Self-mutilation/in the ITT-OTT yearbook for 2008), that unfortunately did not get published in Hungary.

However, this forced me to switch my base of operations to the Minorities Studies center in the Buda castle and later to the National Political Research Institute located also in the castle, but located in the Magyarság Háza on Trinity Square. There, and later on Gellért Street, and then Krisztina Avenue, I became a colleague of an excellent research team led by Zoltán Kántor. On a gratis basis I helped refine their English language publications, particularly *The Hungarian Journal of Minority Studies*. This role raised my standing in the eyes of Hungarian colleagues, and this has led to invitations to panel discussions, conference presentations and workshops dealing with the fate of

Hungarian minorities. This recognition has also led to the invitation by Professor Sándor Szakály to become a member of the advisory council/i.e., Board of Trustees of the Veritas institute whose task is to examine and re-examine the history of Hungary from 1867 to 1989–91. This phase in Hungarian history had been most extensivelly falsified by the Marxist-Leninist historians following the Second World War. Attending the meetings of Veritas and following their research work has been an intellectually rewarding experience.

I have also profited greatly on an intellectual level from the loose affiliation I had with the Rendszerváltás Történetet Kutató Intézet és Archívum (The Research Institute and Archives of Regime Change) under the direction of Zoltán Bíró. Their quarterly periodical and professional meetings have enabled me to keep track of the "népi"(populist) elements in Hungarian political life, particularly as these have been manifested in the work of such key figures as István Bakos, Csaba Kiss Gy., Sándor Lezsák, and the emerging younger generation of Balázs Házy and Zoltán Nagymihály. They have also provided one of the major support groups for the publication of *Hitel* (Credit). Together with the Bethlen Gábor Foundation, they have provided the backbone for national and Christian memorials and recognition throughout Hungary.

In 2014, I was also invited to join the Friends of Hungary which is an outreach civic organization committed to improving the image of the country. Szilveszter Vizi E., the former President of the Hungarian Academy of Sciences is the founder of this group. This organization invites successful professionals from all over the world to provide testimony re the positive contributions of Hungarians. Its annual conventions in May provides a forum for ca. 400 guests to share their experiences on how best to counter the distortions and negative stereotyping that are perpetuated in the mass media of the "West." It is an excellent organization for global networking and disseminating positive information.

Finally, during the summer of 2017 I had the opportunity to attend a meeting organized by Pro Minoritate in the Székely region of Transylvania. Although I had been aware of the existence of this important Hungarian conclave held annually in one of the most scenic parts of the Carpathian basin, for some reason I was never able to attend it. Its proximity in time to our own meeting at Lake Hope, was probably the major obstacle. In 2017 a number of things transpired which now made our presence possible at the Tusványos (combination of Tusnádfürdő and Bálványosfürdő) get-together. First of all I offered my colleagues at the National Research Institute the showing of our recently completed documentary film about the "Shooters" which dealt with a group under the leadership of Zoltán Vasvári during the period immediately after the 1956 Revolution. This documentary I felt, was worth a presentation at the Tusványos conference, because it dealt with the efforts of Diaspora Hungarians in the United States to challenge Soviet control of their destiny in East Central Europe. Daniel Gazsó also thought that it would be worth a showing and he supported my invitation to the Bálványos conference. I went there as part of the NKPI delegation of presenters, but in a separate car with Márika and our friend József Komlossy who was also on the program. This conclave was a great opportunity to share know-how about minorities and at the same time to network with all those interested in their fate. Since the establishment of this annual event, it has also become an important brain-storming session for the leaders of FIDESZ. Besides its founder, Zsolt Németh, inevitably Viktor Orbán, László Tőkes and many other important leaders were on the program using this opportunity to formulate policy. Although the "Lövész" documentary was not presented, our stay was well worth the long and tiring road-trip.

A very similar opportunity was offered to us during the summer of 2019 at Lake Szinevér in Transcarpathian Ukraine. Although on a more reduced scale, this meeting also had as its objective the assessment of Hungarian life in minority status. Here too it brought together local leaders like Ildikó Orosz and László Brenzovics with the top leadership of Hungary related to concern for Hungarians on the other side of the border, including Árpád Potápi, Zsolt Németh and Zoltán Kántor. This time we made the long road-trip with Zsolt Szekeres of HHRF and again were part of an unforgettable experience. Although separated by great distances Lake Hope, Tusnád fürdő and Szinevér Lake are held together with the common will of survival.

My move to Budapest was not just a change of locale, but also a new beginning in my life. As I noted in reference to the responsibilities I obtained as a "Communal Representative" in our apartment house and the new research opportunities that engaged me, I also began to look for ways to publish some of my findings. Now I began to write not just about minority issues, but also general policy questions, particularly with a cultural dimension. Being freed up from the classroom setting and the grading of tests and assignments, gave me much more control over what I really wanted to do. In this sense, retirement has liberated me, but with a focus on activities that I did not have time for during my active teaching career. This led me to more writing and also more involvement in linking my American past to my Hungarian present existence.

Registering the Past in Black and White

A first step in this direction was the editing and publication of Tibor Cseh's writings on the fate of Hungarians living in the Diaspora. Tibor was one of the most prolific writers in our circle of friends. I spent about four years collecting and editing his writings. For me this was particularly a great challenge because up to this point I had done book editing only in English. Fortunately Rozália Kóka, who had been one of our invited guests at Lake Hope, and perhaps the best source for information on Csángó Hungarians as well as the Székelys of Bukovina, helped me with the editing. The book was published by Fekete Sas publishers with a "Foreword" by Zsolt Németh the President of the International Relations Committee of Parliament. Our book hit the bookstores in 2014. It did not become a best-seller, but it is one of the best sources for understanding Hungarian-American Diaspora thinking.

My focus on Diaspora existence also received a boost on the pages of *Korunk* (Our Age), the Transylvanian periodical with a cul-

2017 conference brochure, with theme „Music, Life and Soul"

tural and social commitment. Péter Cseke is on the editorial board of this publication and has been a constant spur for articles and reviews about Hungarians in Canada and the United States. His excellent editing has enabled me to contribute two articles in the last two years in Hungarian. For my English language publishing I have sought out the *Hungarian Review*, a bimonthly journal appearing in Budapest with a Central European focus. During the past few years two of my studies have appeared on its pages, some of which I have quoted extensivelly in my present reflections. The other English language publication to which I have submitted book reviews besides *Nationalities Papers* is the e-journal *Hungarian Cultural Studies*. An additional inspiration for English language publishing has been the emergence of Helena History Press, whose dynamic editor, Katalin Kádár Lynn, has been responsible for the appearance of a whole series of valuable Hungarian related studies and compilations. All in all, since my retirement I have written more in both Hungarian and English for a professional audience then when I was still an active academician.

Fulbright, AHEA and Final Academic Activities

On the academic front I have also remained somewhat active in relation to the Fulbright American-Hungarian exchange program. After all, it was this program that enabled me to become more engaged in research as well as teaching in Hungary. I was particularly grateful for the assistance of Huba Brückner of the Hungarian Fulbright Commission, who had played the most important role in establishing this exchange opportunity between the two countries. Thus, when I heard that he would soon be retired, I began to worry about who his successor might be. Thus, when Károly (Charles) Jokay told me that they were looking for a replacement for Huba, and Károly showed interest in the position, I immediately encouraged him to apply for the position. He had all the necessary qualifications: a strong academic backround, an American Political Science Ph.D., extensive experience with East Central European educational developments and fluency in both English and Hungarian. Furthermore, he had a strong organizational and fund raising background.

Károly Jokay applied for the position. So did a number of other potential candidates with the backing of a number of influential individuals and institutions. I too tried to provide support for Károly's candidacy. This lobbying had to be both low key and subtle, since both the American and the Hungarian governmental and academic circles had different interests and concerns. The selection process dragged on and there were times when Károly was ready to withdraw from the race. Fortunately, his patience held out and he was appointed as Huba Brückner's successor. He has been an excellent selection for the post and the Hungarian Fulbright program continues to be a strong program. The number of Fulbright applications in both directions continues to grow. I know that this is the case, since I have been involved a number of times in interviewing the candidates who have applied to study or teach in the United States. This is a very important responsibility because it establishes foundations for strengthening Hungarian and American linkages and friendships.

Still another "bridge-building" activity since my retirement has been the renewal of my membership and involvement in the American Hungarian Educators Association. I had been among the founding members of this organization in Cleveland, initially under the umbrella of the Hungarian Association in that city during the early 1970s. But my participation became sporadic after my other commitments overwhelmed me. Only after most of our time has been spent in Budapest have I rejoined the work of this organization. With regime change AHEA has tried to hold every third conference in the Carpathian Basin. From our family's Budapest homebase these were easier to attend. Thus, during the past decade I have attended their conferences in Szeged, Budapest, Kolozsvár/Cluj and co-sponsored in Csíkszereda/Miercurea Ciuc. In 2020 their annual conference will be held in Pécs. In planning this get-together I too gained a greater role, since I have been elected to its Executive Committee two years ago. In this capacity I did something that I had never done before in my long academic and organizational career, I proposed myself to be among those who should be considered for Keynote Speaker at the Pécs conference. With my abstention, at its November 5th, 2019 meeting the Executive Committee selected me for this role.

At this conference my focus was to be the Treaty of Trianon. On the hundredth anniversary of this devastating imposed, nay dictated, redrawing of

Hungary's borders, my task was to re-assess what we failed to do during the past hundred years, and how we must try to correct our work in the foreseeable future. For me this was a major challenge, not just because I have accumulated a vast amount of emotional baggage, but because the conditions in the region have been drastically altered by both the passage of time and the traumatic events that have transpired there. At any rate I was not able to present my observations in 2020 because Covid 19 still obstructed the conference. I was able to deliver my keynote presentation via Zoom in 2021 with the changed title: Trianon 101 Years Later. The finalized version of this talk appeared in the 2022 edition of Hungarian Cultural Studies.

For a long time I have assumed that my task would be to write the 20th century history of Transylvania, but the more I have read about it and the more I have studied it, I have realized that others in the Carpathian basin are better suited for this task than I am. So if I receive a few more years after my 82nd birthday, I will write a biography of my father, vitéz Antal Ludányi. I owe this to my daughters and my grandchildren and my brothers' and sister's families. If I receive still one year more, I will help Péter Kovalszki, József Megyeri, Hajnal Minger, Erika Bokor, László Fülöp and Ágnes, and others to write the history of MBK and the ITT-OTT periodical. If I'm given still more time, I will write the history of the Birmingham Hungarian community in Toledo, OH. I do not dare to think beyond that, but we must always have goals and deadlines to keep us going, while we breath, while we see and hear, and while we can still think!

Facing the Coronavirus!

In Hungarian we have a saying: "Ember tervez, Isten rendez!" (Mankind plans, but God puts things in order!) Well, when I wrote the above last two paragraphs I had not considered the impact of this folk wisdom. Since then the AHEA Conference (and my Keynote Address) was delayed for a year and our return to Ada, Ohio was also delayed. But the curfew in Budapest led to the completion and publication of my present autobiography in Hungarian. This was possible due to the generosity of Zsolt Németh's family, the Pro

Lake Hope in 2017

Some of the 2017 Lake Hope conference participants at the last meeting preceding the Covid 19 shut-down. l. to r. Mária Repolski, Csilla Somogyi, (behind Csilla) Péter Kovalszki, Ildikó Forgács, Zsolt Németh, Márika Ludányi, Balázs Somogyi, and András Ludányi

Minoritate Foundation and Méry Ratio publishers. I'm in the process of re-reading and re-thinking everything that I have put to paper. I hope I do not have to revise too much of my past! At present it seems to reflect what it was and the English version of My Roadtrip is heading toward its completion as well. While Covid – 19 has brought an end to my American road trip, it does not end my American life, since both my daughters, my three grandchildren, my former wife and innumerable friends live throughout the United States. However, this virus and now the Russian-Ukrainian war add uncertainty to our plans and our lives on both sides of the Atlantic. This virus also puts a major crimp on international travel. However, my immobility has had a positive side-effect, it has given me the opportunity to re-read my life a number of times and to compare the present prospects of Hungary and Hungarians and the prospects of the USA and Americans in the forseeable future.

Conclusion to my road trip (Some Afterthoughts)

The contemplation of our past has forced me to take a second look at the prospects for democracy in both these settings. In the American superpower at present the prospects actually look dimmer than in the Indiana-sized Central European polity of Hungary. Why? Because at present Hungary has a popular leader who has a clear-cut vision and the organizational skill to mobilize and lead his people to work out their destiny with other East Central European states, particularly the V-4. In the USA, on the other hand, the political order is being de-stabilized both by the polarizing leadership of President Trump and the rampage of covid-19 and the subsequent economic problems and racial confrontations spurred by Black Lives Matter and Antifa activists. The unrest and the vandalism on the streets of American major cities, lasting for weeks, has unhinged political leadership in both major political parties. The toppling and decapitation of symbols and statues, secular and religious, challenges both the content and recording of American history and the very existence of a uniting political culture.

In my opinion this disruption of American political culture, may lead to its total collapse. Like "Topsy, America growed and growed," but failed to integrate and consolidate its peoples and its values. This growth, at least since the Civil War, was driven not by a conscious and self-conscious American elite based on the common good of the commonweal, but by the rapacious profit seeking corporations that dominated the economy of the land. The latter lacked the vision of the founding fathers, whose statues are presently being vandalized or dragged off their pedestals by the mobs dominating the streets. Indeed, the Founding Fathers inherited the values of Western Civilization, including Christian values and traditions. They added to this the natural spirit of the North American continent and combined the two to provide the core and the backbone of American political culture. As opposed to this, slavery, unfair labor practices and discrimination of various sorts were the biproducts of unlimited corporate power and robber-baron capitalism. It was also this expansion of corporate power that led to massive changes in immigration policies following World War II. By the end of the 1950's this was exaggerated even farther by the institutionalization of the military-industrial complex. The end result has been the abdication of control over the future profile of American political culture.

A substitute culture has been developed by the corporate elite which has used the mass media and the entertainment industry to sell the new perspectives to the American public. This substitute culture is called "Liberal Democracy." It rejects the Christian legacy of the Founders and replaces it with a secularized consumer materialism. This substitute political culture is enforced in the public arena by p.c.[39] censorship that controls both the mass media and the entertainment industry. Thus, all traditional values become subject to this censorship. Christmas and the Christ Child are replaced by the fat and jolly figure of Santa who is important for our December spending spree and not religious worship. The same is true for the eclipse of All Saints Day by the orgy of spending that is generated by Haloween and Easter is now overwhelmed by the Easter Bunny. Aside from the market driven objectives undermining tradition, other basic elements of Judeo-Christian values are also under attack. The normal family based on marriage between a man and a woman to procreate and raise children is castigated as a homophobe institution. A patriotic commitment to what America stands for from Bunker Hill, through Valley Forge, Gettysburgh, Appomatox Courthouse, the Allamo, to the Beaches of Normandy are somehow linked to racism and fascistic inclinations.

"Racism" and "fascism" are not defined, but are used to stigmatize any and all individuals and institutions that represent the past going back to the

---

39 *PC or p.c.* is the abbreviation of "politically correct," which is the phrase used to define what is acceptable in public discourse related to race, religion, gender or even personal characteristics. For example, it is not p.c. to say that "My opponent is a fat, Uncle Tom." This phrase casts aspersions on his/her physical characteristics as well as his /her race and political posture. P.C. is an exercise of social and political censorship which frequently infringes on freedom of speech.

1950's, but in some instances all the way back to Christopher Columbus and Jesus Christ.

This same negative brush has been applied in relation to Viktor Orbán and present-day Hungary by liberalist corporate power centers in the USA as well as Western Europe. Hungary and Hungarians, however, are not likely to kneel down in the face of the demands of crazed and primitive mobs. In present-day Hungary the rule of law and constitutional democracy are the guiding principles of state, government and society. This is backed up by a unified national political culture that reflects a millenium of trials and tribulations. The Hungarian survival instinct is strong and well, mobilized by a talented and charismatic leader who has been returned to power by four successive elections with a two-thirds Parliamentary majority.

In the West, particularly in the so-called elite media *(The Economist, The New York Times, Der Spiegel, The Washington Post, The Wall Street Journal)* Orbán is portrayed as a populist autocrat. Particularly during Covid-19, when he requested emergency powers from Parliament, did the feeding frenzy of these media giants exceed fever pitch. Just one dramatic example was Christiane Amanpour on CNN, falsely claiming that Hungary had disbanded its Parliament, to consolidate Orbán's power. Furthermore, when his emergency powers reverted to Parliament after the effective handling of the first wave of this health crisis, not one peep resembling an apology appeared in any of these important sources of opinion formation. Since Orbán cannot be attacked as being anti-democratic, he is dragged over the coals as a violator of the "rule of law." This general charge is leveled without verified specifics and is used without an awareness of the actual constitutional and legal conditions in Hungary.

The rule of law in Hungary has a longer history, both with ups and downs, than in most of the political systems whose corporate media currently criticize Hungary. We can go back to the reign of István I. (Saint Stephen) 1000-1038 who obtained Papal recognition via the Holy Crown that is on display in the rotunda of Parliament to this day. With his crowning, both Canon law and the law of primogeniture and elements of Roman law gained acceptance in Hungary. István I. also provided the guiding principles for his successors, with his "Admonitions" to his son Prince Emeric (Imre). Under King László

I. (Saint László), the separation of Church authority over the right to appoint the higher clergy became the prerogative of the monarch in 1077 and he also issued the first comprehensive legal code in the country. In 1222, just seven years after the Magna Carta was signed in England, King Andrew II. had to accept the limitations of the Golden Bull document. This was followed almost immediately by the granting of autonomous self-government to the Saxon-German cities in Transylvania. During some of Hungary's most challenging confrontations with the Ottoman Turkish empire the famous law codification (Tripartitum) took place under the direction of István Werbőczy (1514). In this same century the Hungarian Princedom of Transylvania issued the Edict of Torda (1568) which was the first general declaration of religious toleration on the continent of Europe. Ottoman Turkish occupation of Hungary interrupted this development and after 1686 Habsburg absolutism also put limits on Hungarian autonomous legal development. However, the independence movements of the nation could not be completely stiffled, and both the rising of Ferenc Rákóczi II. in 1703–12 and the Lajos Kossuth rising of 1848–49, produced important reforms that led Hungary into the 20th century, including the abolition of serfdom in 1853, and Europe's most liberal minority rights law in 1868, and also the introduction of electoral reform laws, including the extension of suffrage to women in 1919. Finally, Hungary's adoption of a new Basic Law in 2012, replaced the Stalinist-Mátyás Rákosi constitution of 1949. Furthermore, since 1990, with the end of one-party Communist rule, all governments have come to power via popular elections. The Orban government has been more successful than its predecessors, since it has gained the support of the majority of the Hungarian electorate with control of two-thirds of the seats in Parliament.

Since Franklin Deleno Roosevelt, no American President has been able to match this in terms of electoral support. In fact, two American presidents (George W. Bush and Donald Trump) were elected by the Electoral College and not the popular vote of the American electorate. However, this has meant frequent dead-lock in decision making because of the separation of powers and the dominance of conflicts among the major corporate interest groups in the country. A similar situation exists in most West European political systems, were the electoral politics have produced fragmentation that leads to coalition governments, whose strongest member party at best has only the plurality support of the electorate.

The corporatist world under the flag of "Liberal Democracy" prefers this kind of indecisive electoral process because powerful interests can muddle through or manipulate, even dominate, the governing process. Of course the possibility of miscalculation, can lead to the self-destruction of the American enterprise. By destroying the traditional democracy based on a balance between the values of liberty and equality, the door is opened to real dictatorship. Either the Antifa/Black Lives Matter dictatorship or its polar opposite, the NRA/threatened Silent Majority dictatorship. The latter is the more likely scenario, but in either case it is the end even of a corporatist dominated democracy.

This brings us to the Presidential elections of 2020 and the ensuing political and legal stalemate which threatens not only the well-being of the United States, but the continuing prospects for democracy in North America as well as Europe. This is not just a political stalemate, it is the polarization of cultural values. Furthermore, this confrontation is being copycatted throughout the so-called Western World. The present confrontation between Joe Biden and Donald Trump is not just a traditional confrontation between Democrats and Republicans. It is now a drama dividing the country and the Western World according to corporatist, consumer oriented materialist goals on the one hand and a tradition preserving Christian world view committed both to family and national values on the other. The results of the present electoral process bear this out. The inconclusive nature of the "results" should warn us that society is dangerously split on key issues that define the political and legal order. A nation divided against itself cannot long survive. During the Civil War the split was geographically defined, today the split cuts through all races, all ethnic groups, all classes in all parts of the country. Furthermore, the results of the elections are called into question because of perceived voter fraud. American democracy is consequently in deep crisis. A great deal of wisdom and tolerance will be necessary to overcome this crisis. If it cannot be resolved through existing institutions, through legal channels, the confrontations in the streets will take over. American prestige and world leadership hangs in the balance.

Hungary's "Illiberal Democracy" or traditional democracy, is more likely to remain intact, because it can muster a solid majority behind a government that reflects its political culture. Stability, security and the protection of the rights of both the majority and existing, particularly historic minorities, is assured by a constitutional order based on majority rule with minority rights! It does not sacrifice the American First Amendment freedoms on the alter of the new dogmatism of Liberal Democracy. Perhaps Hungary's successes in fighting major natural catastrophies (Danube flooding), massive illegal migration and the first wave of Covid-19, will lead not simply to near-sighted envy, but to the adoption of similar policies elsewhere. My 100% loyalty to the American values (work ethic, thrift, openness to innovation, volunteerism, respect for the rights of others, commitment to individual freedom and pragmatism) and my 100% loyalty to Hungarian values (family solidarity, national loyalty, courage to stand up for convictions) will at least have some impact on my friends and family in the USA also. I invite them all to Lake Hope State Park in Ohio to be part of the Hungarian-American revival in August, 2023!

Afterword

One of my respected colleagues at Ohio Northern University, Professor John Lomax, after reading my reflections about myself, wrote the following observation: "You characterize your life in the United States as a road trip. A curious choice of words. Are they simply a literary device, or is it that you were something of a foreign tourist during your years in America? Has your Hungarian identity always predominated? Did you ever feel truly American?"

In one sense it was a literary device, I wanted to sum up, to express in a succint phrase, one person's travels through the vastness and complexity of the American experience. In another sense, now that you have cornered me, dear John, I must admit that it does reflect my uncertainty about my own identity, my "Americanness." It also highlights the certainty of my dual existence in time and space. When does one become an American? Who is really a Hungarian?

Remember when you and Peggy visited us in Budapest, on our tour of the city I took you near the Parliament building where we stopped next to a statue of Attila József, sitting on the parrapet looking down at the Danube. I remember, that I had said that he is one of our greatest poets of the 20th century and that he wrote one of the most perceptive poems about Hungary and its relations to all the peoples who live in the Carpathian Basin. In this context I also reflected on his statement that through his vains courses the blood of Kumans, Székelys, Romanians, Slovaks, as well as Magyars, so the Danube should be a link between all of us and not a barrier to realizing our common interests. As he points out, all ethnic communities in the Carpathian Basin provide the foundations for resolving our common concerns. However, his life also demonstrates that the factor that was most important in providing identity, unity and direction to this community of peoples was the unique possession of a language that was not a racialist, nor ethnic, but a linguistic carrier of values and traditions.

This trait of cultural transmission is in many ways similar to what I (we) encountered in the United States, although on a much larger scale. In the American context the English language was the "force" of unification, with a certain tolerance for language diversity within the context of local community existence. (Aside from short periods of pressure to assimilate, in both contexts linguistic diversity was the case.)

Now what about my identity? For years I claimed that I was a 100% Hungarian and a 100% American! In retrospect I realize that this was a noble (?) lie. Now I contend that no-one can be a 200% person divided right down the middle! So right now in 2020, what do I consider myself? While I was writing my remembrances I had to constantly face this question. In this confrontation of my double identity when I first became conscious of having to define myself, as a youngster my surroundings gave me my self-definition. In the Austrian refugee camps we were simply "Hungarian refugees." (Also "Displaced Persons" or D.P.s for short.) Then when we crossed the Atlantic and settled in Virginia, I was simply the "foreign kid" until I was able to change my short pants with Austrian-like suspenders to jeans. From then on my Americanization moved forward rapidly because the ideals of Partick Henry's "give me liberty or give me death" made chopping wood on Mr. Forester's and the Watkins' farm that much easier. Then when we moved to Astoria in NYC, the world again became more complex as I played soccer with Maltese, Italian, Greek and Ukrainian "immigrant" teen-agers in the shadow of the Triboro and Hell Gate bridges. Here I also became involved with the Exile Hungarian Boy Scout Troop of NYC and the St. Emeric Youth Sports Club on eighty-first Street on the East Side. Then the 1956 Revolution broke out in Hungary!

1956 was a transformative event in my life. Although I experienced it only via radio broadcasts, it led me into the kind of activism that reinforced my Hungarianness. Street demonstrations in front of the Soviet Mission to the UN and assorted other activities reinforced my commitments to be a "fighter" for the rights of the underdog. As a kid I remember when we played Cowboys and Indians, I always role-played Crazy Horse or Geronimo! Now at the age of sixteen my role-playing was more directly tied to my own people, held captive by the Evil Empire. As I already summarized in my recollections, this led to experiences and confrontations which defined my future scholarly, political and emotional allegiences. Thus, my studies at Elmhurst College and my graduate studies at LSU just continued me on this path, including the IREX and Fulbright study/teaching opportunities in former Yugoslavia and Kadarist and post-Communist Hungary. All this within the context of American opportunities and the acquisition of American know-how.

My "Americanness" is part of me in the organizational skills gained from lobbying activities and the election campaigns in which I could participate. These skills were also obtained in the work I did to help organize the ONU faculty union in opposing the arbitrary Loeschner presidency on campus. These practical elements were wedded to conceptions of real democracy enshrined in Lincoln's (and Kossuth's) "Government of, for, and by the people" as opposed to the politics of money and corporations which dominates American politics in alliance with the Military-Industrial complex since the late 1950's. At the same time I admire the Christian ethics associated with the "inner-directed" Americans who dominated our politics until the "other-directed" LBGTQ-Hollywood-Media secular world imposed its p.c. and consumer crazed corporate interests on us in the second half of the 20th century to the present.

As opposed to this, my "Hungarianness" rejects the consumerism and materialism which has invaded East-Central Europe (including Hungary) with McDonalds, Coca-Cola, NIKE, and other like-minded multi-nationals. Instead, I maintain my allegiance to my language, my national culture, my Christian traditions, and my family and community centered values. All these were of course also present in the American-Hungarian communities of Toledo, Cleveland, Chicago, New Brunswick, and Pittsburgh. So, what am I? Hungarian-American? American-Hungarian? In the final analysis I think it depends on which Hungary or which United States we are talking about! It was definitely not the Hungary dominated by the Soviet puppets Mátyás Rákosi or János Kádár or the Nazi dominated Döme Sztojay or Ferenc Szálasi! Nor was it the United States of George W. Bush or Barack Obama dominated by Big Oil and the massive military devastation of Iraq, Libya, Syria under the guise of bringing democracy via the "Arab Spring" but delivered by laser-guided drones. So what am I? You tell me and you need not break it down in percentage points.

With best wishes always,

Andy for you and my ONU colleagues, or Andrew or András for others

APPENDIX

*This essay was written during the Spring of 2018 and presented at the University of Graz in Austria on July 5th of that year. Changes that have occurred since then or criticisms that have led to recent changes are incorporated in the text in italics.

Is Viktor Orbán A Populist ?

Is Viktor Orbán, the current Prime Minister of Hungary, a "populist"? This question deserves attention, because it may help define what is meant by the overused and abused term "POPULISM."[1] Of course journalists are more likely to use the term very loosely, but this does not excuse the scholarly world from doing so as well! With this in mind, plus the appearance of many "populism" related studies, articles and essays,[2] the present reflection will try to

---

1   In formulating my own thoughts on "populism," I owe a great deal to the (yet) unpublished paper presented by Professor Michael Loughlin to the Ohio Academy in April of 2018. The title of his paper was "Trumpism: Fascism, Populism or Something Else?" Loughlin drew particularly on the writings of Jan Werner Müller, *What is Populism* (2016), Benjamin Moffitt, *The Global Rise of Populism: Performance, Political Style, and Representation* (2016), Cas Mudde and Cristóbal Rovira Kaltwasser, *Populism: A Very Short Inroduction* (2017), and Frederico Finchelstein, *From Fascism to Populism in History* (2017). In his discussion, Loughlin seems to side with the elitist interpretation of Richard Hofstadter. However, he does admit that he finds the term populism "no less complex, controversial, and elastic than the term fascism, an inveterate pejorative whose definition continues to arouse debate and whose use seems to prevent objectivity."

2   The Orbán government has come under constant criticism from the elite media both in Western Europe and in the United States. The criticism has also always included the "populist" adjective in a pejorative context. The number of such journalist attacks increased dramatically in the months preceding the national elections of April 8, 2018. Some additional attack articles and reviews followed after Orbán again won a sweeping victory with two-thirds of the seats in Parliament. See: Patrick Kingsley, "As West Fears the Rise of Autocrats, Hungary Shows What's Possible," *The New York Times*, Feb. 10, 2018; "How Hungarian PM's Supporters Profit from EU-Backed Projects," *Guardian*, Feb. 12, 2018; Joseph C. Sternberg, "The EU's Hungary Problem is the EU: Prime Minister Viktor Orbán Masters Europe's Legalisms While Flouting its Democratic Aspirations," *The Wall Street Journal*, March 2, 2018; Griff Witte, "Hungarian Campaign Demonizes Liberal Soros," *The Washington Post*, March 18, 2018; Charles Gati, "Book Review of Paul Lendvai's *Orbán Hungary's Strongman:* Tilting Towards Dictatorship in Hungary: Why Hungary's Prime Minister Blames George Soros for all the Country's Woes," *The Washington Post*, March 25, 2018; Jan-Werner Müller, "Homo Orbánikus: Review of *Orbán, Hungary's Strongman* by Paul Lendvai," *The New York Review of Books*, April

shed light on the meaning of this concept with the specific example of the Orbán phenomenon in Hungary. A case study of this nature must at the same time have a comparative dimension, relating Orbán to others who have been described as populists.

Historical Roots

What are the historical roots of populism? The quest for the popular control of decision-making is as old as humanity, but its realization is mainly a product of the revolutionary movements of the past two hundred and forty-two years. The American 1776, the French 1789 and the Hungarian 1848 and 1956 revolutions are each milestones in this governmental evolution of mankind. Abraham Lincoln's classic phrase from the Gettysburg address of "government of, for and by the people" is just the most succinct definition of this quest! Of course Lincoln's definition related to "democracy" and not to "populism," but when he formulated it "populism" had not yet made it unto the public stage as a movement. Furthermore, as American historian Charles A. Beard points out in *An Economic Interpretation of the Constitution of the United States* (1913), from the very beginning this document was a restraint of rather than an encouragement for popular democracy.

Some elements of popular democracy, however, already appeared in the United States with Andrew Jackson's presidency, but the Populist Movement as a real force only appears in 1892 and gains prominence in the 1896 electoral campaign of William Jennings Bryan.[3] It responds to the period in American history that we tend to associate with the raw capitalism of the post-Civil War decades and the "robber Barons" of the railroad builders, bankers

---

5, 2018; Eleni Kounalakis, "Viktor Orbán's Victory in Hungary Brings Important Lessons to Us Here at Home," *Hungarian Free Press* (Toronto), April 14, 2018. http://hungarianfreepress.com/2018/04/14/viktor-orbans-victory-in-hungary-brings-important-lessons-to-us-here-at-home/ ; Heather A. Conley and Charles Gati, "Why Donald Trump loves Viktor Orbán," *The Washington Post*, May 27, 2018.

3 The two historians who have defined early American populism have been Richard Hofstadter, *The Age of Reform* (1962) and *The Paranoid Style in American Politics and Other Essays* (1967) in a negative light, and Lawrence Goodwyn, *Democratic Promise: The Populist Movement in America* (1976) from a positive perspective.

and mining magnates who dominated the financial and political world of the United States at that time. The names of Carnegie, Hill, Morgan, Harriman and Rockefeller immediately come to mind. Their efforts to control markets and increase profits led to the exploitation of miners and farmers throughout the country. (But also contributed to the dramatic growth of the American economy!) This led to the first, although unsuccessful, rebellion, of the disadvantaged against the forces of economic globalization. The symbol of this struggle became William Jennings Bryan's "Cross of Gold" campaign speech.

The populism of Bryan could not effectively challenge the hold of big money, for at least two major reasons: first, because the frontier was still open and it became a "safety-valve" drawing the discontented ever Westward,[4] and second, because mass immigration from Eastern and Southern Europe provided the needed labor force to replace those who abandoned the mills, factories, mines and railroad yards in the East and Mid-West. The new replacement work force initially did not speak English and could be more easily manipulated and used as strike breakers. Thus, the process of immigration from Eastern and Southern Europe helped to stifle the populist movement in the United States while at the same time providing a "safety-valve" for the social and economic unrest that was surfacing at this time on the European continent. This unrest was the twin brother of Bryan's populism, but based not on "robber Barons" but "landed Barons" who controlled the feudal legacy of the continent.

In the Czarist Russian Empire the analogous *Narodnik* (people's) movement tried to challenge the established landed and monied interests of the empire. Although this movement was not more successful than its American counterpart, it spawned during the late 19th and early 20th century the unrest that ended the Czarist Empire and ultimately led to the Bolshevik seizure of power. The *Narodnik* movement, however, was based on the recently emancipated serfs who constituted the overwhelming majority of the rural population. (However, this movement was led by young people from the cities who had an unrealistic, overly romanticised view of the Russian *muzsik/peasant*.) As opposed to this group, the Bolsheviks were always an urban, St.

---

4   See Frederick Jackson Turner, *The Frontier in American History* (1920).

Petersburg and Moscow centered proletariat and lower-middle class organization. Thus, the Russian peasantry were again excluded from the decision-making process and in fact became the exploited masses of the collectivized Soviet agricultural system.

Hungary's Népi/People's Movement

In the meantime, particularly after the collapse of the three dominant regional empires (Czarist Russian, Austro-Hungarian/ Habsburg and Ottoman Turkish) during and after World War I, social unrest appeared in almost every successor state. For the Hungarian peasantry or agrarian interests, this was spearheaded by the *Népi*/People's movement of Dezső Szabó, Gyula Illyés, László Németh, Péter Veress and Imre Kovács, to name just some of the most prominent writers of the movement. As this listing indicates, the People's movement in Hungary (as in Poland, Romania and other states of the region) was led by "conscience stricken" intellectuals, many of peasant origin, but generally at least one generation removed from the peasantry itself. The movement's main elements were similar throughout the region.

In Hungary the *Népi*/People's movement sought to overcome the backwardness of Hungary's agrarian society and the injustices of the remnants of feudalism in the countryside. Its concern was to revitalize Hungarian society via a thorough land reform that would break up the large latifundia of the aristocracy and the Roman Catholic Church. Its aim was to base the Hungarian political order on the agrarian majority of the land. World War II, however, dramatically altered the agenda. It swept away the old order and replaced it with the Dictatorship of the Proletariate. In Hungary too, this was an import imposed on the country by the expansion of the Soviet state. The Soviet Union's local satraps, Mátyás Rákosi and János Kádár, carried out the "land reform" that never had a chance in the inter-war period. But this reform was not led by members of the *Népi*/People's movement, or by their needs and interests. It was designed to enable the Hungarian Workers Party (Communists), later Hungarian Socialist Workers Party to centralize control over the Hungarian population and economy.

Inadvertently, this dramatic change in Hungarian society really pulled the rug out from under the *Népi*/People's movement. Collectivized agriculture and the state's forced industrialization on the Stalinist model dramatically changed Hungary's social and economic profile. The *Népi*/People's movement was marginalized, and their most prominent representatives were tolerated only in a window-dressing context. Their most important issue, land reform, was swept off the table by the policies of the HWP/HSWP. The dramatic urbanization that was linked to the industrialization process combined with the elimination of the former "ruling classes" (middle- and upper classes), also reduced and transformed the agrarian population of the land.

Orbán's Political Socialization

Viktor Orbán was born into this changed world in 1963. He missed the Hungarian 1956 and the worst of the Kádár dictatorship's years, and in terms of personal experience he witnessed mainly the toned down version of Hungary as the "happiest barack in the Soviet Camp." However, as József Debreczeni points out in his biography of Viktor Orbán, his family was apolitical.[5] Orbán as a youth was not interested or involved in political affairs. His main interests were his studies and in his spare time playing soccer. However, while attending high school in Székesfehérvár, he did get involved in a discussion club that dealt with literature and society and provided him with a network of important friends. But from all available information about his involvement, he did not have access to the *Népi*/People's writers of the interwar period. Tellingly, the family book shelves did not include the writers published by Püski, the main publisher of *Népi* literature.[6] Orbán's one year military service in Zalaegerszeg provided him with a more life changing experience, by exposing him to a system of discipline and order that was beyond his control.

Viktor Orbán's political socialization took place in the context of his law student years in the Law Program of ELTE (Eötvös Loránd Tudomány Egyetem)

---

5   József Debreczeni, *Orbán Viktor*, Budapest (2002), pp. 11, 31-32.
6   Ibid., p. 54. For a good summary of their interwar impact see Nóra Szekér, *Titkos társaság: A Magyar Testvéri Közösség története* (2017), pp. 107–137.

University, particularly as a member and student leader of the Bibó István Szakkollégium.[7] *The activities of this group complemented the formal law studies of the students and provided the opportunity to invite speakers that deal with contemporary issues in Hungarian society. However, this environment was dominated by the emerging opposition groups linked to the samizdat publications like Beszélő. It included mainly leaders and activists of the future SZDSZ, neoliberals like János Kis, Miklós Haraszti, ifj. László Rajk, and János Kenedi, rather than future MDF leaders and activists like Gy. Csaba Kiss, Gyula Kodolányi, Bába Iván or Rudolf Joó. A major influence can be attributed to the Polish Solidarity Movement! This means that the main intellectual influence came from the left, and not a "populist" left, but a "neoliberal" left. Thus, the innitial momentum for the organization of the Bibó Szakkollégium was strongly anti-Communist but not based on a Népi/populist foundation.*

According to Debreczeni, it was an orientation that was closer to the neoliberal, globalist capitalism of the USA and not the more traditional European family, religion and nation focused conservatism of the "old continent."[8] *Viktor Orbán's political socialization by the former orientation, is therefor ideologically linked to ideas that were anything but the populism of the interwar Népi/People's movement. However, the student movement and his circle of friends, including Zsolt Németh, László Kövér and Lajos Simicska strenghtened his anti-Communist and Christian perspective. Furthermore, the "Szakkollégium" network (including the Bibó, Rajk, Németh, Széchenyi, Erdei networks) were really more important for Orbán from an organizational, political perspective*

---

7 Szakkollégium is a special entity/institution that links housing (residence hall/dormitory) life with the "major" studies of students at Hungarian universities. The American "college" is the rough equivalent of the Hungarian "főiskola." "Kollégium", on the other hand, is not the counterpart of the American "college." At the same time, the concept of "szak" relates to what we in the USA would call the "major field" of study. In this way, the members of a "szakkollégium" are simultaneously residents of a particular dormitory and students focused on a certain field of study. Thus, the residence building on Ménesi út #12 was the focal point, convergence center of law students who attended ELTE University in Budapest. However, for them the residence hall was not just where they resided, but also a center for organizing lectures and presentations that related to their academic, social and political interests. It was at the same time a self-governing institution, the closest thing to a democracy, albeit for a small community separated from the rest of society. These were frequently more important for the intellectual and personal development of students than the formal courses they attended at the university.

8 Debreczeni, p. 56; Also: András Lánczi, "The Renewed Social Contract: Hungary's Elections, 2018, *Hungarian Review* (May, 2018) IX,3: 17–19.

in organizing FIDESZ, rather than in terms of ideology. At the same time in the early years the rising significance of the persecution of the Hungarians in Ceaușescu's Romania and Milosević's Serbia and elsewhere led to a greater commitment to national solidarity for the defense of cultural and civil rights across borders. The clash of these different values came to a head first in 1992 around the formulation of the Democratic Charter, but finally in 1994 after a split in FIDESZ and the fragmentation of MDF and parties with a national orientation, which led to the electoral victory of MSZP (Hungarian Socialist Party). It also led to a Coalition between MSZP and SZDSZ, the erstwhile neoliberals, who up to this point had been the major opposition allies of FIDESZ.

This Coalition of the Left leads to Orbán's political transformation. From this point on, he becomes a centrist in Hungarian politics. This paper has already demonstrated that his Hungarian political roots do not go back to the *Népi*/People's movement. Since there is no ideological connection, is there any other factor that makes him a "populist"? To answer this question I have consulted a number of Hungarian studies that have appeared on populism since the 1994 elections and the emergence of Orbán as the most important political actor on the Hungarian political scene. These studies,[9] together with the accusatory sources already mentioned, and the actual policies that he has pursued may provide the answer to the question posed by the title of this paper.

Populist Revival?

The earliest document I have consulted concerning Orbán's alleged populism is a study written by András Bozóki in the critical year of 1994. In this analysis Bozóki points out that populism in Hungary is not a likely scenario, because the political culture in the country does not support it. Bozóki lists the

---

9   András Bozóki, "Vázlat három populizmusról: Egyesült Államok, Argentína és Magyarország," *Politikatudományi Szemle* (1994), III/3: 33–68; Péter Cseke, "Népiség-populizmus-nacionalizmus az ezredvégén," *Korunk* (1995) 4: 95–102; Ákos Bartha, "Tojástánc a populizmusok körül: A magyar népi mozgalom keretei és regionális dimenziói," *Múltunk* (2014), LIX/4: 58–104; András Körösényi and Veronika Patkós, "Liberális és Illiberális populizmus: Berlusconi és Orbán politikai vezetése," *Politikatudományi Szemle* (2015), XXIV/2: 29–54; Attila Antal, "A populizmus vizsgálata demokráciaelméleti perspektívában," *Politikatudományi Szemle* (2017), XXVI/2: 129–148.

following reasons: the Kádár era has turned the majority of the population into following their self-interest and thereby they can avoid the appeal of political demagogues; in spite of reduced economic opportunities the majority of the population will not support such leaders; the extremist appeals of both fascists and communists have been costly and the population is not likely to follow similar appeals in the future; the patron-client relationships of the Kádár era established informal mechanisms for individual problem solving; the "cult of personality" of the communist years has made the population suspicious of all personalistic leadership; the small size of Hungary and its dependence on the global economic order does not favor nationalism; the economic well being in the West is seen as the only alternative for Hungary; there seems to be no significant opposition to Western capital investment in the country; most of the intelligentsia is committed to democratic values; wide-spread acceptance seems to exist for liberal and democratic values and their relationship to capitalism; economic leveling does not seem to be a concern for significant groups in society; society lacks confidence in the state as a neutral agency and in fact there is a strong anti-state mentality, which is also a problem for democratic governance.[10]

With all these obstacles to "populism," do the opponents of Viktor Orbán have a leg to stand on when they claim that he is a "populist?" Here we must ask whether or not the term has become simply a "bad word" to stigmatize our political opponents.[11] This pejorative function of the term is definitely part of the arsenal of those who want to discredit Orbán. The disbelief of his opponents that he had actually won the elections with a sweeping two-thirds majority for the third time (2010, 2014, 2018) enabled them to justify organizing demonstrations against the results claiming that they, the opposition, are the real majority. This is reminiscent of the majority-controlling "minority," the Mensheviks, having their legitimacy challenged by the minority-controlling "majority," the Bolsheviks.[12] At this point it is worth

---

10 Bozóki, "Vázlat három populizmusról...", pp. 57–58.
11 Bartha, "Tojástánc a populizmusok körül...", p. 61.
12 See: Ibid., footnote 49 based on Ákos Szilágyi's concept of the resort to "Veto-cracia," i.e., refusal to accept the decision of the electorate. Also: Gáspár Gróh, "Parliamentary Elections in Hungary, 2018," *Hungarian Review*, (May,2018), IX,3: 9.

raising the question does the two-thirds majority, the real majority, actually feel that what Orbán represents is not only a reflection of their will, but also in the interest of the Hungarian people and the Hungarian state? This is the very question that was raised by Dani Rodrik within the context of American politics in his recent reflections in *The New York Times*! Is it possible to have a populism that is both positive and beneficial? At least in the case of FDR's New Deal, he concludes that this was the case, even if FDR was not characterized as a populist.[13]

Elections and Media

The organizers of these anti-Orbán demonstrations use the label "populist," but contend that it is an autocratic commitment and not a democratic one. In their eyes the elections were "fixed." Orbán used the "devious" electoral system that benefits a two-party set-up, rather than the more democratic proportional system that would enable even miniscule parties to obtain representation in Parliament. According to this criticism the elections in the United States, the United Kingdom and the Federal Republic of Germany would also be "devious." Patrick Kingsley in a New York Times *article also contends that electoral laws were manipulated to favor the ruling party.[14] Kingsley does not provide specific examples, but maintains that some electoral district boundaries in Budapest were drawn in such a way that it reduced the chances of "the democratic opposition." This is highly misleading, particularly if we compare the Hungarian electoral laws with those in Ohio or Texas or almost anywhere else in the USA where the dominant party (either one) has a chance to gerrymander electoral districts. A comparison of the electoral map of Hungary following the April 8, 2018 elections with those in Ohio, will show nothing like Marcy Kaptur's elongated district in northern Ohio, which was established by the Republicans to eliminate their "favorite" Democratic opponent in Cleveland.[15]*

---

13 Dani Rodrik, "What Does a True Populism Look Like? It Looks Like the New Deal," *The New York Times*, February 2, 2018.
14 Kingsley, "As West Fears the Rise of Autocrats, Hungary Shows What's Possible" op.cit.
15 See: "Választás 2018," *Magyar Demokrata* (April 11, 2018), XXII/15: map, pp. 10–11.

The other favorite charge is that the election results were only possible because the media and political communication was dominated by pro-Orbán forces. According to Médianéző, *one of the most respected and systematic media commentators in Hungary, this charge is unfounded. The most blatant examples of this charge have recently appeared at the Toronto based* Hungarian Free Press. *On the pages of this internet portal two articles appeared after the April 8th election claiming that the "lack of press freedom" was crucial to Orbán's victory. One was written by a Danish student journalism major who visited Hungary just prior to the election, the other was the product of Eleni Kounalakis' (U.S Ambassador to Hungary, 2010-2013) post-election reflections.[16] Neither of these observers speaks, reads or understands Hungarian, therefor it is not unreasonable to assume that they received their information from the anti-Orbán opposition. According to the* Médianéző *research site, prior to the election, both in terms of access to the printed as well as the electronic media coverage, effective information dissemination was close to 50-50% between the government and the opposition.[17]*

*Since Orbán's sweeping victory in April, one important opposition printed source (*Magyar Nemzet*) has folded, due to lack of popularity and falling subscriptions. In the area of electronic media the* RTL-KLUB, ATV, *and* HÍR-TV *still provide the opposition with popular outlets to the public. While the flagship opposition daily* Népszava *also folded earlier, it is now back with a reduced readership. However, opposition voices can be heard loud and clear on* INDEX, 168óra, 444, Új Szó, Fidesz figyelő, Magyar Narancs, Vastagbőr, Hír24, Napi Gazdaság, Átlátszó, Ténytár, Gépnarancs, Cink, Bors, Nyugati fény, Újegyenlőség, Zsúrpubi, Klubrádió, SlágerFM, *and* INFORÁDIÓ.[18] *In addition, the internet challengers are ever present, as attested by the above*

---

16 Jeppe Bjerre Trans, "Lack of press freedom crucial to Orbán's victory," April 29, 2018; and Eleni Kounalakis, "Viktor Orbán's victory in Hungary brings important lessons to us here at home," April 14, 2018; in http://hungarianfreepress.com/2018/04/14/viktor-orbans-victory-in-hungary-brings-important-lessons-to-us-here-at-home/

17 Médianéző, "Ellenszélben: Magyarország nemzetközi médiaképe 2017-ben," February 16, 2018; in hpps://rendezveny.nezopontintezet.hu/event/ellenszelben-magyarorszag-nemzetkozi-mediakepe-2017-ben/

18 Georg Spöttle, "És akkor most mit szeretnétek?—A tüntetés margójára," April 16, 2018; and Péter Krekó, "Hungary is a Post-Truth Laboratory," interview by Anita Kőműves, *Transitions Online,* June 8, 2018. From opposite sides of the political spectrum both state that the Hungarian public has access to media of all political persuasions.

quoted Hungarian Free Press. Furthermore, in Orbán's Hungary not one political critic has yet landed in jail. Not one opponent or opposition reporter has been eliminated by a convenient accident. The media controlled by the left opposition, as for example ATV *or* RTL-KLUB, *or by the right opposition, as for example the recently folded* Magyar Nemzet, *have(had) free rein to print any scurrilous material about Orbán and his administration. A good example of this was the poster campaign of Jobbik financed by Gábor Vona's millionaire sponsor Lajos Simicska, presenting Orbán and his administration as a den of thieves. Or street demonstrations that have tried to disrupt the March 15th celebration (Hungary's 4th of July) where Orbán was the keynote speaker. Or better yet, the demonstration where Orbán's effigy was beheaded and one opposition leader actually played soccer with his head for the benefit of the TV reporters who were present. (Note: the* Magyar Nemzet *has now returned to the Conservative fold!)*

CEU / KEE

Besides stifling the freedom of the press, freedom of assembly and free expression of political views, Orbán's "populist autocracy" has also been accused of limiting freedom of religion, infringing on academic freedom, following a racist and anti-Semitic and anti-Roma policy, and that it has obstructed the free flow of refugees and migrants into Europe and wants to weaken the NGOs that act as facilitators of this flow. The freedom of press and assembly has already been dealt with above, so I will turn to the academic freedom issue next, for two reasons: First, because of time limitations, second because this is an academic scholarly conference and this audience in particular, has been activated by the fate of CEU to exert pressure on the Orbán government. One of my medievalist colleagues at Ohio Northern University forwarded the following appeal to me from the "Medieval Academy of America" dated April 3, 2017: "In solidarity with our colleagues at Central European University, threatened by action by the Hungarian government, the governance of the Medieval Academy of America sent a letter this morning to the Hungarian Minister of Human Capacities. We urge our members to sign the petition or send a letter of support. You will find more information about this urgent situation here: hpttps://www.ceu.edu/node/17842".[19]

My colleague asked "What's this all about?" I did not respond immediately, because I wanted to provide the facts, rather than succumb to the hysteria that surrounded the fate of CEU at that time. A good example of the hysteria was Anne Applebaum's April 7th article: "Hungary's Attack on CEU Should Inspire Bipartisan Outrage," *The Washington Post*. The article is filled with distortions and half-truths that paint Orbán and his administration in the image of "populist," "authoritarian," "anti-academic freedom," "anti-critical thinking" part of the "Russian-Iranian-Hungarian-nationalist paranoia" which targets George Soros as a scapegoat, who is conveniently "a Jewish financier." What then are the facts?

In its cyclical, regular review of higher educational institutions the Ministry of Human Capacities found that CEU had been operating in Hungary with criteria that were not in line with the operational requirements of other foreign higher educational institutions in the country. The review revealed that New York State certified CEU in 1991, one year after regime change in Hungary. This was certification *in abstentia* since there was no such university in New York State at that time. It existed only on paper and did not acquire a physical being, aside from a mailing address at the headquarters of George Soros' "Open Society Foundation" in NYC. After this paper accreditation (without a base institution or students) in New York State, a second university was established in Budapest in 1993. This second institution had real students, a campus on Nádor utca in Budapest, named Közép Európai Egyetem (literal name translation of the name acquired in New York State). It was accredited in Hungary with this name. It has become a highly respected institution for graduate studies with a broad cross-section of international students. (Only 10-20% of the student body is composed of Hungarians.) Now comes the rub! The Közép Európai Egyetem (KEE) provides a Hungarian Diploma (M.A. or Ph.D.) for its students. However, the physically non-existing University (CEU) in New York State issues a duplicate American Diploma (M.A. or Ph.D.) for these students.

---

19   The Medieval Academy <info@themedievalacademy.org >, April 3, 2017.

Thus, these students acquired both a Hungarian and an American diploma which they have earned only at KEE in Budapest. This double granting of diplomas automatically disadvantages all Hungarian institutions which can issue only a Hungarian M.A. or Ph.D. This favoritism, discrimination, in favor of the CEU paper institution in New York State, is what the Hungarian government wants to terminate. Why doesn't CEU affiliate or become incorporated into Columbia University's Central European program or NYU's European Studies program? Then it would have real institutional roots to grant American diplomas on an exchange studies basis. (Since the controversy erupted, KEE/CEU has now established such a relationship with Bard College in New York State. Does this mean there will be Bard College M.A. and Ph.D. diplomas?)

Hungary cannot abolish CEU which has its offices at the headquarters of the Open Society Foundation in NYC, and it does not want to abolish KEE in Budapest. It values the existence of this institution. It simply wants to eliminate the double-dipping in diplomas that exists at present. It is not in the interest and is not the objective of the Orbán government to terminate either institution. That demonstrators claim that he wants to destroy them is simply a continuation of the concerted campaign to discredit and ultimately overthrow the Orbán government.[20] Behind this campaign stands a network of international NGOs (Amnesty International, Helsinki Watch, Transparency International and refugee and immigrant service organizations) that are financed by international fund raising efforts as well as the Open Society Foundation. These organizations all have a vested interest, both financial and ideological, in the continuous flow of migrants from the Middle East and North Africa into Europe.[21] Orbán is an obstacle in the path of this flow, so both his policies and government are targeted by these NGOs in demonstrations and lobbying efforts in Brussels, Paris, New York and Berlin.

---

20   Part of correspondence written to Professor John Lomax at Ohio Northern University, April 9, 2017.
21   See particularly the thorough exposé on this issue by Udo Ulfkotte, *A Menekültipar* (trans. by Andrea Rimaszombati from the original German *Die Asyl-Industrie*) Budapest: 2016.

LIBE Accusations and NGO Activities

Most recently the European Parliament's Commission on Citizenship Rights and Internal and External Justice (LIBE) has held hearings and calls for disciplinary action against Hungary for attempting to restrain the activities of these externally financed NGOs. At this time the Hungarian government is focused on making it illegal for any NGO, financed significantly from outside the country, to hinder the government's efforts to determine who can and who cannot settle in the country. The Orbán administration feels that the NGOs that support the refugee/migrant flow into Europe are a threat to the cultural characteristics and national identities of European states. Orbán does not support the EU and UN effort to try to define the right to migrate as a "human right." To this end, it has adopted laws that limit the activities of these groups within Hungary, particularly those activities which encourage illegal and undocumented entry into Hungary. This is not a limitation on all NGOs (there are over 61,800 such civil groups in Hungary), only on those with foreign funding and a foreign agenda that threatens Christian European values and national traditions. Is this a "populist" agenda or simply a commitment to national sovereignty?[22]

Is a commitment to cultural values and Christian traditions a populist characteristic? Is opposition to open borders a populist or a state concern? The Green, Liberal and Socialist parties that have pushed for the LIBE sanctions have also added other accusations to discredit the Orbán government. Charges of anti-Semitism and anti-Roma racism have been leveled without any effort to provide specific examples and documentation. Like the Anne Applebaum article in *The Washington Post* of April 7, 2017, which maintained that "Soros is conveniently a Jewish financier," the goal is simply to smear, not to prove that anti-Semitism is actually the case. Or Charles Gati's comment that Orbán called the Roma (gypsy) citizens "internal migrants." A falsification without any reference to source or event! Or that Orbán built a wall on the country's southern border "to keep out Muslim refugees." Not

---

[22] Letter from László Csizmadia of the Civil Összefogás Közhasznú Alapítvány (Foundation for Civil Solidarity) to Claude Moraes, President of LIBE, Brussels, June 7, 2018, in info@civiloszszefogas.hu

the fact that unlike Greece or Italy, Orbán took the Schengen requirements of the EU seriously to keep out "undocumented migrants."²³ These cute little twists of facts and emphasis have been thrown into the couldron of discreditation. -- And these charges are made in the face of a government that has carried out more programs in favor of minorities than any of its predecessors, inluding Holocaust memorials, increased educational opportunities for Roma youth, a policy of zero tolerance for racist manifestations, and testimonials and declarations from both Jewish and Roma communities that they have confidence in the programs of this administration. Furthermore, Benjamin Netanyahu's recent visit to Budapest demonstrates no ill will between Israel and Hungary.

(The questionable accusations of anti-Semitism and discrimination on religious grounds goes back to the period of regime change, but gained a particularly offensive aggressiveness when Hillary Clinton became the U.S. Secretary of State. It came to a head at the time that Hungary adopted new regulations and guidelines regarding the legal status of religious communities in Hungary. At this time the influence of former Ambassador András Simonyi and former interim Prime Minister Gordon Bajnai (both from the former MSZP administration) together with professor Charles Gati composed an influential cabal in Washington which encouraged the anti-FIDESZ orientation of the Obama administration. It was probably also linked to generous campaign contributions to the Democratic Party from financier George Soros. At any rate, the new law on churches came under scrutiny as a violation of religious liberties because the new regulation reduced the number of "acknowledged religious groups" from 358 to 32. The rationale for the new law was to eliminate the paper "churches" that were simply created for "business" purposes to obtain state subsidies and tax benefits such as Scientology and The Faith Church. While the latter made the final listing and is included in the 32 recognized and accepted denominations, Scientology did not.)²⁴

---

23 Anne Applebaum, "Hungary's Attack on CEU Should Inspire Bipartisan Outrage," *The Washington Post*, April 7, 2017; Charles Gati, "Book Review of Paul Lendvai's Orbán Hungary's Strongman...," op.cit.
24 See: "The New Law on Churches," *Kormányzati Médiamonitor* (2012.3.7), 2–4 in info@medianezo.hu

United States-Hungarian relations, began to sour already during President Bill Clinton's administration when Hungary purchased Swedish Grippen fighter planes rather than the used American fighters they were offered. In spite of active efforts to try to improve relations, from 2010 to the present even international events conspired against closer ties. The American interventionism and exceptionalism of the George Bush administration in the Middle East after the 9/11 attack on the World Trade Center, and the following "democratization" campaign of the Barack Obama administration in North Africa and the Middle East, put the real interests of Hungary on a collision course with the United States. (This became particularly clear with the massive migrant flow through Hungary during the summer of 2015.) It is also this interventionalim that leads to the earlier interferences with Hungary's domestic policies regarding the regulation of its own church-state relations. A close reading of the official Hungarian statement on church-state relations reflects both the rejection of the anti-religious ideology of the previous Soviet world and the secularism and materialism of the present multi-Corporation dominated West.[25]

"Bad Word" Populist or "Popular" Populist

The above developments and events are the cause for the bad image Hungary has in the Western elitist media and in the governmental circles of these states. In these circles the "bad word" populism is attached to Viktor Orbán. Now let us look at the policies that have made him a popular populist at home. In other words, why has the Hungarian electorate given him a sweeping two-thirds majority mandate in Parliament three times, in 2010, 2014, and 2018?

First, because Orbán has *not* bought into the guilt-ridden perspective that nations, particularly nation-states, were the cause for the miseries of the 20th century (World War I, the Great Depression, World War II, the Holocaust, the Cold War and everything in between!). Global imperialism, com-

---

25 Ibid.

petition for energy and other resources, and colonialism carried out by the "great" powers were closer to the root cause of this misery than the national loyalty that peoples focused on their respective nations. Hungarians were victims of these great power confrontations and the most dramatic evidence of this is the dictated Treaty of Trianon (1920), the side effects of the above misery causing events, including the Holocaust and 1956, in which Hungary sustained more than its share of destruction and loss. Thus, for Orbán, the defense of Hungary's sovereignty is his number one concern.[26] The vast majority of the Hungarian electorate trusts him on this score.

Second, Orbán views Hungarian families as the backbone of the nation. He has undertaken policies that strengthen families. This has been achieved through a two-pronged strategy that supports the educational role of family-friendly Christian churches and Jewish synagogues and provides generous economic and financial assistance to young families. The latter includes very generous tax breaks for families with children. The more children you have the less taxes you pay. Furthermore, you are given long-term credit advantages for the purchase of family homes depending on the number of children you raise. These children also benefit from a program that provides free textbooks and free school lunches. Finally, disadvantaged and poor families also benefit from government supported summer camps for their children.[27]

Although these policies have not yet turned around the demographic decline, they have increased the birth rate of Hungarian families. These expensive state-supported policies have been made possible by a new taxing system instituted by the Orbán government targeting multi-national and transnational corporations. According to the July 2017 Tusnád summary, during the previous year Hungary collected 272 billion forints from the international banking sector, 31 billion forints from the international insurance corporations, 120 billion forints from the energy sector, and 55 billion forints from the telecommunications industry. This close to 500 billion total was used to build the programs for Hungarian families that were summa-

---

26 Lánczi, "The Renewed Social Contract..." op.cit., 23–24.
27 A. Ludanyi, "Viktor Orbán: Europe's Putin, Erdogan or Trump?" Presentation at Ohio Northern University to the Phi Beta Delta International Honor Society Forum on September 13, 2017.

rized above.[28] These policies have also received the support of an overwhelming part of society.

Third, national economic policies have resulted in reducing the national debt of Hungary. Orbán inherited an 80.2% of GDP national debt in 2010 from his predecessors. During the eight years of his administration Orbán's policies have been able to reduce this to 73.6% of GDP.[29] Hungary began to regain control over its own economic destiny when its government sent the IMF packing. The preceding Socialist governments had transformed Hungary into a debtor nation. This enabled the outside world to interfere constantly in Hungary's internal affairs. It kept Hungary weak and dependent. Since the country regained control over its financial and economic affairs, it has re-gained its independence. This has made it possible, according to Orbán, for Hungary to defend its interests and become a strong and respected member of the international setting. A side effect of these policies has been to slow down the outmigration of young workers to Western Europe and the United States. Newly instituted development programs have increased the GDP growth rate in Hungary to double the average in countries of the European Union. As he pointed out in his talk at Tusnád, when he was elected in 2010, only 3.6 million Hungarians were gainfully employed out of a population of ten million. Of this number, only 1.8 million paid taxes. In 2017, 4.4 million Hungarians were gainfully employed and 4.4 million paid taxes. Furthermore, according to data released at the end of 2017, Hungary's unemployment rate at 4.2% was one of the lowest in Europe.[30] People work that is why Hungary is strong, contends Orbán. Most of the population supports this result.

Fourth, Hungary is also more in control of its own destiny because under Orbán it has regained control over its strategic services. As he pointed out in his Tusnád talk, his government has spent more than a thousand billion forints during the past few years to obtain majority control in the energy producing industries, in the banking sector, and in the mass media. In reference

---

28 Ibid.
29 Sándor Szarka, "Adósságválság fenyegeti a világot: Magyarország az árral szemben," *Magyar Demokrata* (June 20, 2018), XXII/25: 16–17.
30 Ludanyi, "Viktor Orbán: Europe's Putin, Erdogan or Trump?" op.cit.

to the latter the squeals of the oppositon have been picked up by the corporate elitist alliance in Brussels as an indication that Orbán is consolidating his "autocratic dominance" of the country. What these observers do not admit is that this policy replaces or at least reduces their own "corporate financial dominance" in Hungary. (Regarding the media it should be added that these policies have actually leveled the playing field, which up to this time had been dominated by the post-Communist elite who were closest to the media establishment when their Communist Party parents and relatives had to give up power in 1989-91.) This result has also been viewed positively by the voting public.

Fifth, under Orbán Hungary has remained loyal to its historical legacy. This means that it has stood firm in its defense of national cultural values including Hungary's commitments to its thousand years of Christian civilization. In Hungary the Christian legacy of the country is taken seriously. In spite of being a small country with limited financial resources it has stepped up its support for persecuted Christians in the Middle East and North Africa by supporting the speaking tours of their clergy in Europe and by providing the Syrian Christians with financial aid to rebuild their churches destroyed during the recent internal war sponsored by the outside major powers.[31] Similarly it has provided financial assistance to the Copt Christians of Egypt for the reconstruction of their churches that had been damaged by Islamist terrorist bombs. (This is an aspect of Orbán that Brussels rejects because it runs counter to the secularism that dominates the Western European elites.) At the same time, the traditional sectors of society also back Orbán on this front.

Sixth, the Orbán administration has not abandoned the Hungarians who have been scattered to all parts of the world by the cataclysmic 20th century or those separated from their homeland by border changes. For both categories of Hungarians his administration has created an activist outreach program. For Diasporic Hungarians (those beyond the Carpathian Basin), the Kőrösi Csoma Sándor Program was established to help sustain them in their cultural commitments and to enable them to be constructive representatives

---

31 Dániel Bodnár, "A gyermekek generációja nem élt még békében: Adománygyűjtés szír keresztényeknek," *Új Ember* (June 10, 2018) LXXIV/23: 9.

of Hungary and its global interests. For the Hungarians in neighboring states that have been detached from historic Hungary, the Petőfi Sándor Program was created to help them retain their identity within nation-states with different *Staatsvolk* than their own. Here Kin State and minority community relations are institutionalized via special cross-border programs such as the Status Law and Dual Citizenship. These commitments have also strengthened Orbán's popularity with the people.

Seventh, Orbán has established himself as a leader in resisting the refugee/migrant waves unleashed onto the European continent during the past decade and most aggressively since 2015. His strong stand against George Soros and the corporatist elitists in Western Europe has made him popular at home as well as abroad. He has undertaken policies that run counter to the will of most transnational and multinational corporations to obtain a cheap work force from the Third World. Instead of importing a work force from Africa and the Middle East his policies have focused on strengthening the native work force of Hungary. To this end he has restricted mass immigration into and through Hungary by building a defensive fence on the Serbian-Hungarian border, which was the main avenue of migration through the Balkans. His policy has put an end to undocumented illegal immigration into Hungary and also reduced the number of undocumented immigrants into the rest of Europe. (This is a responsibility that Hungary has accepted as a Schengen border country of Europe.)

Eighth, Viktor Orbán has also undertaken active alliance building to be able to withstand this modern migrant invasion. He has built on the common historical roots and experiences of Central European states. The Visegrád 4 states (Poland, Czech Republic, Slovakia, Hungary)[32] all had been victims of the Nazi and Communist totalitarianisms of the 20th century. After the collapse of the USSR, these former satellites of the Soviet Empire came together at Visegrád on the initiative of the Hungarian Antall government.

---

32 Visegrád-4 or V4 are the four East-Central European states (Poland, Czechia, Slovakia and Hungary) that met in the historic Hungarian settlement of Visegrád on the invitation of Prime Minister József Antall in 1991, to coordinate their policies regarding their admission into NATO and the EU. (At their first meeting there were only three members, but Czechoslovakia split into two states shortly thereafter.) The V-4 have continued to coordinate their policies ever since.

Their commitment to inform, consult and coordinate their policies has continued even after all four became members of NATO and the European Union. The V4 has become Orbán's major support system in the face of bullying from Brussels, Berlin or Paris and the refugee/migrant threat to the continent. The solidarity of the V4 has provided Orbán with the strength to resist the hare-brained policies that the new corporatist vision of George Soros tries to impose on Europe. These international alliance efforts on Orbán's part are also popular in Hungary.

Ninth, to be able to achieve all these things Viktor Orbán's government has restructured the Hungarian constitutional system. However, this too has led to major criticism from the outside world, particularly from those who are unfamiliar with the previous order that Orbán's reforms have replaced. The New Hungarian Basic Law replaced the 1949 Communist Mátyás Rákosi constitution which had been patched up and manipulated to provide for regime change after 1991. Yet, this document contained all the flaws of its origin and remained an obstruction to effective government. In its symbolism it was also alien to the legacy of Hungary's long and proud constitutional legacy development from St. Stephen's Admonitions, through the Golden Bull (1222), the Torda Edict of Religious Toleration (1568), the Reform Acts of the 1840's and the Nationality Law of 1868. In both its symbolism and streamlining the new Basic Law fits the Hungarian needs and expectations for the 21st century. Its main focus includes a defense of the Graeco-Roman legal and cultural traditions and the Christian centered traditions of the Hungarian nation. This responsibility relates to the defense of the linguistic and cultural diversity of the world in the face of the globalizing assault of profit driven corporatist interests.

Finally the tenth consideration is his ability to lead both on the international and the domestic front. Viktor Orbán has leadership skills that few leaders have in present-day Europe. He has the admiration of the majority of his countrymen as the sweeping electoral victories attest. This admiration is based on results, not smoke and mirrors. It is definitely not based on a "Cult of Personality." His posture at the victory gathering of FIDESZ/KDNP on April 8th 2018, was reserved and generous, telling his followers that the results should be accepted responsibly and with humility. Furthermore, that his role is to serve all Hungarians, including those who voted against him in the elections. He is not a demagogue and his speeches are factual presentations and avoid bombast. In his relations with his own administration, he is a demanding taskmaster and removes or replaces those who do not measure up to the standards he sets. However, in addition to the many achievements, there are problems which are linked to Lord Acton's truism that: "Power corrupts and absolute power corrupts absolutely." In his oversight of some members of his following, the time has arrived to set examples, by dramatic removals of those who are responsible for the violation of public trust.

Concluding Observations

The "bad word" populist labeling of Orbán by the elitist Western media, leads these sources to put him in the company of such past "populists" as Juan Perón of Argentina and Huey Long of Louisiana, as well as such contemporaries as Vladimir Putin, Donald Trump and Recep Tayyib Erdogan. But even scholarly treatments are guilty of such inaccurate categorizations. For example, such highly respected institutions as Cornell University, Swathmore College and Johns Hopkins University have faculty members who have jointly produced a "study" that puts the leaders of Poland, Hungary, Marine Le Pen, and Geert Wilders in the same populist club as Hugo Chávez and Recep Tayyib Erdoğan.[33] Are any of these individuals really populists in the sense that William Jennings Bryan was a populist? No they are not, and neither are they comparable to Viktor Orbán. Only in one sense can the populist label fit Orbán and that is in the same sense that it also fits William Jennings Bryan. Both of them have stood up to the "Robber Barons" created by the concentrated money power of their time. In this sense Viktor Orbán is indeed a populist, a popular populist, who has taken off his gloves to take on the oligarchical interest clusters, like Big Oil, Monsanto, and the Pharmaceu-

---

33 Robert C. Lieberman, Suzanne Mettler, Thomas B. Pepinsky, Kenneth M. Roberts and Richard Valelly, "Trumpism and American Democracy: History, Comparison, and the Predicament of Liberal Democracy in the United States," pp.11–23, in – https://papers.ssm.com/sol3/papers.cfm?abstract_id=3028990

tical giants, for whom national cultures and Christianity are simply obstacles. For Orbán these "obstacles" provide meaning for survival.

Andrew Ludanyi
Emeritus Professor of Political Science
Ohio Northern University

Index of Names

Numbers in italics refer to photo captions

Adam, Christopher, 156
Ady, Endre, 5, 70
Ahern, Jack, 110
Alexander, Robert, ix, 103, 147
Alexander, Shelleigh, ix
Almay, Vörner Katalin, 116
Amanpour, Christiane, 174
Andreánszky, Jenő, 58
Andreánszky, Károly, 33, 80
Andrew II., 175
Antall, József, 200n32
Applebaum, Anne, 192, 194
Atzél, Endre ("Bácsi Bandi"), 122–24

Bacevich, Andrew J., 157
Baden-Powell, Lord Robert, 23
Badertscher, Patricia, 103, 162
Bajnai, Gordon, 150, 153, 156, 195
Baker, Kendall, 126
Bakos, István, 165
Balogh, Edgár, 97
Balogh, Judy, 101
Banes, Gay, 113, 114
Barber, Benjamin, 158
Bart, Panni, 78
Bartus, Alexander, 75
Basa-Molnár, Enikő, 110
Bashar, al-Assad, 154
Beard, Charles E., 182
Begin, Menahem, 128
Bellemore, Walter, 43
Benes, Eduard, 136n34
Benko, Stephen, 114, 115
Bennet, Steve, 102
Béres, Ferenc, 78
Bertalan, Imre Sr., 112, 154
Bhattacharya, Amar, 87
Biden, Joseph, 157, 176

Billig, Pamela, 110
Bíró, Zoltán, 165
Blair, Tony, 127
Bobango, Gerald J., 108
Bodnár, Gábor, 33, 40
Bodoni, Ildikó, ix, 113, 116
Bognár, Béla, ix, 133, 134
Bognar, Steve, 101, 134
Bokor, Erika, 90, 137, 170
Boros-Kazai, András, 94
Boros-Kazai, Mary, 94
Borsody, Stephen, 109
Bozóki, András, 187
Bozoki, Antal, ix, 135
Bőjte, Csaba, 123, 145
Bőjtös, László, 79
Brezhnev, Leonid, 82
Brogyányi, Gábor, 27
Brogyányi, Jenő, 110
Brückner, Huba, ix, 106, 168, 169
Bryan, William Jennings, 182, 183, 203
Buchanan, Patrick J., 158
Bulganin, Nikolai, 27
Bush, George W., 111, 126–30, 149, 153, 154, 175, 180, 196

Cadzow, John F., 108
Calvin, John, 110n30
Carnegie, Andrew, 183
Carpenter, Richard, 170
Carr, E.H., 157
Carter, Jimmy, 84
Ceauşescu, Nikolai, 79–83, 122, 123, 142, 187
Chászár, Edward, 80
Chavez, Hugo, 203
Chomsky, Noam, 158
Ciszka see Layton, Ludányi, Nárcissza

Index of Names

Clemanceu, Georges, 29
Clinton, Bill, 117, 118, 153, 154, 196
Clinton, Hillary, 150, 157, 195
Cohn (history Teacher at L. I.C. High School), 32
Columbus, Christopher, 174
Combs, Cindy, 127, 128
Compton, Phillip, 104
Connor, Walker, 110
Cornstein, David, 157
Countess Kastell of Hochburg, 12
Crawford, Russ, 147
Csajka, Tamás, 151
Cseh, Gábor, ix
Cseh, Tibor, 23, 77, 80, 85, 88, 91, 94, 136, 167
Cseke, Péter, 125, 136, 168
Cseke, Irénke, 125
Csepeli, György, 125
Csíkszentmihályi, Mihály, 40, 43
Csomay, György (George), 71, 77

Danko, Steve, 43, 111
Darlington, Oscar, 102
Davis, Robert, 86, 104, 126
Dávid, Ferenc, 145
Dávid, Lajos, 125
Deák, István, 108
Debreczeni, József, 185, 186
Deloria, Vine Jr., 69
Dewey, Thomas, 24
Domokos, Géza, 80
Domonkos, László, 108
Dreisziger, Nándor, 109
Dulles, John Foster, 29

Egyed, Csilla, 43
Egyed, Zsuzsa, 43
Eisenhower, Dwight D., 24, 27, 28, 63, 64, 152
Éltető, Áron, 75
Éltető, Erzsébet, 75
Éltető J. Lajos Jr. (Lou), 4, 64, 74, 75, 78, 79, 80, 85, 91, 92, 94, 108–10, 160, 161

Éltető, Lajos Sr., 75
Éltető, Zsuzsa (Sharon), 75
Engdahl, F. William, 158
Erdogan, Recep Tayyib, 203
Érdy, Lily, 150
Érdy, Miklós, 80
Erős, Gusztáv, 21, 23, 26, 136

Fabricy Kováts, Mihály de, 66
Farkas, Árpád, 80
Fejős, Zoltán, 110
Fekete-Győr, András, 132n33
Fischer-Galati, Stephen, 110
Fischer, Viktor, ix, 22, 23, 25, 80
Fisk, Robert, 128
Fliess, Peter, 46
Ford, Gerard, 82–84
Forester, Mr. (farmer near Victoria, VA), 16, 18, 19
Forgács, Ildikó, ix, 161
Formisano, Ron, 158
Frecska, Márta, 71, 7, 79
Frecska, Tamás, 80
Freed, DeBow, 104
Für, Lajos, 109

Gati, Charles, 150, 153, 194, 195
Gellérd, Judit, 110
General Blachford (U.S. Navy transport), 15
Gilbreth, Terry, 104
Glasser (Home room and English teacher at L.I.C. High School), 32
Glenn, John, 117
Goltz, Thomas, 111
Göllner, András, 156
Gore, Albert, 117, 118
Görömbei, András, 106, 136
Grimes, Eddie, 162
Gulden, Marika, 115
Gyurcsány, Ferenc, 132–34, 156

Hajdú, Győző, 80, 81
Hamza, András, 80, 90, 92

Index of Names

Hámos, László, 86, 112, 114, 115, 118, 119, 154
Hanák, Péter, 109
Hanley, Bernard, 114, 116
Haraszti, Miklós, 186
Harriman, E.H., 183
Harrington, Donald, 110
Harsányi (Reformed Minister in Hawthorne, New Jersey), 45
Hassell, George, 103
Hegyi, Klára, 110
Held, Joseph, 108
Henry, Patrick, 19, 178
Hilliard, Robert, 75, 86
Hill, James P., 183
Horthy, Miklós, 9n1, 68
Horváth, János (John), 33, 109, 116, 131
Hutchings, Robert, 115

Illyés, Gyula, 184
Iohannis, Klaus, 143
Irwing (American history teacher at L.I.C. High School), 32
István I. (Saint Steven), 174

Jackson, Andrew, 182
Jackson, Stonewall, 19
Jackson (Student at Victoria public school), 18
„János" (Pseudonym of local Catholic priest in Subotica), 56
Jászi, Oszkár, 109
Jefferson, Thomas, 19
Jeszenszky, Géza, 109
Johnson, Lyndon Baines, 72, 82
Jókay, Károly (Charles), ix, 1, 109, 110, 168, 169
Jókay, Lajos, 40
Jónás, Paul, 109
Joó, Rudolf, 96, 97, 109, 110, 186
József, Attila, 178
Juhász, Katalin, 151
Jurevicz, Ed, 101

Kádár, Géza, 118
Kádár, János, 40, 180, 184, 188
Kádár Lynn, Katalin, ix, 168
Kaiser, Terry, 104
Kálmán, Szabolcs, ix
Kántor, Zoltán, 164, 166
Kányádi, Sándor, 80, 97, 99
Kaptur, Marcy, 110, 119, 189
Károly, László, 151
Károlyi, Mihály, 67
Kató, Béla, 143
Kazella, Ignatius, 101
Kenedi, János, 186
Kennan, George F., 14
Kennedy, John Fritzgerald, 64, 72
Kertész, Imre, 106
Kertész, Stephen, 108
Khaddafi, Muammar, 154
King, Martin Luther Jr., 69, 72
King, Robert, 4, 44
Kingsley, Patrick, 189
Király, Béla, 109
Kis, János, 186
Kiss, Gy. Csaba, 165, 186
Kissinger, Henry, 82, 83, 85
Klausewitz, Karl Maria von, 127
Kodolányi, Gyula, 186
Kóka, János, 156
Kóka, Rozália, 136, 167
Kormányos, Erzsébet, 55
Korossy, Mária, 146
Kőrösi, Csoma Sándor, 138
Kossuth, Lajos (Louis), 66, 149–51, 175
Koszorús, Ferenc vitéz, 9n1
Koszorús, Frank, 112, 119
Köteles, Gyöngyi, 94
Kounalakis, Eleni, 190
Kovács, Árpád, 92, 125
Kovács, Beáta, 112, 113
Kovács, Béla, 90
Kovács, Imre, 184
Kovács, József, 40
Kovács, László, 113
Kovács, Melinda, 90

Kovalszki, Péter, 79, 119, 170, 171
Kövér, László, 186
Krushchev, Nikita, 38
Kun, Béla, 67
Kuncze, Gábor, 156
Kun Szabó, István, 80
Kurek, Rosemary, 101

Langhorst (coach at Elmhurst College), 44
Lantos, Tom, 115
Latkóczy, Emese, 112, 119
Lauer, Andrea, 41, 42, 114
Lauer, Edith, ix, 112, 113, 114, 116, 118, 125, 154
Lauer, John, 118
Layton, Howard Manton, 45
Layton, Ludányi Narcissza, ix, 9, 11, 31, 45, 91, 116, 155
Layton, Paulette, 106, 116
Lázár, György, 156
Leamon, Jim, 44
Lee, Robert E., 19, 60
Lezsák, Sándor, 165
Lieven, Anatol, 158
Lincoln, Abraham, 149, 152, 179, 182
Lippert, Anne, 104
Lipták, Béla, 96, 97, 119
Litván, György, 109
Litvinenko, Alexander, 111
Loeschner, Raymond, 89, 102, 104, 179
Lomax, John, ix, 103, 104, 109, 177, 193n20
Long, Huey, 203
Loughlin, Michael, 103, 104, 109, 111, 118, 150, 181n1
Lőrik, Matild, 51, 52
Ludányi, Antal vitéz, 9, 26, 170
Ludányi, Antal Jr., 9, 15, 73
Ludányi, Csilla Anna, ix, 94, 95, 98, 99, 100, 105, 106, 119, 123, 137, 138, 151, 161
Ludányi, Gaál Anna Mária, ix, 120–22, 125, 131, 134, 136, 144, 146, 155, 161, 162, 166, 171

Ludányi, Lizy, 144
Ludányi, Lona, 144
Ludányi, Madelaine, 73
Ludányi, Pál (Paul), ix, 9, 11, 15, 21, 40, 48, 73, 80, 91, 144–46, 162
Ludányi, Prileszky Erzsébet, 9, 21, 28, 73, 91, 95
Ludányi, Réka, 141
Ludányi, Tamás (Tom), 9, 11, 15, 17, 21, 43, 73, 77, 140, 141, 144
Ludányi, Theresa, 144
Ludányi, Nádas Julianna, ix, 76
Lukács, Tibor, 80

MacArthur, Douglas, 24
Madarász, Géza, 80
Magyar, Kálmán, ix
Makay, Árpád, 23, 25
Makay, Csilla, 25, 43, 116, 171
Malcolm X, 69
Mara, Ernő, 143, 145
Mara, Márta, 143, 145
Márika see Ludányi, Gaal Anna Mária
Masaryk, Thomas, 136n4
Matuska, Márton, 57
Matthias Rex, 144, 145
Mauksch, Péter, 22
McCarthy, Joseph, 24
McIntosh, Pringle, 89
Megyeri, József, 90, 137, 170
Mertus, Julie, 119
Metzenbaum, Howard, 85
Meyer, Samuel, 89, 102
Mihályfy, László, 101
Milnar, Anthony, 104
Milosevic, Slobodan, 134, 187
Minger, Hajnal, 170
Molnár, August, 40, 43, 80
Molnár, Mária, 25, 32
Moore, James, 103
Morgan, J.P., 183
Morgenthau, Hans, 157
Mossadegh, Mohammad, 149
Mubarak, Hosni, 154

Nádas, Gabriella, 116
Nádas, Julius, 76
Nádas, Ibolya, 76
Nádas, Julianna Rose see Ludányi, Julianna
Nagy, Gáspár, 92
Nagy, Imre, 81
Nagy, Emmi, 93
Nagy, Károly, 80
Nagy, Károly Endre, 80, 93
Nagy, Margit, 134
Nagy, Nagybaczoni Vilmos vitéz, 9n1
Nanyó see Ludányi, Prileszky Erzsébet
Nasser, Gamal Abdel, 28
Nemes, Árpád, 116
Németh, László, 184
Németh, Zsolt, ix, 166, 167, 170, 171, 186
Némethy, Péter, 25
Netanyahu, Benjamin, 195
Nixon, Richard M., 30, 34, 82
Nogge, Burl, 59
Nusi see Cseh, Gábor Anna

Obama, Barack, 61, 129, 149, 150, 153, 154, 157, 180, 195, 196
Orbán, Viktor, 133, 138, 144, 145, 153, 155–57, 166, 174, 175, 181, 182, 185–203
Osama bin Laden, 127, 129

Pacepa, Ion, 142n35
Pahlavi, Reza Mohammad Shah, 149
Panni see Ludányi, Julianna,
Papp, László, 44
Pastor, Peter, 108
Paulo, Renate, 73
Pen, Marine le, 203
Pereszlényi, Márta, 116
Perkins, John, 158
Perón, Juan, 203
Péter, László, 27n8
Pigniczky, Réka, 41, 42
Pók, Attila, 109

Politkovskaya, Anna, 111
Previte, Peter, 76
Prileszky, Csilla, 94
Prileszky, Gyöngy, 146
Purger, Tibor, 117, 158
Putin, Vladimir, 111, 127, 203
Putnam, George, 47, 49, 58
Püski, Ilus, 90
Püski, István, 90
Püski, Sándor, 80

Rajk, László, 27, 186
Rajk, László Jr., 186
Rákóczi II., Ferenc, 175
Rákosi, Mátyás, 27, 33, 68, 175, 180, 184, 201
Rankovic, Aleksandar, 49, 58
Rehák, László, 57, 58
Riesman, David, 63
Rockefeller, John D., 183
Rodrik, Dani, 189
Roider, Karl, 108
Roosevelt, Franklin Deleno, 175
Rosapepe, James C., 125
Rózsa, Sándor, 51
Rubin, Diana, 115
Russell, John, 111

Saffell, David, 102, 104, 109, 126, 146
Salmone, Tony, 86
Sass, Magda, 80, 106
Sass, Márton, 80, 91, 92, 116, 120, 131, 138
Sass, Rozál, 120
Satterwhite, James, 111
Savoy, Eugene, 50
Schade, Rudolf G., 45
Schmidt, Royal J., 45
Schöpflin, George, 125
Schuck, Raymond, 103, 147
Scott, JoAnn, 103, 104, 147
Scrimger, Kay Randle, 114, 116
Sefton, David, 102
Servetius, Michael, 110n30

Index of Names

Shannon, Wayne, 59
Sharon, Ariel, 127, 128
Simicska, Lajos, 186, 191
Simon, de, László, 26, 77
Simonyi, András, 150, 153, 195
Sinor, Denis, 109
Smith, David, 103, 147
Smith, John, 19
Soltay, László, 78, 80
Soltay, Mária, 78, 80
Somogyi, Balázs, 85, 171
Somogyi, Csilla see Makay, Csilla
Somogyi, Ilona, 116
Soros, George, 153, 157, 192, 194, 195, 200, 201
Spira, Thomas, 109
Stalin, Joseph, 13, 27, 49
Stephen, I (saint), 93
Stevenson, Adlei, 24, 27
Sütő, András, 80, 97, 110, 115
Swett, Brett, 162
Swett, Ludányi Anikó Ilona, 95, 162
Szablya, Helen (Ilonka), 118
Szabó, Dezső, 184
Szabó, Katica, 151
Szakály, Sándor, 165
Szálasi, Ferenc, 180
Szathmáry, Lajos (Louis), 94, 110
Szász, János, 97
Szekeres, Zsolt, ix, 85, 112, 166
Szendrey, Thomas, 110
Szent-Iványi, Sándor, 90
Szentkirályi, Endre, 151
Szemerkényi, Réka, 116
Szilágyi-Ovaitt, Katalin, 42
Sztojay, Döme, 180

Taft, Robert, 24
Taliga, Miklós, 21
Tamas, Bernard, 114
Tito, Josip Broz, 49, 52, 53, 58
Tokay, János, 92, 94
Tőkés, László, 123, 166
Tollas, Tibor, 69, 70

Tóth, Csaba, 80
Truman, Harry, 13, 24
Trump, Donald, 157, 172, 175, 176, 203
Turner, Frederick Jackson, 62

Ujvagi, Bernadett, 110, 150
Ujvagi, Peter, 89, 100, 101, 110, 112, 116, 119, 150
Ujvagi, Krisztina, 119
Ulfcotte, Udo, 158
Unghváry, Alexander S., 110

Vago, Raphael, 110
Vardy, Stephen B., 108, 109
Varjú, László, 42
Vasvári, Enikő, 42
Vasvári, Zoltán, 4, 21, 22, 32, 33, 40, 41, 47, 166
Veres, Ferenc, 80
Veress, Bulcsú, 88, 109
Veress, Péter, 184
Verseghy, István, 32, 44
Vizi E., Szilveszter, 165
Vona, Gábor, 191

Washington, George, 19, 66
Waters, Robert, 147
Watkins, Jimmy, 19
Watkins, Marvin, 19
Werbőczy, István, 175
Whyte, William, 63
Wilders, Geert, 203
Williams, George M., 110
Wilson, Charles E., 152
Wilson, Ellen, 102, 103, 104, 109, 146, 147, 150
Wilson, Jimmy, 147
Wright, Gene, 94, 95
Yeltsin, Boris, 111

Yesahanu, Yitzhak, 142n35

Zangwill, Israel, 66
Zarb, Ronnie, 26

Index of Names

Zarb, Savier, 26
Zemin, Jiang, 127
Zolibá see Vasvári, Zoltán,

Zoltáni, Ildikó see Bodoni, Ildikó
Zoltán, Piroska, 119
Zoltán, Sándor, 119

www.ingramcontent.com/pod-product-compliance
Lightning Source LLC
Chambersburg PA
CBHW042048280426
43673CB00087B/481/J